CULT ARCHAEOLOGY
AND CREATIONISM

D0881796

CULT ARCHAEOLOGY & CREATIONISM

Understanding Pseudoscientific
Beliefs about the Past

An Expanded Edition

Edited by Francis B. Harrold
and Raymond A. Eve

University of Iowa Press Ψ Iowa City

University of Iowa Press, Iowa City 52242
Copyright © 1995 by the University of Iowa Press
All rights reserved
Printed in the United States of America

Printed on acid-free paper

Library of Congress Cataloging-in-Publication Data
Cult archaeology and creationism: understanding pseudoscientific beliefs
   about the past / edited by Francis B. Harrold and Raymond A. Eve.—
   An expanded ed.
      p.   cm.
   Includes bibliographical references.
   ISBN 0-87745-513-9 (pbk.)
   1. History—Errors, inventions, etc. 2. Creationism. 3. History—Study
and teaching—United States. 4. Archaeology and history. I. Harrold,
Francis B., 1948–   .   II. Eve, Raymond A., 1946–
D10.C84   1995
001.9—dc20   95-8515
                                                              CIP

01 00   P 5 4 3 2

For John, Jim, and Susan

Contents

Preface to the
Expanded Edition

We humans tend to be interested in our past. Books, articles, television shows, and films about human origins and past civilizations are often very popular. Some of the most popular ones, unfortunately, make claims about the past which are simply wrong—sometimes spectacularly so. For instance, the books of Erich von Däniken (1970, 1972, 1974) claiming that extraterrestrial visitors guided the course of human development, sold in the millions and are apparently still believed by vast numbers of people. Yet the assertions about the past which they present are ludicrously incorrect (for instance, see Stiebing 1984). This book is concerned with unsubstantiated beliefs about the human past, beliefs which can be readily divided into two categories.

One category is *creationism*, which involves an account of human origins taken more or less literally from the opening of the Book of Genesis in the Bible. According to creationists, the earth is only a few thousand years old, and humans, along with all other living things, were directly created pretty much as they are today. Creationists deny the scientific concept of the evolution of humankind and other life forms via descent with modification from ancestral species. Most of them argue that the fossil and geological records really show that evolution never happened.

The other category of pseudoscientific beliefs about the past is *cult archaeology*, which includes a whole variety of fanciful claims. Examples include von Däniken's "ancient astronauts," as well as the belief that a great civilization once existed on the continent of Atlantis before it sank beneath the waves in a giant cataclysm, or claims that Romans, Phoenicians, and many other Old World visitors left rock inscriptions all over North America.

Claims in both categories, however, are unsupported by scientific study of the available evidence and furthermore fly in the face of what we *do* know about the human past. This picture of the past has been built up gradually by the efforts of archaeologists, physical anthropologists concerned with the human fossil record, geologists, paleontologists, historians, and other specialists. We are far from completely understanding the human species' career, but it is clear that the evidence does not allow claims like those noted above.

Those advocating these beliefs, however, typically do claim scientific validity for their ideas and use terms associated with science, like "data," "theory," and "hypothesis." Nonetheless, they do not actually use scientific method, which involves careful consideration of all relevant evidence and the proposal and testing of hypotheses to explain the evidence. For this reason, such claims are typically called "pseudoscientific." As with many other kinds of pseudoscientific beliefs—such as those concerning UFOs as extraterrestrial spacecraft, astrology, and the Loch Ness Monster—their supporters claim scientific support but do not merit it.

Our use of the term "pseudoscientific" is typical but not universal. Trefil (1978), for example, notes that a precise line between science and pseudoscience may be hard to draw in some cases. He prefers to speak in terms of concentric circles, with established science in the center, beyond which are a "frontier" of concepts and procedures which may or may not win eventual acceptance (as has continental drift in geology) and finally a "fringe" of more outlandish claims which will probably never be accepted. It is even argued (Truzzi 1979) that "pseudoscience" is itself a vague and value-laden term which should be replaced by something more neutral, such as "unconventional." A full discussion of this issue would be beyond the scope of this book—as would a comprehensive sorting-out of the many other terms used to refer to some or all of the beliefs under study here, such as "paranormal," "occult," "superstitious," and "fantastic." However, we defend our use of the term "pseudoscientific" as a reasonable characterization of the beliefs we studied, beliefs which are unjustifiably claimed by their advocates to have solid scientific support.

The articles in this book are concerned with pseudoscientific beliefs about the human past. They are *not* primarily concerned with showing how and why these beliefs are wrong. Such refutation is an important task, one probably undertaken too tardily by scientists. The scientific community was slow to realize the popularity and implications of these beliefs and was concerned that discussing them with the public would give them more attention and credence than they deserved. However, many excellent books and articles written for the general public have shown what is so seriously wrong with creationism (e.g., Kitcher 1982; Godfrey 1983) and cult archaeology (e.g., Stiebing 1984).

Instead, this book is concerned primarily with two tasks relatively neglected by the scientific community: *understanding* these beliefs and *dealing* with them. Just how popular are such pseudoscientific beliefs, especially among college students—i.e., those who will eventually be among the most influential members of our society? In a relatively well educated, scientifically sophisticated nation, why are these beliefs so popular? What do they say about our educational system and cultural values? Finally, what can and should be done in the areas of science education, mass communications, and future research to deal with such claims? These and related questions will be discussed by our authors.

This book grew from a symposium at the 1986 meeting of the Society for American Archaeology. Its organizers, anthropologists Kenneth Feder, Luanne Hudson, and Francis Harrold, were concerned enough about the preceding questions to bring together specialists from archaeology, physical anthropology, sociology, history, and psychology to examine pseudoscientific beliefs about the past from the perspectives of several disciplines. The symposium also reported the results of a unique coordinated research project conducted by the organizers and Raymond Eve, himself a sociologist. Nearly a thousand college students at five campuses across the country answered detailed questionnaires concerning pseudoscientific beliefs, as well as many background factors such as school experience, religious beliefs, and geographical region of origin. The analysis of the resulting data is reported in chapters 4, 5, and 6. The other chapters are revised and enlarged versions of papers presented at the symposium, except for those by Kehoe and Ortiz de Montellano, which were invited contributions.

For this new edition, we have added the chapter by Bernard Ortiz de Montellano on the increasingly prominent and controversial topic of "Afrocentric" readings of the human past. We have also rewritten (with Geertruida de Goede) the final chapter to bring up to date our discussion of pseudosciences of the past, and we have updated the contributors' biographies. The other chapters, as informative and thought-provoking as when they were originally published, are unchanged.

We owe debts of gratitude to many people who have helped us realize this volume. Special thanks must go to Ken Feder and Luanne Hudson, our collaborators in the research project which provided the impetus for the symposium and this book. Without their hard work, patience, and collegiality, the project, symposium, and book would never have been completed. We also thank the other contributors to this volume, who despite the heavy demands of fieldwork, teaching, and other duties, produced excellent papers.

Our colleague at the University of Texas at Arlington, Theodore N. Greenstein, gave us invaluable aid in various technical matters. We also thank Deborah Wood for her tireless efforts as a research assistant over the period of the research project; Faye Self, who typed the manuscript; and Yafit Avizemal and John Taylor, who drafted the figures. We also wish to thank colleagues and students on five campuses for their cooperation in making possible the study reported in chapters 4, 5, and 6. And finally, we are grateful indeed to our spouses, Trudy de Goede and Susan Brown Eve, for the patience and good humor which so eased our tasks, and to our parents: Francis and Eileen Harrold, for their love and support, and Ida and Arthur Eve, who never failed to encourage their son's interest in science.

References

Godfrey, Laurie R., ed.
1983 *Scientists Confront Creationism*. New York: Norton.
Kitcher, Phillip
1982 *Abusing Science: The Case against Creationism*. Cambridge: MIT Press.
Stiebing, William H., Jr.
1984 *Ancient Astronauts, Cosmic Collisions, and Other Popular Theories about Man's Past*. Buffalo, N.Y.: Prometheus Books.
Trefil, James S.
1978 A consumer's guide to pseudoscience. *Saturday Review*, April, 16–21.
Truzzi, Marcello
1979 On the reception of unconventional scientific claims. In Seymour H. Mauskopf, ed., *The Reception of Unconventional Science*, pp. 125–137. AAAS Selected Symposium No. 25. Boulder, Colo.: Westview.
von Däniken, Erich
1970 *Chariots of the Gods*. New York: Bantam.
1972 *Gods from Outer Space*. New York: Bantam.
1974 *Gold of the Gods*. New York: Bantam.

catastrophes in historical times. Older theories see pyramids as possess-
ing mysterious powers and hiding cosmic secrets in their measurements;
trace all civilization to refugees from Atlantis; or contend that human cultural development was interrupted by a universal flood (Feder 1980;
McKusick 1984; Stiebing 1984). Despite their differences, these and
other popular ideas have common features which allow us to treat them as
a single phenomenon. Cole has enumerated nineteen of these features
of cult archaeology (1980:4–9), but I feel that they can be grouped into
three basic areas: (1) the unscientific nature of cult archaeology's evidence
and methodology, (2) its tendency to provide simple, compact answers to
complex, difficult issues, and (3) the presence of a persecution complex
and ambivalent attitude toward the scientific Establishment.

Perhaps the most striking feature of cult archaeology is its rejection or
ignorance of the results of modern stratigraphic archaeology. Individual
artifacts, sites, or archaeological "mysteries" are often claimed as supporting evidence by pseudoscientific theorists, but the contexts for these
items, especially the evidence for their dates, is almost always ignored. It
is usually impossible to reconcile the kinds of cultural and historical explanations desired by pseudoarchaeologists with chronologies for archaeological deposits and artifacts which have been scientifically built up over
generations of excavation and study. So archaeological chronology must
be dispensed with.

In place of professionally gathered archaeological evidence, a variety of
other material is used. One of the most common types of "evidence" used
by cultists consists of generalized cultural comparisons. For example,
those who believe that there was one origin for all civilization, whether it
be Atlantis, Mu, Egypt, ancient spacemen, or some other source, commonly point to similarities between civilizations of the Old and New
Worlds to prove their point. The existence of pyramids in both hemi-
spheres, common worship of the sun and moon, and similarities in sound
between some vocabulary items in various American Indian languages and
the corresponding words in Japanese, Chinese, or other Old World tongues
have all been cited as evidence for various popular theories (see, for example, Donnelly 1882; Berlitz 1975:151–168). Others draw support for
their views from American "inscriptions" which are supposedly written in
Phoenician, Celtic, Greek, Latin, and other Old World languages (for example, Fell 1976, 1980). And still others rely on their subjective impres-
sions of art works or other artifacts. Probably the best-known instance of
this latter type of "evidence" is Erich von Däniken's interpretation of a
complex, stylized Maya bas-relief from the site of Palenque as a depiction
of an astronaut in a rocket ship (in fact, it depicts a dead king entering the
underworld). The archaeological dates and cultural contexts for such so-

called evidence usually disprove the claims made for it by the cultists (Stiebing 1984). Nevertheless, popular theorists continue to sway the public with such material.

But cult archaeologists' favorite type of evidence seems to be their special interpretations of ancient myths and legends. Supporters of a worldwide flood, Atlantis, ancient astronauts, recent cosmic catastrophes, pre-Columbian voyages to the New World, and a number of other pseudo-archaeological theories draw extensively on myths from around the world. However, their interpretations of these myths are quite subjective and usually ignore the cultural contexts in which the various accounts arose.

For example, ancient Egyptian myths which are sometimes cited as flood stories like those found in the Bible and in Mesopotamia actually refer to noncatastrophic local flooding of the Nile River or to the chaotic ocean (not a flood), from which, according to Egyptian belief, all gods and created things arose (Stiebing 1984: 18). And Immanuel Velikovsky used the Aztecs' beliefs about the ferocity of their war god and legends about their migrations as evidence for a cosmic catastrophe which he claimed took place in the seventh and eighth centuries B.C. (Velikovsky 1950: 253–54, 269). But the myths and legends to which Velikovsky refers are fairly late (about A.D. 1100–1300), and there is no evidence that the Aztecs even existed as a tribe as early as the seventh century B.C. (Davies 1979: 177).

Such problems with cultists' misuse of mythology are quite common. More fundamentally, the belief of most cult archaeologists that the vast majority of myths are simply distorted remembrances of historical events is contradicted by modern research into the nature and origins of mythology (Grimal 1965, especially pp. 13–14; Fredericks 1978: 81–82).

Other problems with evidence and methodology abound (using non-sequiturs and other faulty logic, misusing references, especially out-of-date or untraceable sources, confusing possibilities with probabilities, etc.), but space does not permit detailed discussion of all of them. Michael Carroll, a sociologist and a student of myth, summed up the situation when he commented that the evidence presented by cult archaeology "is so impressionistic that it serves a function analogous to the inkblots on a Rorschach test, namely, such evidence serves as an ambiguous stimulus onto which the subject can project what he wants to see" (Carroll 1977: 542). Or, to put it another way, many people believe in cult archaeology not because of the evidence but despite its ambiguous and questionable nature.

A second characteristic of cult archaeology is its propensity to provide relatively simple explanations for extremely complex events and difficult questions. The pseudoarchaeologists present issues in absolutes. They see scholarship as a conflict between Light and Darkness, Truth and Falsehood (Cole 1980:6). Their oversimplification of the issues makes the choices between alternative explanations seem clear-cut and easy to make.

One issue many pseudoarchaeologists deal with in one way or another is the origin of civilization. Did humans develop civilization on their own or did they receive it from some outside source, such as extraterrestrial visitors? Did all civilization have a common origin? Some go beyond questions about civilization and concern themselves with issues normally reserved for religion: Is there some superior being or supernatural power present in the universe, and has it interacted with humanity?

In answering such questions, cult archaeology functions in the way myth does in primitive cultures (Carroll 1977). It resolves psychological dilemmas and provides answers for the unknown or unknowable. As Isaac Asimov has recently put it (1986:212), "Inspect every piece of pseudoscience and you will find a security blanket, a thumb to suck, a skirt to hold. What have we [professional scholars] to offer in exchange? Uncertainty! Insecurity!" The objective methods of modern scholarship cannot provide immediate, simple answers to all questions or absolutely certain explanations for all phenomena. Yet it is natural for individuals to want to know why things are the way they are. Unresolved issues produce a degree of psychological discomfort which often spurs on intellectual curiosity and the desire to learn. However, those who have a low tolerance for the psychological discomfort caused by unanswered or unanswerable questions become prime candidates for the new mythologies (some of which, of course, are continuations of very old mythologies). Cult archaeology provides the "answers" that traditional scholarship cannot. Or, where answers have been given, cult archaeology can often provide ones that are more psychologically satisfying to many individuals.

Of course, from childhood almost everyone in Western society has been taught that he or she should make decisions based on logic and reason, so some "evidence" must be adduced by the cultists. But as we have already stated, the evidence favoring a given popular theory need only be strong enough to provide a rational pretext for those who already want to believe. And the mythlike character of pseudoscientific theories may account for their tendency to use traditional myths as evidence. Perhaps subconsciously, modern cult archaeologists recognize their kinship with the mythmakers of the past.

The third major characteristic of cult archaeology is what Cole has called "an ambivalent antielitism: vilification of the Establishment coupled with an inordinate respect for and envy of it" (Cole 1980:7). A common claim of archaeological cultists is that professional scholars are so blindly committed to a prevailing dogmatic view that they cannot recognize the validity of new concepts. For example, statements such as the following can be found in almost any cult archaeology book:

It took courage to write this book, and it will take courage to read it. Because its theories and proofs do not fit into the mosaic of traditional archaeology, constructed so laboriously and firmly cemented down, scholars will call it nonsense and put it on the Index of those books which are better left unmentioned. (von Däniken 1968:vii)

All the lights in the House of the High Priests of American Anthropology are out, all the doors and windows are shut and securely fastened (they do not sleep with their windows open for fear that a new idea might fly in); we have rung the bell of Reason, we have banged on the door with Logic, we have thrown the gravel of Evidence against their windows; but the only sign of life in the house is an occasional snore of Dogma. (Gladwin 1947:361)

Yet it is paradoxical that authors who complain so much about scholarly blindness and ignorance almost always point with pride to any support they receive from members of the Establishment. Archaeological cultists frequently quote statements by leading scholars showing real or (more commonly) fancied approval of their ideas. Harold Gladwin, author of the quotation immediately above, saw no contradiction in having the preface to his *Men Out of Asia* written by one of the "High Priests of American Anthropology," Dr. E. A. Hooten (then professor of anthropology at Harvard University and curator of physical anthropology at the Peabody Museum). And Barry Fell includes in his books many photographs of scholars who supposedly agree with his theories (Fell 1980:6–8, 39–41). The ridicule and scorn cultists heap on the "dogmatic" scholarly Establishment seems to be a psychological defense against rejection by authorities whose approval they desperately would like to have.

This "us against them" stance is a natural outcome of the previously mentioned tendency of cult archaeology to see issues in black and white. It leads pseudoarchaeologists to write as if they were presenting an exposé—"Brave Defender of Truth Reveals Facts Despite Attempted Scholarly Cover-up." When, as predicted, most scholars do reject the fantastic claims (and the insufficient evidence behind them), pseudoscientific archaeologists usually declare that they have been persecuted and proclaim themselves martyrs for truth. Galileo and Einstein frequently are cited as examples of theorists whose ideas were also attacked by their conventional-thinking contemporaries. The parallel, of course, is very inexact. Though regarded as radical by some authorities of the time, the theories of Galileo and Einstein were accepted fairly quickly by their scientific colleagues, for the evidence was on their side. However, it is precisely the faulty nature of the evidence and methodology of cult archaeology which causes it to be opposed by professional scholars.

Two recent instances of "radical" proposals which have won widespread scholarly support disprove claims about the invincibility of scholarly dogma. A couple of decades ago, few geologists supported continental drift, the idea that the continents were floating on the earth's surface and moving away from one another. But today a revised version of that hypothesis, known as plate tectonics, is almost universally accepted by earth scientists. Evidence from a variety of sources, including study of the ocean floors and data from orbiting satellites, indicated that the continents were moving (Hallam 1973). And the recent hypothesis that a massive asteroid or comet impact caused the extinction of the dinosaurs is also an idea which would have found few adherents a generation ago. But more and more earth scientists and paleontologists are accepting that theory today because of physical evidence which seems to support it. Whichever theory best explains the evidence is the one which the majority of scientists will accept. There is no "dogma" which can stand in the way of persuasive evidence. This is a fact which cult archaeologists do not recognize. Their theories are rejected by scholars not simply because they are new or radical; they are rejected because there is little or no valid evidence to support them.

Moreover, the supposed scholarly persecution of pseudoarchaeological theories is not very systematic. While it is true that the views of cult archaeologists are not usually included in university textbooks (but see Williams, this volume), they are well represented on the shelves of almost any bookstore, on television specials, and in movies which favorably present them to the public. This is certainly unlike any censorship or persecution of the past.

But if cult archaeology is so deficient, why is it so popular? Many accept it because to the layman the claims of Immanuel Velikovsky, Erich von Däniken, Barry Fell, and others appear to be accurate and well documented. Those who know little about archaeology, linguistics, and other scholarly disciplines have difficulty recognizing the erroneous nature of supposedly "factual" claims of pseudoscience and pseudoarchaeology. When told that pyramids appeared simultaneously in many areas of the world, that some American Indian tribes speak a Semitic language, or that the Easter Island statues could not have been carved with stone tools, the average person does not recognize immediately that these assertions are false. But such individuals can be educated by reasoned debunking and a nontechnical presentation of the evidence.

On the other hand, the strong emotional attachment some people have for various pseudoscientific theories must have a different explanation. For these individuals it would seem that the unscientific, quasi-religious, anti-Establishment nature of the theories is what is important. Western civilization has a built-in tension between the demands of human reason (derived from our classical Greek heritage) and those of revealed Truth (derived from our Judeo-Christian roots). Just as throughout the ages there have been some who abandoned all religious faith in favor of reason alone, so there have always been those who chose blind belief over the human intellect. Today many people seem to feel that science and reason have failed them. The "knowledge explosion" has not solved the world's problems and produced a utopia. So there is often a favorable reaction to attacks on science and traditional scholarship. Antiscientific and even anti-intellectual movements ranging from traditional biblical Fundamentalism and its recent offspring, "scientific creationism," to astrology and mystical Eastern religions are currently quite popular. And, as we have seen, cult archaeology often fulfills the same psychological needs that these other movements do.

Desire to be part of a community that possesses special knowledge may be bound up with the antiestablishment facet of cult archaeology. Organizations whose members share secret rituals, arcane knowledge, and mystical symbols have long been popular. They supply a sense of belonging, of community identity, that many of their members cannot find elsewhere. In the same way, those who accept cult archaeology become part of a special community. They see themselves as believers in the Truth that dogmatic scholars won't accept. For such individuals, rejection of their favorite theory by the scholarly community is not a problem to be overcome; it is a mark of honor to be borne proudly. It proves that they are part of a small elect persecuted because of their superior insight. Being part of such a community of believers who share a rejected Truth appeals to many, especially when the "persecution" doesn't involve threats to life, limb, or property.

In 1962, Robert Wauchope noted that professionals considered pseudo-archaeologists a danger "only to the extent that their extremely popular writings persuade so many intellectually unwary people that research is simply a process of manipulating facts, intuition, and imagination in approximately equal parts" (Wauchope 1962 : 134). But over the past twenty-five years we academics have done little to make the public less "intellectually unwary" than they were before. During that period, many science, archaeology, and ancient history books have been written for interested laymen, but few of them mention the claims made by cult archaeologists. Most professionals seem to feel that discussing a pseudoscientific theory would make it seem more worthy of serious consideration than it really is.

However, the relative silence of scholars is at least partly responsible for the widespread followings these belief systems attract. In the public's mind, the reluctance of professional scholars to discuss the claims of cult archaeology may be an indication that the specialists cannot disprove these claims and lends credence to charges of Establishment dogmatism. Professional scholars need to heed Cole's advice: "There is a huge public that is more or less open-minded, and it is short-sighted to cede arguments to cultists by ignoring them. . . . If scientific archaeology is shown to have answers to unanswerable challenges, many people will be swayed, including opinion shapers in the mass media" (1980:24).

The movement in a number of states to pass laws requiring the teaching of scientific creationism as well as evolution in science courses in public schools indicates how urgent it is that professional scholars learn to communicate their subject matter and methodology to laymen. Many people see these proposals as a fair way to give students a choice between alternative theories of origins. Suddenly scientists are finding it necessary to explain to the general public (and its representatives in various legislative and judicial bodies) what science is and how its conclusions are reached. For, of course, evolution and creationism are not really comparable—labeling both theories makes them sound more alike than they actually are. The evolution of species is a scientific concept supported by vast amounts of evidence from a variety of fields, including genetics, comparative anatomy, and paleontology. On the other hand, creationism is a religious belief that is not scientific at all. It attempts to make the physical evidence conform to ideas derived from the biblical book of Genesis. To present both theories equally in a classroom would give students a false conception of the scientific method and of the nature of scientific evidence.

Anthropologists, archaeologists, and historians should learn from this controversy over evolution and creationism, for the average person doesn't really understand the methodology of the social sciences either. Laymen think of the past in terms of "facts." By digging in the ground or rummaging through old documents, scholars discover these "facts." But few people understand the details of how this process works. So when a von Däniken or a Barry Fell comes along, announcing the discovery of new and different "facts" about the past based on his own study of ancient myths, strange inscriptions, or archaeological monuments, it is difficult for the average person to judge the validity of the claims.

Professional scholars may not have the time or the inclination to extensively discuss every pseudoarchaeological theory that appears. Nevertheless, we must deal with those which achieve the most widespread popularity or risk having supporters of one or more of these views become politically potent enough to use the state to promote their cause. That surely is a situation which we must resist at all costs (Asimov 1986:214).

If we spent a little more time making our methodology understandable, maybe the public would be able to recognize the problems that characterize cult archaeology without professional help. What is needed are more works written without scholarly jargon that not only describe what is known about the past but also tell how we know it. We need more authors who can communicate scholarly problems to laymen and explain the ways various proposed solutions have been developed. We need to translate some of the spirited debates which take place in our scholarly journals into common English and discuss them in popular magazines so the public can see how foolish the idea of a scholarly conspiracy or dogma actually is. We need more television series like *Nova* and *Odyssey* to show what archaeology is really like, countering the false impression people get from sources such as *Raiders of the Lost Ark*. And we need more emphasis in college classrooms on proper use of written sources and archaeological evidence and on constructing logical arguments.

There will always be some fervent believers in Atlantis, ancient astronauts, or recent cosmic catastrophism, no matter how effectively scholars present the case against such ideas. But perhaps with concerted effort we can reach the majority of the people and make them less intellectually unwary than they have been heretofore. If so, it is to be hoped that cult archaeology will be much less popular in the future.

References

Asimov, Isaac
1986 The perennial fringe. *The Skeptical Inquirer* 10(3):212–214.
Berlitz, Charles
1975 *The Mystery of Atlantis.* New York: Avon Books.
Carroll, Michael
1977 Of Atlantis and ancient astronauts: A structural study of two modern myths. *Journal of Popular Culture* 11:541–550.
Cole, John R.
1980 Cult archaeology and unscientific method and theory. In Michael B. Schiffer, ed., *Advances in Archaeological Method and Theory,* vol. 3, pp. 1-33. New York: Academic Press.
Davies, Nigel
1979 *Voyagers to the New World.* New York: William Morrow.
Donnelly, Ignatius
1882 *Atlantis: The Antediluvian World.* Modern revised edition (1949). New York: Harper.
Feder, Kenneth L.
1980 Psychic archaeology: The anatomy of irrationalist prehistoric studies. *The Skeptical Inquirer* 4(4):32–43.

2.

Scientific Creationism: World View, not Science

Alice B. Kehoe

Science and religion are popularly opposed, though for some they are complementary means to understanding our world, and for others they represent dire conflict between Truth and Error. There is in fact a very broad middle ground between empirical science and pure spiritual revelation, a middle ground broad enough to contain both Albert Einstein and the Reverend Jerry Falwell. Because the middle ground is the playground for unspoken premises, for slogans and social labels, for politically framed agendas and maneuvers, it is the arena in which debates are waged and brickbats thrown. To understand the attacks, flurries, and crusades, we must disentangle the expedient groupings and analyze what the clichés signify. Only fools think it is easy to separate the benighted from the enlightened.

One contemporary American movement illustrates very well the real questions and the real political threat thrashing about in that middle ground between replicated empirical observations and wholly personal orgastic visitations of divine light. Scientific creationists claim to be able to scientifically support statements in the King James English Bible, which they believe to have been dictated by God. This would be merely curious if it were not part of the credo of a political movement that advocates measures many opponents consider unconstitutional and policies tending to harden international hostilities. The movement hinders the emancipation of women from traditional constraints and fosters a pessimistic view of human nature that some followers interpret to justify harsh treatment of children and the indigent. Rooted in a cultural tradition that has already persisted for millennia, the Fundamentalist Protestant Christian political movement, including scientific creationism, will not melt away under simple pronouncements that it isn't scientific.

Argument of Scientific Creationism

Scientific creationists are, for the most part, conservative Protestant Christians who assert that there are no discrepancies between scriptural statements and reasonable scientific interpretations of geological, paleontological, physical, and biological data. They also assert that their belief in a supernatural Creator who worked as recorded in Scripture is not incompatible with scientific explanation.

By no means are all persons who believe that the God of the Old Testament created the world scientific creationists. The great majority of Christians and Jews are most comfortable with the position of theistic evolution, that God set in motion the processes described by mainstream science, among them biological evolution and the physical and geological effects of several billions of years. Theistic evolutionists usually also accept scholarly analyses of the sources and history of the Bible as legitimate aids to better understanding of its spiritual teachings and see the canonical Bible as essentially a set of human documents, although blessed with a wealth of passages of divine inspiration or revelation.

In addition to theistic evolutionists, there are persons who believe the God of the Old Testament created the world but are unconcerned with scientific discussions of paleontological or geological data. In other words, most Jews and Christians are creationists in the sense that they accept the attribution of the origin of the world to the will of the God of the Old Testament, but this faith does not mean rejection of the principle of evolution, of an earth billions of years old, or of the explanations developed by mainstream biologists, geologists, physicists, paleontologists, and anthropologists. The majority of Christians and Jews either have no problem reconciling the Bible with mainstream science or have no problem maintaining two systems of knowledge, religious and secular.

Scientific creationists insist that the Book of Genesis is a recitation of events that happened just as described in the King James translation and is entirely compatible with scientific interpretations of observational data. To make this claim, they define science as "knowledge." Henry M. Morris, leader of the contemporary "creation movement," as he has termed it, asked, "Whoever decided that 'science' should be defined as 'naturalism,' anyway?" He countered, "The word *science* comes from the Latin *scientia*, meaning 'knowledge.' True scientists are supposed to 'search for truth,' wherever that search leads . . . It is inexcusable for evolutionists (whether they are atheistic evolutionists or 'theistic' evolutionists) to arbitrarily exclude even the consideration of special creation as a scientific model from public institutions, when it might well be *true*, and therefore profoundly and perfectly scientific" (Morris 1982:23–24; his italics). Morris' etymology is correct, but the *Oxford English Dictionary* says that to define science as knowledge is archaic. Modern usage, says the OED, considers science "systematic and formulated knowledge . . . , pursuit of this or principles regulating such pursuit." "Truth" does not enter into these definitions. (For a glimpse of the thorny thicket philosophers of science thrash about in discussing the question of truth, see Suppe 1977:262–263, 642–643, etc.)

Mainstream science is not a search for "truth" but the proposal and testing of hypotheses that seem in accordance with empirical observations. Scientists are not so arrogant as to think they can discover truth; several decades of work in the history and philosophy of science have demonstrated the influence of traditional cultural biases on scientists' interpretations (for example, Kuhn 1962; Laudan 1983:13; Levi 1974). What scientists hope to achieve are valid theories, explanatory constructions well grounded in empirical observations others can replicate and free from apparent (or at least inexplicable) contradictions. Theories are constructed, not discovered; they are not lying around out there like fruit fallen from Newton's apple tree. Ideally, a theory is parsimonious in using a few terms to explain a great deal of data and is elegantly written; realistically, theories are acceptable if they clearly are built from tested hypotheses presented in such a manner that they are falsifiable; that is, a test to disprove the hypothesis is offered or easily inferred. Two basic requirements of science are that (1) the scientist has no *a priori* commitment to any particular explanation before working to explain the data collected, and (2) there is no recourse to absolutely unique or nonmaterial factors for the explanation. Who decided that science should be "naturalism"? A very large number of thinkers over several centuries who realized that some questions are amenable to investigation on principles of naturalism while other questions are not. The former set of questions has been assigned to science, the latter to philosophy and theology.

Henry Morris states, "It is precisely because Biblical revelation is absolutely authoritative and perspicuous that the scientific *facts*, rightly interpreted, will give the same testimony as that of Scripture. There is not the slightest possibility that the facts of science can contradict the Bible"

(1974:15; his italics). Morris and his fellow creationists are committed to an *a priori* explanation before they begin to study data: there is "not the slightest possibility" of contradicting statements in the Bible. Morris points out that "by its very essence, true creation involves processes no longer in operation" (1982:12). This statement removes the study of "true creation" from the domain of science, because science can only proceed from studies of present processes. George Gaylord Simpson, the doyen of twentieth-century paleontology, explained in a magisterial review,

Interpretation of the past involves confrontation of its record and of comparisons of its present results with knowledge of relevant processes. The general procedure of historical research has three phases: (1) obtaining and ordering historical data [by "historical," Simpson means geological, paleontological, and astronomical data resulting from events in the past]; (2) determining present processes; (3) confronting (1) and (2). The result is largely retrodictive . . . Retrodictive interpretation and explanation are almost unique to the historical sciences, astrohistory, geohistory, and biohistory, and are not characteristic of science in general. They require application of uniformitarian principles. (Simpson 1970:90–91)

Simpson also commented on naturalism: "Naturalism is a basic postulate of science as now almost always construed, a necessity of method and procedure in science regardless of what theological or philosophical stand may be taken on it. If only on heuristic grounds, scientific explanation must not invoke the supernatural, non-natural, noumenal, or any other preternatural factor" (Simpson 1970:61).

Henry Morris and his colleagues differ from mainstream scientists in their conception of what science permits as science. Philosopher of science Larry Laudan concluded a discussion over how to recognize "pseudo-science" as contrasted with "real science," saying that "the problem of demarcation between science and non-science is a pseudo-problem (at least as far as philosophy is concerned). I am manifestly not denying that there are crucial epistemic and methodological questions to be raised about knowledge claims, whether we classify them as scientific or not . . . Ask questions like: when is a claim well-confirmed; when can we regard a theory as well-tested; what characterizes cognitive progress?" (Laudan 1983:29).

In other words, *all* claims to knowledge should be supported ("confirmed") by clearly stated grounds for confidence, and there should be careful consideration over whether claims to knowledge are mere repetitions of dogma or truly helpful in deepening our understanding. Mainstream science is naturalistic and uniformitarian (that is, repeatable, not unique, singular events are looked for) because accepting these constraints has strengthened efforts to find strong confirmation and heuristic fertility in scientific research. To abandon these constraints would set us back in the medieval period fruitlessly pursuing issues that are simply beyond contemporary human capability to resolve by empirical investigation. The issue of First Cause, Simpson remarked (1970:61), is by consensus of scientists one of these issues beyond our methodologies. Morris and other scientific creationists insist on a concept of the domain of science like that of medieval times, when theology and philosophy were classed as sciences; that is, on the archaic definition of science as knowledge. The real question is, why do these reasonably intelligent and well-read persons reject the contemporary mainstream view of the domain of science?

Roots of Scientific Creationism

Scientific creationism and creation research are promoted by a number of persons who are members of conservative Protestant Christian churches. As they frequently affirm, scientific creationism is not directly tied to Christian faith. A creationist need only believe in a Creator; it need not be the God of the Old Testament and, conversely, a creationist who believes that the Creator is the God of the Old Testament needs no scientific support for that faith. (This alleged independence of biblical from scientific creationism is the basis for the movement to require the public schools to teach the "Creation Model" as well as biological evolution.) However independent the two varieties of creationism may appear to be, it is a fact that the Creation Research Society was founded in 1963 by ten men who openly witnessed their allegiance to "Jesus Christ as Lord and Savior" and to faith that the "Holy Scriptures are the inspired Word of God." All who wish to join the Creation Research Society must sign assent to the description of the society as "an organization of Christian men of science, who accept . . . that salvation can come only through accepting Jesus Christ as our Savior." It is a fact that Henry M. Morris was for some years, until 1980, president of Christian Heritage College (San Diego, California), leaving that post to direct the Institute for Creation Research, described as the research division of the college. Bob Jones University of Greenville, South Carolina, perhaps the leading strict Fundamentalist college, actively fosters scientific creationism both on and off campus. Not all scientific creationists are conservative Protestant Christians, but the majority are.

Scientific creationism descends from the historic Christian concept that

God can be glimpsed through his works. Eighteenth-century Christians suggested that God has revealed himself in two media, the Holy Bible and the Book of Nature. Theologians and scientists were reading two books by the same author. One problem much discussed in the eighteenth century was the disagreement among philosophers over the proper method for discovering truth. Thomas Reid, a Scottish philosopher, urged the use of what he called the Baconian method, from Francis Bacon's writings, of empirical observations from which general laws could be inferred by induction. Reid hoped that empirical orientation would produce confirmable (that is, scientific) understanding of God's world, a set of First Principles on which this world was created and according to which it ought to operate. Once the First Principles became known, people could build social institutions and a moral code conforming to God's design. Reid's "Scottish Realism" contrasted with the purely intellectual deductive logic indulged in by some of his competitors. Scottish Realism was carried into the nineteenth century by Reid's disciple, Dugald Stewart.

Many Scots emigrated to the United States, and among them were educated men, quite a few of them Presbyterian ministers familiar with Scottish Realism. This philosophy's emphasis on empirical observation to discover First Principles was peculiarly congruent with an aspect of nineteenth-century American engineering and industrial development that at the time was called the American system of analyzing processes and products to distinguish necessary components from mere customary embellishments or ornamentation. Stripped-down but highly serviceable processes and products could be sold cheaply to the mass market, enriching entrepreneurs. The European system, by contrast, kept fine craftsmanship and elaborate ornamentation, thereby restricting its market to the rich. The contrast had strong political overtones of participatory democracy versus a class system that suppressed the workers. Scottish Realism was the philosophy preferred by leading American Presbyterians, whose followers made up the influential bourgeoisie of America outside of New England. Princeton College was the fountainhead of wisdom for this class, and it was staunchly Presbyterian.

Early in the twentieth century, conflicts between liberal and conservative Presbyterians forced the 1910 Presbyterian General Assembly to bring debate to a head. The assembly defined five fundamentals of orthodox Protestant Christianity: that Christ really performed miracles, that he was born of a virgin, that he was bodily resurrected, that his sacrifice on the cross has atoned for human sin, and that the Bible is the "inerrant" Word of God. (Note that "inerrant" means "without error"; it can be construed somewhat broadly to allow, for example, seeing Genesis as a myth telling spiritual, although not literally factual, truth.) Wealthy laymen popularized these fundamentals through a series of booklets distributed free in enormous quantities. A Fundamentalist expresses faith that these five miracles really occurred; the first four obviously are the core of the Christian message of salvation, and the fifth serves to validate that message. Millions of Christians are Fundamentalists insofar as they profess this faith. Some of these Fundamentalists are convinced that it is not enough to accept that the messages of Scripture are essentially true; conservative Fundamentalists reject critiques distinguishing secular legends, history, elements from pagan myths, mistranslations, and copyists' errors and claim that the entire canonical Bible must be literally true—or, more precisely, that "when the plain sense makes common sense, we seek no other sense," as an independent Baptist pastor phrased it in an interview with me. "Commonsense Realism" is a label applied to the nineteenth-century American version of Reid and Stewart's Scottish Realism, to the dominant philosophy of Princeton College and its Presbyterian associates. Commonsense Realism's modern child is scientific creationism, the philosophy that promotes the Book of Nature as the alternate form of Scripture, open to all to read through Baconian science, the methodology emphasizing empirical observations. True to its eighteenth-century origins, scientific creationism allows *a priori* statements to exist unchallenged (the most familiar example of this eighteenth-century habit is Thomas Jefferson's "We hold these truths to be self-evident . . ."). Scientific creationism is not pseudoscience, but an archaic out-dated version of science.

World View of the Scientific Creationists

More than an archaic conception of sciences is involved in scientific creationism. Its most zealous promoters are truly evangelists who have accepted what they call the "Great Commission" to "go into the whole world and preach the gospel" (Mark 16:15). In common with those other conservative evangelists whose coalitions and parallel movements have been dubbed the New Religious-Political Right, the leaders of scientific creationism see the world as the battleground between the forces of evil, led by Satan, and the forces of God. The favorite theologian of many of the conservative evangelists is the late Francis A. Schaeffer, who wrote, "There really are such things as absolutes . . . in the area of Being (or knowledge), and in the area of morals . . . Absolutes imply antithesis . . . right or wrong . . . true and false . . . Historic Christianity stands on the basis of antithesis" (Schaeffer 1968:14–15). Out of this world view, this perception of the world consisting of antitheses, comes the statement by Henry M. Morris, "There are only two possible ultimate world views—evolutionism or creationism" (1982:30).

A world of absolute right or wrong has no place for evolutionary change: everything is as it is, subject at most to minor variation. When the scientific creationists argue that evolution cannot "be either confirmed or falsified by the scientific method, since neither [evolution nor creationism] can be tested or observed experimentally" (Morris 1982:9), they reject the wealth of data confirming evolution from experiments on fruit flies and microorganisms; that is, on short-lived species whose generations pass rapidly under human observers' eyes. This rejection is the result of the world view structured on antithesis, on either/or, the world view that categorizes small changes as "variation." What Morris and his colleagues demand as possible evidence for evolution are "transitional or incipient structures, such as half-scales/half-feathers on reptiles/birds" (Morris 1982:28), but they should know that it is unlikely genes could work that way. Actual transitional species (and all species are basically transitional, since all species have, from the point of view of evolution, evolved from another and are probably going to give rise to yet others) cannot exist in the extreme creationists' world because the creationists will classify them into one or another species. Data are, literally, "givens," and it is what one does with the givens that constitutes "facts" (the word "fact" is derived from the Latin *facere*, "do"). The *a priori* commitment by scientific creationists to the premise of special creation of each "kind" (their usual term) of organism by God channels all their observations into already-fixed categories; their premise that this creation occurred only once in the past precludes them from creating, as it were, new categories for data. Bound by their acceptance of the position that the world has a fixed structure that will endure until the final apocalypse, conservative Fundamentalist Protestants, including most scientific creationists, cannot abandon the notion of fixity of species because their world view of absolutes and antitheses ties fixity of moral standards to the general principle of fixity. "Satan himself is the originator of the concept of evolution," says Henry Morris (1975:75), so for Morris to resist the concept of evolution is to resist evil. Archaic "science" encompassed moral as well as material investigations.

Scientific Creationism Compared to Cult Archaeology

A tendency to set up antitheses bedevils more than conservative Protestants. Mainstream scientists sometimes assign all maverick or opposing claims to science to the trashbasket labeled pseudoscience. This easy action masks the important differences between ideas that are poor science in being poorly confirmed (for example, parakinetics or astrology) but are politically inconsequential, and ideas that, like scientific creationism, are the tip of an iceberg mass of premises and principles threatening to sink the constitutionally-based structure of American society. Between merely entertaining charlatans on the one hand and political movements within the New Religious-Political Right on the other are more or less openly racist groups who denigrate American Indians, or non-European peoples in general, by supporting the notions that these peoples could not have produced great monuments or art or science and that such achievements found in their homelands must have been the work of Europeans (Barry Fell's "Celto-Iberians," for example) or extraterrestrials (for example, von Däniken's "gods"). A willingness to suppose that Lord Pacal of Palenque, as pictured on the lid of his own sarcophagus, was not a Maya king but an ancient astronaut is insulting to the Maya but unlikely to spur maneuvers in Congress.

Scientists properly expose ill-founded, ill-confirmed interpretations within mainstream science or in pseudoscience. Archaeologists should marshal all they have learned about Lord Pacal and his kingdom (which is considerable) or about Colonial/nineteenth-century versus prehistoric stone constructions in New England, or about petroglyphs and historic graffiti on rocks and present the information in popular publications. Some readers will gladly learn the professional archaeologists' interpretations; some will adamantly refuse to discard their racist stereotypes, painting their own ancestors as superior to others; some will continue to hold everything to do with prehistory as no more than leisure-reading trivia. Professionals have an obligation as scientists, and to the public that supports them through taxes and foundations, to make the best-founded opinions accessible. Yet scientists do not, should not, must not have dictatorial powers to blot out differing opinions, however poorly founded.

Scientific creationists are part of a movement that seeks to establish through governmental policies a particular religious doctrine contrary to the principles of the United States Constitution. The movement is strongly authoritarian, patriarchal, militaristic, and opposed to public support of social welfare programs. This New Religious-Political Right represents not just a disagreement about scientific interpretations but a serious effort to buttress the economic and political power of the traditional American bourgeoisie. The debate over evolution versus creation is at once a side effect of the movement's world view of antitheses and a means of identifying those who will follow authority in the movement. To put one's signature to a declaration that one accepts on faith the "absolute inerrancy of the Bible" is public witness of one's willing submission to authority. Nothing scientists outside the movement can say can change the minds of those who have declared their *a priori* commitment to "Biblical revelation [as] absolutely authoritative." Scientists who feel compelled to challenge the movement must look to the political arena.

Conclusion

Henry Morris himself sums up "creation and evolution. Each model is essentially a complete world view, a philosophy of life and meaning, of origins and destiny" (1982:9). It is this holistic commitment that distinguishes scientific creationism from most cult archaeology and other pseudoscience followings. Though few mainstream scientists think, as scientists, much about philosophy of life and meaning, not to mention "destiny," the scientific creationists will have nothing less. In their world of antitheses, the eternal fate of their, and our, very souls depends upon choices between Satan and God. Their world has no place for compromise. Citizens who disagree with the conservative New Religious-Political Right, including scientific creationists, must realize that it is not a controversy over good science versus pseudoscience, but over, as Morris tells us, complete world views.

References

Kuhn, Thomas S.
1962 *The Structure of Scientific Revolutions.* Chicago: University of Chicago Press.
Laudan, Larry
1983 The demise of the demarcation problem. In Rachel Laudan, ed., *The Demarcation between Science and Pseudo-science*, pp. 7–35. Blacksburg: Center for the Study of Science in Society, Virginia Polytechnic Institute and State University.
Levi, Albert William
1974 *Philosophy as Social Expression.* Chicago: University of Chicago Press.
Morris, Henry M.
1974 *Scientific Creationism.* San Diego: Creation-Life Publishers.
1975 *The Troubled Waters of Evolution.* San Diego: Creation-Life Publishers.
1982 *Creation and Its Critics.* San Diego: Creation-Life Publishers.
Schaeffer, Francis A.
1968 *The God Who Is There.* Downers Grove, Ill.: Inter-Varsity Press.
Simpson, George Gaylord
1970 Uniformitarianism: An inquiry into principle, theory, and method in geohistory and biohistory. In Max K. Hecht and William C. Steere, eds., *Essays in Evolution and Genetics in Honor of Theodosius Dobzhansky*, pp. 43–96. New York: Appleton-Century-Crofts.
Suppe, Frederick
1977 *The Structure of Scientific Theories.* 2nd ed. Urbana: University of Illinois Press.

3.

Educational Experience and Belief in Paranormal Phenomena

Thomas Gray

Recent national poll results, many of the other contributions to this volume, and recent research findings (for example, Gray 1985) indicate that surprisingly high percentages of people believe in phenomena for which there is no evidence that would meet generally acceptable criteria of trustworthiness. Why?

Belief in various paranormal phenomena has spread into all areas of life. Businessmen have become embroiled in suits brought by psychic advisors trying to collect unpaid fees; some police forces have apparently followed the advice of psychic detectives; psychic archaeologists promise quick location of artifacts (do they have friends who can psychokinetically remove sand and rocks?); some physicists are prepared to talk about conscious decision making on the part of subatomic particles, and I know of an accredited psychologist who consults a palmist for advice. Why do so many otherwise generally sensible people believe in such unsubstantiated claims? There is no easy answer to this question. Essentially circular answers such as "people have a need to believe" or, as one student extravagantly phrased it, "paranormal belief is a product of man's insatiable desire to believe in the unknown," are clearly question begging and not very useful.

There is now a large scientific literature concerned with the way humans reason and make judgments. Flaws in the application of what are considered to be elementary probability rules and failures to take crucial information into account (for example, too much reliance on confirmatory instances—single occurrences which seem to confirm one's beliefs) are well documented (see, for example, Jenkins and Ward 1965; Kahneman and Tversky 1973; Nisbett and Ross 1980; Tversky and Kahneman 1983). There appears, for instance, to be too much reliance by people on only confirmatory instances that fit in with previously conceived ideas. Although the research has tended to concentrate on fully documenting the kinds of reasoning errors and the nature of the more intuitive, everyday, nonstatistical heuristics (aids to problem solving and decision making) that subjects do use, some researchers have also been concerned with finding ways to remedy the situation. Recent reports indicate, for example, that formal training increases the use made of statistical heuristics (Nisbett et al. 1983). As will become clearer, I believe that the problem is more fundamental than the misuse or avoidance of either formal or informal heuristics.

The guiding hypothesis in this preliminary research involved the assumption that people, at least in part, believe in what we know to be scientifically unsubstantiated claims because they are ignorant of what constitutes good versus bad evidence. They believe because they think they have evidence to support their beliefs. I believe that the problem is much more fundamental than a failure to use the statistically sound heuristics that were mentioned above in connection with the work of other researchers. The majority of people, including those attending colleges, do not even know of the existence of such heuristics. Although it may be the case, as Nisbett et al. (1983) claim, that some statistical understanding is part of an individual's intuitive equipment, it is also the case that very few people ever get even the most rudimentary exposure to basic principles of research methodology that might help them assess the reliability of information they are given. Most people do not know anything about the unreliability of eye-witness testimony or how our perceptions and memories are subject to distortion from our preconceptions and expectations. Few possess the necessary information about motion parallax to correctly interpret distant, apparently stationary, bright lights in a featureless night sky as a distant jet approaching for a landing. How many, for example, know why the full moon seems so much larger on the horizon than at its zenith? How many are aware of the research that discounts various physical explanations and strongly supports the notion that its huge appearance is an optical illusion?

I have argued, then, that part of the reason why people believe in paranormal phenomena is because they do not know that the "evidence" they have is poor. They have not learned to automatically think of questions to raise that would help them check the reliability of reports, such as those of sightings of UFOs or ghosts, and they have not been introduced to alternative, nonparanormal explanations. Following such arguments would lead to the prediction that people would tend to believe less in paranormal phenomena to the extent that they were more sophisticated in assessing the reliability of information. We would certainly be led to suppose, for example, that university students who had taken courses specifically dealing with research methodology and statistical analysis would be more sensitive than others to the quality of the evidence with which they were presented as documentation for supposed paranormal events. We might expect that just going through three years of university, an experience which presumably is supposed to hone critical abilities, would decrease willingness to endorse poorly supported claims. Would we not predict that students specifically trained in scientific areas would be especially skeptical of claims about events that contradict otherwise well-established natural laws?

What I have to report is not, in general, good news. I will show results of surveys that assess levels of belief in students with different backgrounds; namely, natural science, social science (psychology), and humanities (English). The results will be disconcerting to those who, like myself, expected to see dramatic differences in the level of belief in the paranormal as a function of university experience.

The Surveys of Student Belief

The questionnaires used were quite simple. Students were asked to indicate the strength of their belief in each of ten phenomena. The phenomena were presented on a single page and respondents could indicate the strength of their belief by checking one of four levels of yes or no. A 1 indicated a weak response while a 4 indicated a strong response. Subjects could then indicate the intensity of either their yes or no responses.

For the sake of brevity and simplicity I will present here only the data showing the percentages of the respondents who checked the yes categories. Analyses on the data that take into account the strength of the yes do not lead to any different overall conclusions, but they do allow for a finer-grained analysis. I will mention the results of these analyses where appropriate.

I will present only the data for the following five phenomena: ESP (for example, telepathy and clairvoyance), UFOs (extraterrestrial spacecraft), astrology (the supposed effect of the position of the planets at birth on our lives), reincarnation, and von Däniken's theory of extraterrestrial intervention in Earth history. I also surveyed belief in ghosts, the Bermuda Triangle, psychic healing, miracles, and biorhythms. Overall levels of belief in the latter five phenomena were quite high, ranging from about 40 percent checking yes to ghosts to about 55 percent checking yes to miracles and biorhythms.

Responses to the questionnaire were anonymous. The students were asked only to indicate their sex, their program of concentration, and the number of credits they had completed at the university. The questionnaire took only about ten minutes to describe and administer. It was emphasized that we were interested in whether they believed in the reality of the phenomena, not merely the theoretical possibility. The surveys were done in the various classes (respondents were therefore not self-selecting). Over the course of very many surveys only two students declined to take part. One student simply said, "I don't want to do it" and another refused to participate because I would not engage with him in a detailed discussion of what I meant by a "ghost."

All of the surveys reported here involved students at Concordia University in Montreal, Quebec, Canada. Concordia is a very large, English-language, urban university with undergraduate and graduate programs in the usual areas.

It is important to note that in the province of Quebec students enter a three-year undergraduate program after two years of collegial studies. At the collegial level students follow either a science profile or a humanities profile. The students who have completed the science profile have done a number of one-semester science courses—three physics, two chemistry, two biology, and calculus I and II. Students in the humanities stream have usually had no science since high school. In order to enter a university program leading to a bachelor of science degree, students must have completed the science profile at the collegial level. Psychology students typically enroll in the bachelor of arts program and hence have not completed the collegial science program. However, in contrast to the humanities students, psychology students have done collegial math (at least precalculus functions) and collegial biology.

Students were surveyed in first-year courses or in third-year courses in biology and chemistry, English literature, and psychology. I refer to the different samples as introductory versus advanced. The advanced students in the natural science courses (biology or chemistry) and the humanities courses (English) were completing their final-year credits, while the introductory students were still completing first-year credits. The professors teaching the various courses in biology, chemistry, English, and psychology were very cooperative in allowing access to their classes to present the questionnaire.

In the case of the social science (psychology) samples, the distinction between introductory and advanced was made in terms of whether the students had completed their required research methods and statistics courses. These methodology courses are required of all students in their first year and must be completed before students can take upper-level courses.

In summary, then, I am presenting results of surveys from students who were early or late in their undergraduate programs, and I am looking at students who differ markedly in their scientific sophistication. With regard to the advanced psychology samples, we are dealing with students who have been specifically acquainted with problems concerning evidence collection and how to avoid erroneous conclusions. These students are supposed to specifically learn how to take a critical approach to the information they encounter.

Overall Levels of Belief

Figure 1 presents the overall data showing the percentage of more than four hundred respondents who were willing to say yes to belief in the various phenomena. These average levels are representative of most of the different subsamples (that is, the different classrooms) that were surveyed. Belief in ESP always appears as the most frequently endorsed phenomenon. Clearly, skeptics are in the minority. Perhaps the good news

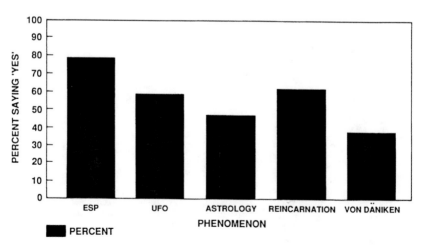

FIGURE 1. Overall percentage of respondents endorsing belief in the phenomena.

here for readers who are mostly concerned with paranormal beliefs that are related to history and archaeology is the finding that belief in von Däniken's theories of extraterrestrial intervention in Earth history is relatively low. Only about 40 percent of the students in a modern urban institute of higher learning are willing to endorse ideas such as the ancient Egyptians built the pyramids only with the help of spacepersons. A large majority of the respondents have no problem believing that thought transmission and clairvoyance can take place.

The total sample of 419 respondents breaks down into 241 males and 178 females. There were 166 from the natural sciences, 151 from psychology, and 102 from the humanities (English).

The Effect of Three Years of University

Does going through three years of university have an effect on the willingness to endorse such beliefs? I think the answer is self-evident from Figure 2, which presents overall findings concerning the differences between first-year and final-year students. The small differences between the introductory and the advanced levels are not statistically reliable. Figure 3, which presents a slightly more detailed analysis showing the effects of field of study (discipline) and university level for each of the five phenomena, is hardly any more encouraging. The only statistically reliable difference between advanced and introductory levels was obtained for the psychology students' belief in ESP. However, it should be noted that 72

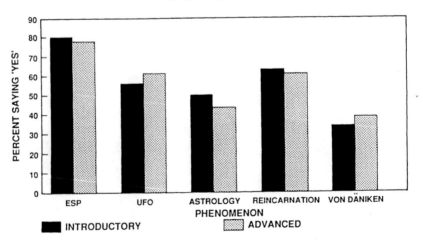

FIGURE 2. Percentage of believers as a function of university level.

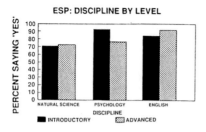

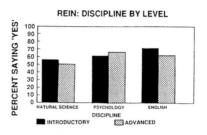

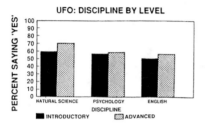

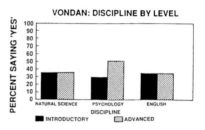

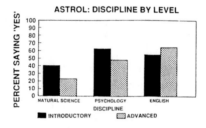

FIGURE 3. Percentage of believers in each phenomenon as a function of area of study (discipline) and university level. (ASTROL = astrology, REIN = reincarnation, VONDAN = von Däniken's "ancient astronauts.")

percent of psychology students who have had courses in social science methodology and statistics still believe in ESP.

Examination of Figure 3 also shows that in general the lowest levels of belief are to be found in the sample of students in natural science. These are the students who have completed a science profile at the collegial level before entering the university. A notable exception to the generally lower levels of belief for this group is in connection with UFOs—the science students, particularly males, more often endorse belief in UFOs as extraterrestrial spacecraft.

An overall analysis taking gender into account is presented in Figure 4. The differences between males and females were statistically reliable for ESP, UFOs, astrology, and reincarnation. Notice that the percentage say-

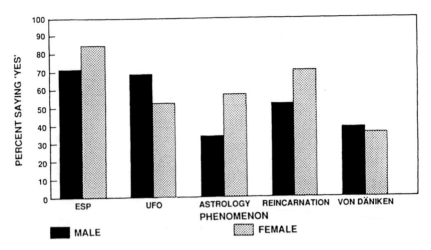

GENDER DIFFERENCES (N=419)

PERCENT SAYING 'YES'

ESP   UFO   ASTROLOGY   REINCARNATION   VON DÄNIKEN
PHENOMENON

■ MALE   ▦ FEMALE

FIGURE 4. Overall percentage of believers among male and female respondents.

ing yes is reliably higher for males in the case of UFOs. Figure 5 presents the gender differences separately for each of the academic areas. I want to emphasize that I am not presenting these male versus female differences as sex differences. I suspect that the consistent differences that are found (for example, the higher male belief in UFOs as spaceships) are possibly the result of different reading and viewing preferences. I hope soon to begin a study that will be looking at belief in paranormal phenomena in young children, but at the moment I don't know how early these gender differences appear.

Do They Really Believe?

I am often asked if the respondents really believe in the phenomena. It is clear that they are not merely saying yes to all of the phenomena so as to appear open-minded, because there are large differences in the percentages saying yes to various phenomena. I have also obtained survey results from questionnaires that included a fictional phenomenon. Only 19 percent of a class of advanced psychology students were willing to believe in "Lyman Harper's magnetic resonance theory of pre-cognitive ability," a theory which does not exist. The lowest level of yes for a "real" phenomenon was obtained from male natural science students with regard to astrology—only 25 percent of this group checked yes.

Perhaps more compelling evidence concerning the reality of the stu-

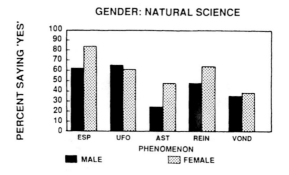

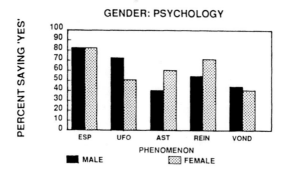

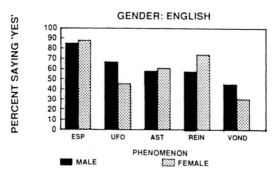

FIGURE 5. Male versus female response patterns for students in the different university disciplines.

dents' beliefs is portrayed in Figure 6. Do the respondents think there is good evidence for the beliefs they endorse? Instead of asking students to indicate their belief I asked a sample of psychology students "how good do you think the evidence is for . . ." Respondents could indicate o meaning no evidence, or 1, 2, 3, or 4. They were instructed that a 1 meant some

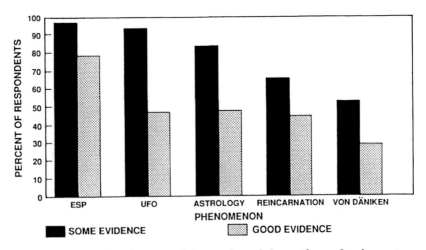

FIGURE 6. Respondents' rating of the quality of the evidence for the various phenomena.

evidence, 2 meant good evidence, and 3 and 4 correspondingly stronger evidence. It is clear from Figure 6 that the respondents believe that there is evidence for the phenomena. Almost 80 percent think that the evidence for ESP is good or better. These findings are consistent with the idea that people believe because they think there is evidence for the reality of the phenomena.

I think it is clear that students do not in general leave university more skeptical about claims of paranormal phenomena. Even the social science research methodology and statistics that are part of the training for psychology students do not seem to have much impact. Perhaps, however, a university course that specifically dealt with the reliability of the evidence for paranormal phenomena would be more effective in reducing the students' willingness to endorse belief in unsubstantiated phenomena.

The Effects of a Specific Intervention

My own interest in belief in unsubstantiated phenomena began in connection with my teaching of an introductory-level course that introduced students to general principles of what constitutes good versus bad (unreliable) evidence. The course, which stressed what I call the "control-group-way-of-thinking," attempted to improve the students' ability to assess the reliability of the information they receive. The control-group-way-of-thinking stresses the need to always ask questions that will help to rule out alternate explanations. In the context of belief in the paranormal the students are encouraged, for example, to consider whether a particular supposedly paranormal phenomenon could be a chance or coincidental event. The course drew attention to certain basic principles of evidence collection and critical thinking that would allow them to be better able to discriminate sound claims from mere propaganda. Most of the examples used in the course involved what are commonly called paranormal phenomena; for example, ESP, astrology, UFOs, reincarnation, and the like.

I was understandably interested in whether students who had taken my course were less willing to endorse belief in various paranormal phenomena. The results of a properly controlled study of the changes that occurred in the students' beliefs have been reported elsewhere (Gray 1985), but Figure 7 here summarizes the general nature of some of the results. The figure shows data for the same five phenomena that were discussed earlier. The study was basically the same as described earlier but involved students who were enrolled in my course called "The Science and Pseudoscience of Paranormal Phenomena."

Students were asked to fill in a simple questionnaire that allowed them to indicate no (don't believe) or yes (do believe). They could also indicate

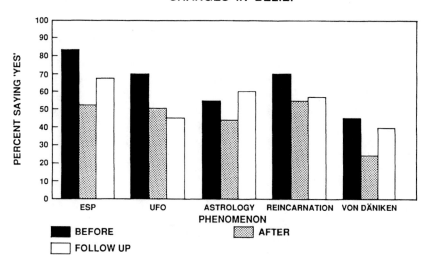

FIGURE 7. Changes in percentage of students expressing belief as a result of a university course specifically addressing the issue of belief in paranormal phenomena. The follow-up was conducted one year after the end of the course.

the strength of their belief by checking a 1 (weak yes), 2, 3, or 4 (strong yes). I have shown here the percentage of students checking yes. The figure summarizes findings from three successive classes (1981–83), each of which had about thirty-three students. The questionnaire was given at the beginning of the semester, at the end of the semester, and, for two of the samples, by telephone one year later. The five phenomena I have presented here are ESP, UFOs, astrology, reincarnation, and von Däniken. The respondents were told that we were interested in whether they believed in the reality of these phenomena, not merely their theoretical possibility.

There were statistically significant decreases in the percent saying yes at the end of the semester, but clearly the immediate gains dissipated (except in the case of UFOs) over the course of the year the students spent back in the generally proparanormal environment. There were no decreases over the course of the semester in the percentages checking yes for students who were enrolled in control groups taken from two other university classes that were not concerned with belief in the paranormal.

Although the percentage of believers was lower at the end of the course, there were many students who still believed in the reality of some of the phenomena. Half the class, even immediately after a course with content specifically aimed at "debunking," still claim to believe in ESP. It was not the case that the students disliked the course. The results of routine, anonymous course evaluations showed that students liked the course and professor a lot and found the course informative and interesting. The drift back toward precourse levels of belief was substantial in the case of ESP, but the percentage saying yes was still statistically significantly lower than originally even after the one-year interval.

The finding that a course specifically dealing with evidence for the paranormal has only modest and not very durable effects on beliefs makes it less surprising that a more general university education has virtually no effect. It does not, however, make me more comfortable with what appears to be a failing in our attempts to improve students' critical abilities.

Conclusion

The overall picture that I have briefly presented is not encouraging, but there is some evidence that the stronger the students' background in science the lower the levels of belief. This has to be qualified for the female samples and it does not apply to UFOs. Three years of university does not in general produce more skepticism with regard to belief in unsubstantiated phenomena. I was surprised that there was not a dramatic drop in levels of belief on the part of the psychology students as a result of the emphasis we place on methodology and statistical analysis in the domain of evidence collection.

It appears that to bring about moderate changes in paranormal beliefs we have to specifically address the particular claims in question. Even with such specific efforts (see Figure 7) the effects of the intervention are not permanent. General training in how to collect and evaluate data does not seem to produce people who automatically ask the appropriate questions to evaluate the information and so-called evidence with which they are presented.

The lessons of the laboratory and lecture hall are not carried over to the "real world." I have other preliminary data which I have not presented here which show that even sophisticated, final-year honors students have not incorporated what I call the control-group-way-of-thinking into their cognitive armamentarium. They are still swayed by individual, personally compelling occurrences that fit their preconceptions. The power of the single confirmatory instance still seems to far outweigh disconfirmations.

I am afraid that the occasions when a "psychic archaeologist" says "dig there" and an artifact is uncovered will stay in people's minds. The unsuccessful attempts, as you know, rarely make the news.

References

Gray, T.

1985 Changing unsubstantiated belief: Testing the ignorance hypothesis. *Canadian Journal of Behavioural Science* 17:263–270.

Jenkins, H. M., and W. Ward

1965 Judgement of contingency between responses and outcomes. *Psychological Monographs* 79(1).

Kahneman, D., and A. Tversky

1973 On the psychology of prediction. *Psychological Review* 80:237–251.

Nisbett, R., and L. Ross

1980 *Human Inference: Strategies and Shortcomings of Social Judgement.* Englewood Cliffs, N.J.: Prentice-Hall.

Nisbett, R., D. Krantz, C. Jepson, and Z. Kunda

1983 The use of statistical heuristics in everyday inductive reasoning. *Psychological Review* 90:339–363.

Tversky, A., and D. Kahneman

1983 Extensional versus intuitive reasoning: The conjunction fallacy in probability judgement. *Psychological Review* 90:293–315.

4.

Cult Archaeology and Creationism: A Coordinated Research Project

Kenneth L. Feder

My participation in the symposium that inspired this publication can be traced back to my junior year in college. During spring break I went to get my hair cut and it was my misfortune to be saddled with a rather talkative barber. After determining that I was majoring in anthropology and specializing in archaeology, my barber asked me, "Hey, what do you think about this guy who says that the pyramids were built by men from outer space?" Needless to say I was taken aback. Also needless to say I had no intention of pointing out the absurdity of such a claim to someone holding a sharp pair of scissors close to my head. This was the first of unfortunately many subsequent exposures to popular pseudoscientific ideas about archaeology.

It was not until I entered graduate school that I began to take an active interest in the speculative (or "cult," or "pseudo-," or "fantastic," or any of the prefixes or epithets enumerated by William Stiebing in this volume) varieties of archaeology. I began keeping track of the ways in which archaeological data were misused in attempts to "prove" all sorts of extreme claims concerning either the human past itself or how we can learn about that past. The list was remarkably (and depressingly) long. Some of the claims that have attained a certain amount of popularity include:

1. Ancient astronauts (von Däniken 1972, 1974, 1982)
2. The lost continent of Atlantis (Donnelly 1971; Berlitz 1969)
3. The lost continent of Mu (Churchwood 1932)
4. Pre-Columbian visitation of the New World by Celts, Phoenicians, etc. (Fell 1976, 1980)
5. "Ark"eology (LaHaye and Morris 1976)
6. Out-of-place artifacts—Ooparts (Noorbergen 1978)
7. Psychic archaeology (Goodman 1977; Jones 1979)
8. Archaeological dowsing (Hume 1974)
9. Electromagnetic photofields (EMPF—essentially, dowsing for no longer existing above-ground structures) (Hunt 1984)
10. American genesis (Goodman 1982)
11. Creationist archaeology (Gish 1973; Morris 1980)
12. The Shroud of Turin (Stevenson and Habermas 1981)
13. Velikovskian prehistory (Velikovsky 1950, 1952, 1955)
14. King Tut's curse
15. Pyramid power (Tompkins 1978)

I am certain there are many others.

It should be abundantly obvious to all of those who work in archaeology that our field seems to attract more than its share of unsupported speculation (the fields of psychology and astronomy could probably make the same claim). There are at least two reasons why archaeologists in particular need to understand the etiology of such beliefs. First, clearly archaeology, more than most other disciplines, relies on public support and understanding. The danger posed by public misconceptions and inaccurate expectations concerning our research and results should be apparent. Second, as anthropologists we should be concerned by and interested in folk knowledge of our discipline. Again, as anthropologists we should want to know not only what people believe about the past, but also why they believe.

The 1983 Study

To better understand both the nature of popular misconceptions about the past as well as the professional response to such speculative constructs (and to begin to quantify both) two surveys were instituted in the spring of 1983 (Feder 1984, 1985/86). A questionnaire survey was administered to approximately two hundred undergraduate students at Central Connecticut State University concerning their understanding of scientific reasoning, general science knowledge, acceptance of unverified claims related to all branches of science, and, in particular, acceptance of speculative claims related to the human past. A second survey was sent to 610 teaching professional archaeologists in the United States and Canada asking them about their reactions in the classroom to such extreme claims.

The student questionnaire was in two parts: a personal background section that included family as well as coursework data, and an opinion section wherein fifty statements related to scientific knowledge, pseudo-scientific belief, and general world view were presented. Students were asked to express their opinions on these fifty statements using a five-part scale. Responses were: (1) strongly believe, (2) mildly believe, (3) don't know, (4) mildly disbelieve, (5) strongly disbelieve. The student survey showed that, at least in Connecticut, there was little strong belief in any pseudoscientific claims related to the human past, though general belief levels (that is, combined strongly believe and mildly believe responses) were much higher, ranging up to nearly 30 percent who expressed some level of belief in the reality of ancient astronauts and the lost continent of Atlantis. Perhaps the most remarkable result was the extremely high levels of students' admitted ignorance on most of the science as well as the pseudoscience topics in the survey, including everything from the existence of ancient astronauts to the age of the earth, to which 48 percent and 58 percent, respectively, responded "don't know."

I concluded from the results of this research that among our students there were few true believers in pseudoscientific archaeology. On the other hand, with such high levels of ignorance concerning the human past (and attendant high levels of interest), our students presented a fertile field for those wishing to purvey extreme claims about that past.

Eve and Harrold (1986) conducted a similar study of student beliefs among undergraduates at the University of Texas at Arlington. Their results were in most ways remarkably similar to the data generated from the Connecticut group. The most significant differences in these two geographic samples centered on creationism, not surprisingly, with higher belief levels in Texas. Here, also, there was an attempt to understand the nature of student beliefs related to the past from the perspective of sociological theory. Eve and Harrold concluded that creationist-related beliefs were highly correlated with an entire world view and value system (termed *cultural fundamentalism*), while other unverified claims about the human past seemed not to be rooted in basic values.

At the same time, Luanne Hudson was investigating similar questions among undergraduate students in California at Occidental College and the University of Southern California. These students exhibited both similarities to and differences from the Connecticut and Texas samples. In terms of evolution/creation, they were more similar to the Connecticut group (about a 70 percent level of acceptance of the concept of evolution). On some topics they were more skeptical than either of the other groups (for example, concerning the existence of ghosts), but on other claims they were more credulous (for example, astrology as a valid predictor of personality). The California students also exhibited interesting contradictions concerning religion and its role in understanding the human past; over one-third believed that Adam and Eve were the first human beings and that the Bible is literally true, but only 8 percent accepted the Flood related in the Book of Genesis as a historical fact (that compares to close to 50 percent in Connecticut, and 65 percent in Texas).

A discussion between the California and Texas contingents resulted in a commitment to continue, coordinate, and integrate this research. A letter to me from Frank Harrold initiated my participation in the present project.

The Cult Archaeology/Creationism Project

Since May 1985, Harrold, Eve, Hudson, and I have been coordinating our efforts. The results of these efforts include a student survey instrument amalgamated, reworked, and improved from our prior efforts (see appendix). Principal improvements of the current instrument include:

1. More detailed personal background questions
2. Questions on students' use of and trust in various types of mass media (based on the suspicion that some media coverage may encourage pseudoscientific beliefs)
3. More detailed questions on evolution and creationism
4. A larger variety of cult archaeology topics included in the opinion questions
5. Redundancy built into the survey to determine how carefully students were actually reading the questions, and
6. A reworked set of responses to opinion items.

The revised responses, on a modified Likert-type scale, were (1) agree strongly, (2) agree somewhat, (3) disagree somewhat, (4) disagree strongly, (5) undecided because the available evidence is inconclusive, and (6) never heard of it/don't know enough to have an opinion. This last change is a significant improvement over previous surveys. It allows for differentiation of those who neither agree nor disagree with a statement because they really cannot decide (a response based on at least some sort of thought process) from those who neither agree nor disagree because they have heard little or nothing of the topic or claim (a response based on more or less complete ignorance).

The Sample

The current survey was distributed to students in Texas (a sample of 409 at the University of Texas at Arlington and 34 at Texas Christian University), California (a combined sample of 367 at Occidental College and the University of Southern California), and Connecticut (a sample of 169 at Central Connecticut State University). The total sample size is 979. One exciting aspect of this research rests in the fact that for the first time (to my knowledge) a large sample of students in different geographic regions of the United States has been questioned on acceptance of extreme claims related to the human past. Since the same instrument was used for each subset, the data are entirely comparable; geographic differences and cross-cutting consistencies should be apparent.

The institutions included in the survey vary greatly. Central Connecticut State University is a public institution located in New Britain. Central has a student body of about 13,000 and tuition of approximately $1,300 per year for full-time students who are Connecticut residents. The average combined score on the SAT (Scholastic Aptitude Test, taken almost universally by college-bound high school seniors) is about 880, and a C grade or better in college-preparatory high school courses is a prerequisite for admission. Texas Christian University, located in Fort Worth, is a private institution with a student body of some 4,800 undergraduates. TCU's tuition is about $4,000 per year. The average SAT score for incoming freshmen is 1,060. The University of Texas at Arlington is a public institution with a student population of about 23,000 and tuition of approximately $1,000 per year. There is a sliding scale of minimum SAT scores required for admission based on high school class standing; those in the bottom quarter of their graduating class must have a combined SAT score of at least 1,000; the SAT average for incoming freshmen, though, is about 895. Occidental College is a private school located in Los Angeles. It has a student body of about 1,600 and annual tuition in the neighborhood of $10,000. Average SAT score for incoming freshmen is placed at 1,150. The University of Southern California is another private institution located in Los Angeles with a student population of 17,000 and tuition in the vicinity of $10,000 per year. The SAT average for incoming freshmen in 1,050. Thus, the students in the sample not only represent people from different regions of the nation; they represent people from different socioeconomic backgrounds and with varying levels of academic achievement.

It is useful at this point to briefly describe the demography of the sample. Differences and similarities in the subsamples may help us understand differences and similarities in opinion responses of the students within the subsamples. Some of the more important statistics are presented in Table 1 and they will be summarized here.

Females slightly outnumbered males in both the California and Texas subsamples; males outnumbered females by about two to one in the Connecticut group. The California group was, in general, the youngest; the Connecticut students were a bit older; the Texans, most of them attending a school whose median student age is about twenty-five, were significantly older. Most of the students in all three subsamples (at least 72 percent) identified themselves as being white. The California group had a substantial number of students of Asian heritage. Class standing, by and large, reflected the age differences in the subsamples (there were more upperclassmen in the Texas group). Most of the students in all three groups, however, were freshmen or sophomores.

Academic majors varied among the three subsamples, but not extremely so. Texas had the highest percentages of social science and architecture majors, Connecticut was highest in business and engineering, and California had the most in material science. In all three cases, the widespread trend for students to major in preprofessional or career programs is evident.

Grade point averages are difficult to compare across different institutions. California seemed to have either the highest percentage of academically talented students or the greatest degree of grade inflation.

The statistics concerning the levels of education achieved by students' parents show a great deal of similarity between the Texas and Connecticut groups. A little less than one-third of the mothers and a little more than one-third of the fathers were college educated in the subsamples from these two states. On the other hand, the parents of the students in the California subsample were clearly more highly educated. For example, almost two-fifths of the fathers of the California students had been to graduate school. Unsurprisingly, then, the students at the private schools in California had better-educated, and probably more prosperous, parents than the public university students of the other two samples.

Religious affiliation and ideology and degree of commitment to religion varied among the schools in the sample. There was a higher proportion of Catholics in Connecticut, of Protestants in Texas, and of people with no expressed religious preference in California. The Texans were more conservative in their religious ideology and said that religion plays a more important role in their lives than it does for either the California or Connecticut groups. Politically, the Connecticut students seemed to be a bit more liberal than either of the other two groups.

While about one-third of the students in the sample as a whole had pre-

TABLE 1. Background Characteristics of the Three Samples

	California	Texas	Connecticut
Sex			
Male	46.3%	44.4%	66.9%
Female	53.7	55.6	33.1
Age			
Under 22	95.6%	68.4%	88.2%
23–29	3.6	20.3	8.9
30–39	0.3	6.3	2.4
Over 40	0.5	5.0	0.6
Race			
White	72.1%	82.5%	94.7%
Black	4.5	7.3	1.2
Hispanic	8.2	5.0	0.6
Asian	15.2	4.3	3.0
Other	.0	0.9	.0
Class			
Freshman	33.8%	19.6%	38.8%
Sophomore	39.5	34.6	30.3
Junior	18.0	28.1	24.2
Senior	8.3	17.7	6.7
Major			
Anthropology	1.7%	5.9%	7.1%
Other Social Sciences	17.7	24.6	10.1
Humanities	21.5	19.9	13.0
Engineering	5.5	4.1	10.7
Business	23.2	19.0	34.3
Architecture	0.6	8.1	0.6
Material Science	20.4	13.1	12.4
Other	9.4	5.2	11.2
Grade Point Average (on 4-point scale)			
0–.99	0.8%	0.9%	1.3%
1.0–1.99	0.8	5.2	9.6
2.0–2.49	8.7	18.9	24.4
2.5–2.99	25.9	28.5	26.3
3.0–3.49	36.0	30.1	28.2
3.5–4.0	26.2	16.4	10.3
Mother's Education (highest level attained)			
Elementary	4.4%	8.6%	5.9%
High School	26.0	42.6	47.9

TABLE 1. *(continued)*

	California	Texas	Connecticut
Technical School	8.8	11.3	8.3
College	46.8	32.0	30.2
Graduate School	14.0	5.4	7.7
Father's Education			
Elementary	4.4%	10.2%	6.6%
High School	12.4	30.1	30.5
Technical School	5.5	9.0	13.8
College	39.4	36.7	35.9
Graduate School	38.3	14.0	13.2
Religion			
Catholic	32.6%	27.1%	53.7%
Eastern Orthodox	2.8	1.1	1.9
Jewish	5.2	0.2	1.9
Mormon	1.1	0.7	0.6
Moslem	0.8	0.7	0.6
Protestant	30.1	53.5	18.5
None	18.8	8.0	13.6
Other	8.6	8.7	9.3
Religious Ideology			
Fundamentalist	2.5%	7.3%	1.8%
Conservative	20.3	22.2	13.0
Moderate	27.9	34.6	37.3
Liberal	23.1	25.2	24.3
Nonreligious	26.2	10.8	20.1
Importance of Religion in Life			
Unimportant	29.2%	12.1%	24.6%
Somewhat important	42.2	44.2	47.9
Very important	26.2	43.7	24.6
Political Ideology			
Conservative	30.9%	34.3%	18.3%
Moderate	37.8	25.0	41.5
Liberal	27.1	27.1	34.1
Radical	4.1	2.7	6.1
Books Read outside Class Assignments			
0–2 yearly	23.1%	40.1%	37.5%
3–10	50.3	35.6	43.5
Over 10	26.6	24.3	19.0

TABLE 1. *(continued)*

	California	Texas	Connecticut
Watch TV News?			
Never	1.6%	1.1%	2.4%
Rarely	11.8	9.3	16.0
Sometimes	42.7	35.4	42.2
Often	43.8	54.2	33.1
Read Daily Newspapers?			
Never	2.2%	3.4%	5.6%
Rarely	12.7	18.4	16.0
Sometimes	42.7	33.8	30.2
Often	42.4	44.4	48.5
Read National Enquirer *(or Similar Papers)?*			
Never	67.4%	66.9%	60.9%
Rarely	21.6	23.6	20.1
Sometimes	8.5	8.4	13.0
Often	2.5	1.1	5.3
Were You Taught Evolution in High School?			
Yes, with creation	82.8%	33.1%	31.1%
Yes, alone	8.6	42.5	45.5
No	8.6	24.4	22.2

vious coursework in anthropology, far fewer had prior coursework in archaeology. Previous coursework in a number of academic disciplines is summarized in Table 2. As can be seen, only history and psychology courses had been taken by at least half our students.

The number of books which students reported reading on a yearly basis outside of classroom assignments varied, but none of the institutions had too much to brag about; far too many students read far too few books (see Table 1). The Californians read a bit more than either the students from Texas or Connecticut but, as can be seen in Table 1, about three-quarters of the students in each of the subsamples read fewer than ten books a year.

In general, most of the students in the sample watch television news and read newspapers, at least sometimes. Thankfully, not too many of them read weeklies like the *National Enquirer* (see Table 1). It is encouraging to report that when asked to rate reliability of various sources of information, students tended to rate highly professional science journals, PBS science programs, and popular science magazines like *Discover*. It is also instructive to point out that, as a source of reliable information, stu-

TABLE 2. Previous Coursework

Field of Study	% Students
Anthropology	34
Archaeology	6
Astronomy	17
Biology	48
Chemistry/Physics	37
Geology	17
History	71
Logic	17
Psychology	50
Religious Studies	24

Note: Percentages of students (in all three subsamples combined) who reported completing at least one course in each of the subject fields.

dents rated science fiction books more highly than the *National Enquirer* (one could argue that by providing separate categories of science fiction books and the *Enquirer*, we were being redundant).

One final statistic should be mentioned here. Students were asked if they received instruction in evolution in high school. Three coded responses were provided: (1) yes, with creationism, (2) yes, without creationism, and (3) no.

As can be seen, the great majority of students (over four-fifths) in the California subsample were taught evolution alongside creationism (see Table 1). In Texas and Connecticut not far from one-third were taught both approaches. In both Connecticut and Texas, more than one-fifth of the students had not been taught evolution at all in high school. These figures are certainly not terribly encouraging.

In summary, the sample as a whole includes a wide variety of college students representing differing regions and social classes, races, and religions. They are predominantly young, white, politically moderate, and somewhat religious. They tend to read little, and many are in preprofessional programs. In all likelihood, our group is a fairly representative sample of college students in the United States. The results of the survey will be reported in the next two papers.

Why Bother?

It is perhaps useful to anticipate the reaction of those who might feel that our concern is misdirected, at least regarding what we are here calling pseudoarchaeology. As can be determined from the data generated by the

TABLE 3. Introductory Archaeology Courses Confronting Various Pseudoscience Topics

Course Topic	% Coverage
Ancient astronauts	58
Creationism	57
Hyperdiffusionism	57
Atlantis	42
Bigfoot	34
Noah's Ark	14
Tut's curse	22
Psychic archaeology	27
Archaeological dowsing	21
Loch Ness monster	10
Human/dinosaur footprints contemporaneous	16
Early human evolution in New World	39

Note: Percentage of polled archaeology faculty who deal with the following topics in their introductory courses (from Feder 1984).

questionnaire survey sent to professional teaching archaeologists in 1984, most recognize the importance of responding to irrationality concerning our discipline (see Table 3). However, a substantial minority remain unconvinced.

Certainly, we must all be aware of the very real threat of the creationist agenda to any of us who teach that the world was not created six thousand years ago, that human beings did not first appear suddenly in the Garden of Eden, and that subsequent human history cannot be best understood by reference to a catastrophic universal deluge. But, it might be posed, are not the cult archaeology claims already passé? Was not their popularity at a peak in the 1960s, and are they not irrelevant to our students in the 1980s? For example, Dutch (1986) has shown a drastic decline in the numbers of titles published in just about all the categories of pseudoscience (including archaeological pseudoscience) since 1981.

The example of ancient astronauts is informative in this regard. Erich von Däniken, chief purveyor of this brand of cult archaeology, certainly was at his own literary (I use the term advisedly) peak in the late 1960s and early 1970s. The softcover English translations of his books *Chariots of the Gods, Gods from Outer Space,* and *Gold of the Gods* were published in 1970, 1972, and 1974, respectively. The English version of *Chariots of the Gods* has sold well in excess of four million copies. In the twenty-four hours after the first showing on national television of a documentary based on the premise in his books, Bantam Publishing Company received 350,000 orders for his works.

However, von Däniken has clearly fared not nearly as well in recent years. Neither G. P. Putnam and Sons (his hardcover publisher) nor Bantam (his paperback publisher) would provide even ballpark estimates of sales figures for von Däniken's subsequent books (I was told this was "privileged information"). However, a representative at Bantam did mention the figure of "between five and ten million" for total sales of all of his softcover books. He also stated that all of his books are currently out of stock; he further indicated that current low levels of interest could not justify their being restocked. Von Däniken's most recent book, *Pathways to the Gods*, published in 1982, has not sold nearly as well as his previous works. His name is not as familiar as it once was. So, the question must be asked, why are we still concerned?

While von Däniken's personal fortunes might not be what they once were, it is my contention that the idea he helped popularize has become a part of "pop-science" and, therefore, part of our culture. Few may recognize his name and fewer still may read his books, but most of our students are aware of, and many are sympathetic to, the ancient astronaut hypothesis. By the same token, how many students are familiar, at least in passing, with the Atlantis story? Probably most. But how many have heard of, much less read, Ignatius Donnelly, or, for that matter, Plato?

More recently, a best-selling autobiography of sorts, Shirley MacLaine's *Out on a Limb* (in its thirteenth printing as I write) extols the work of von Däniken. In support of the ancient astronaut hypothesis, MacLaine mentions the Great Pyramid at Gîza, Stonehenge, Machu Picchu, Nazca, the Old Testament, Tiahuanaco, cuneiform texts, the Maya calendar, etc. She states, after reading von Däniken and a number of other, unidentified sources, "It was true that I had heard much of what I read in dribs and drabs throughout my life, but somehow having it compiled and organized in written form with respected and credible researchers and scientists and archaeologists and theologians backing it up—it was different" (1983: 246–247). She neglects to specify which "credible researchers" are being referenced.

Interestingly, when first exposed to ancient astronauts (the hypothesis, not the extraterrestrials themselves), MacLaine asked an intelligent question concerning the ultimate source of the human intellect that had produced great cultures: "[The source of] that intelligence could have been extremely advanced civilizations right here on earth . . . Why does superior intelligence have to come from some other world?" (1983:240). Her guru (someone named David who has regular conversations with an extraterrestrial alien named Mayan—get it?) cleared that right up by telling her: "But you see, there wasn't just one example of superior intelligence. It happened all over the world and at different times" (1983:240).

Recently, during the on-location filming in South America of *Out on a Limb* for a television mini-series, publicity about MacLaine's claims of an extraterrestrial connection for the Nazca ground drawings and Machu Picchu understandably upset the government of Peru. Did MacLaine really mean, they wondered, that ancient high cultures in Peru could be explained only by reference to visits from ancient astronauts, rather than the achievements of native peoples? MacLaine had to back off publicly, saying something to the effect that *if* ancient extraterrestrials ever really had landed on earth, they would certainly have selected Peru as a landing site since it had such a "splendiferous" prehistoric culture. Whether or not most people think MacLaine is a kook is not entirely the point; her books sell in the millions and, at the very least, people are are once again being exposed to the ancient astronaut hypothesis.

In fact, in our combined sample of 979 students, very few (only about 4 percent) responded to our opinion statement, "Aliens from other worlds are responsible for ancient monuments like the pyramids, which primitive people could not have built," with the coded response "Never heard of it/don't know enough to have an opinion." Similarly low figures for the never heard of it response were seen for statements concerning Atlantis (about 12 percent have never heard of the lost continent), archaeological evidence for the existence of Noah's ark (23 percent have never heard of this), the Shroud of Turin (25 percent), and others. In fact, our data show quite clearly that our undergraduate students in Texas, California, and Connecticut largely are aware of these extreme claims. To what extent they accept them is a question to be answered in the following two chapters.

In closing, I would like to note that I have been paid the ultimate compliment accorded to debunkers of pseudoscience. In a book that must rank among quintessential speculative archaeological works—*Treasures of the Lost Races* by René Noorbergen (1982)—I have been quoted. In his first chapter the author discusses psychic archaeology and the claim that artifacts whose existence was predicted by psychics show that modern human beings were walking around in Arizona more than 100,000 years ago. These people were, by the way, refugees from the lost continents of Mu and Atlantis. Noorbergen quotes me—an unattributed reference taken from a short *Science Digest* piece (1981) in which I was quoted in a telephone interview—as saying: "Psychic archaeologists don't want to play by the same rules that scientists play by. They don't set out to test their hypotheses; they set out to prove them." To this Noorbergen responds, "But is that so bad?" To him I believe we all should respond with a resounding "Yes, indeed it is!" The question remains, however, how many of our students would actually agree with Noorbergen and MacLaine and von Däniken and Gish (1973) and Morris (1980) and the rest? This, in turn, raises the question of why they accept muddleheaded thinking and speculative claims about the past? Finally, we are left with the question of what we who are professional educators can do about it. Certainly, excellent books like William Stiebing's (1984) *Ancient Astronauts, Cosmic Collisions, and Other Popular Theories about Man's Past* and semester courses like Luanne Hudson and Suzanne Engler's "Myths, Monsters, and Mysteries" and Stephen William's "Fantastic Archaeology" are making important contributions. It is hoped that our coordinated research project, the symposium that resulted, and this publication will similarly contribute to our understanding of, and our formulation of a response to, the nonsense that is attracted to our discipline.

Acknowledgments

I would very much like to thank the Central Connecticut State University Alumni Foundation for the grant they awarded me in support of my participation in the research project that led to this publication. I would also like to express my appreciation to my colleagues in the Department of Anthropology at CCSU for allowing me to distribute the questionnaire survey to their classes. Also, a special thanks is owed to my wife, Melissa, who assisted in the computer analysis of the Connecticut subsample. I should also thank Joshua, whose two-weeks-late birth allowed me more time to work on this manuscript. A note of appreciation is, of course, due to the editors of this volume, Frank Harrold and Ray Eve. Finally, we must thank the students who participated in the survey. We greatly appreciate their time, their concern, and their candor.

References

Berlitz, Charles
1969 *The Mystery of Atlantis.* New York: Norton Publications.
Churchwood, James
1932 *The Lost Continent of Mu.* New York: Ives Washburn.
Donnelly, Ignatius
1971 *Atlantis, the Antediluvian World.* New York: Harper and Row (originally published in 1882).
Dutch, Steven
1986 Four decades of fringe literature. *The Skeptical Inquirer* 10(4):342–351.
Eve, Raymond A., and Francis B. Harrold
1986 Creationism, cult archaeology, and other pseudoscientific beliefs: A study of college students. *Youth and Society* 17(4):396–421.

Feder, Kenneth L.
1984 Irrationality and popular archaeology. *American Antiquity* 49(3):525–541.
1985/86 The challenges of pseudoscience. *Journal of College Science Teaching* 15(3): 180–186.
Fell, Barry
1976 *America B.C.: European Settlers in the New World.* New York: Quadrangle/New York Times Book Co.
1980 *Saga America.* New York: Quadrangle/New York Times Book Co.
Gish, Duane
1973 *Evolution: The Fossils Say No!* San Diego: Creation-Life Publishers.
Goodman, Jeffrey
1977 *Psychic Archaeology: Time Machine to the Past.* New York: Berkley Books.
1982 *American Genesis: The American Indian and Origins of Modern Man.* New York: Berkley Books.
Hume, Ivor Noel
1974 *Historical Archaeology.* New York: Knopf.
Hunt, Karen
1984 Point Cooke homestead electro-magnetic photo-field survey for Melbourne and metropolitan board of works, Melbourne, Victoria, Australia. Unpublished ms.
Jones, David
1979 *Visions of Time: Experiments in Psychic Archaeology.* Wheaton, Ill.: Theosophical Publishing House.
LaHaye, Tim, and John Morris
1976 *The Ark on Ararat.* San Diego: Creation-Life Publishers.
MacLaine, Shirley
1983 *Out on a Limb.* New York: Bantam.
Morris, John
1980 *Tracking Those Incredible Dinosaurs and the People Who Knew Them.* San Diego: Creation-Life Publishers.
Noorbergen, René
1978 *Secrets of the Lost Races.* Indianapolis: Bobbs-Merrill.
1982 *Treasures of the Lost Races.* Indianapolis: Bobbs-Merrill.
Science Digest
1981 Psychic archaeology: Update. (January/February):37.
Stevenson, Kenneth E., and Gary R. Habermas
1981 *Verdict on the Shroud.* Ann Arbor: Servant Books.
Stiebing, William H., Jr.
1984 *Ancient Astronauts, Cosmic Collisions, and Other Popular Theories about Man's Past.* Buffalo, N.Y.: Prometheus Press.
Tompkins, Peter
1978 *Secrets of the Great Pyramid.* New York: Harper Colophon Books.
Velikovsky, Immanuel
1950 *Worlds in Collision.* Garden City, N.Y.: Doubleday.
1952 *Ages in Chaos.* Garden City, N.Y.: Doubleday.
1955 *Earth in Upheaval.* Garden City, N.Y.: Doubleday.
von Däniken, Erich
1970 *Chariots of the Gods.* New York: Bantam.
1972 *Gods from Outer Space.* New York: Bantam.
1974 *Gold of the Gods.* New York: Bantam.
1982 *Pathways to the Gods.* New York: G. P. Putnam's Sons.

5.

East Is East and West Is West? A Regional Comparison of Cult Belief Patterns

Luanne Hudson

While in the midst of preparing my symposium presentation, which focused on regional patterns in levels of beliefs among college students in pseudoscientific and paranormal claims, I received the spring 1986 issue of the *Skeptical Inquirer*. This issue commemorated the tenth anniversary of the Committee for the Scientific Investigation of Claims of the Paranormal, which publishes the journal. It contained essays on science and the paranormal by Isaac Asimov, L. Sprague de Camp, Carl Sagan, and Paul Kurtz, all of whom discussed the need for more critical inquiry into paranormal and pseudoscientific claims. In addition there were articles on creationist evangelism. All of these issues were also dealt with in the symposium.

One could ask whether ESP or other psychic vibes moved us to have this symposium at the same time as the publication of this issue. Sadly, many people would be "amazed" at the remarkable coincidence. It is not surprising nor is it a coincidence that two different groups of scholars would be coping with the same issues. Rather, it reflects an attempt by the scientific community to deal with the growing acceptance of paranormal and pseudoscientific claims based on unverified and misleading information. This acceptance is taking place in a supposedly educated, rational society. In addition, these claims are reported to the public by uncritical and sensationalistic media. This is underlined by the fact that, on any given day, one can pick up issues of weekly newspapers or journals with headlines that cry out "I was raped (substitute attacked, assaulted, bitten, etc.) by Bigfoot (substitute alien invaders, Martians, etc.)." Not only do people read this information, but they are willing to accept it as "possibly" true.

One encouraging report is that the *National Enquirer*, one of the more avid reporters of paranormal and pseudoscientific occurrences, will be "straighter," relatively speaking, in its future news coverage (Sheaffer 1986:210). Why? Have they seen the light and found that it is not a UFO? Unfortunately not. Their motives are totally pragmatic; they are not attracting the larger national advertisers because of the perception that people who buy the *Enquirer* are not exactly affluent. Thus for economic reasons they are starting to scale down the sensationalism aspect in order to entice "Yuppies" to buy the rag.[1] Their perception that the *National Enquirer* is low on the reading list of future Yuppies is supported by the results of the survey of student beliefs conducted by my colleagues and myself. In our survey only 12 percent of respondents stated that they read the *Enquirer*, while only 6 percent stated that they believe in its contents to any degree.

It appears that a great number of people profess to believe in the paranormal, the occult, and the existence of strange beings and occurrences. Therefore, there is a need to assess which claims are strongly held and which are believed in only peripherally or not at all. The administering of the Student Belief Questionnaire (see appendix) to college students around the nation is part of the attempt to determine what people believe and how they obtain their information.

Prior surveys have been conducted by Bainbridge (1978), Feder (1984), Eve and Harrold (1986), and Means (1985) on the level of belief in cult claims, but this is the first one to involve an interregional study with students from three states and five colleges and universities (see Feder, this volume). This survey allows us to discover what the students believe and how these beliefs might be influenced by sex, region, reading practices, and many other social and cultural variables. In addition, the professional scientific community is given an opportunity to analyze how effective it can be in the future by knowing what issues to speak to and the best methods to use in order to educate people to critically evaluate cult claims.

The term *cult beliefs* encompasses a belief or beliefs, based on nonscientific criteria, in unexplainable or otherwise unfounded beings, events, or behavior. For purposes of this paper it includes the labels *pseudoscience*, *paranormal*, *occult* and *cult archaeology*, which are often used interchangeably in the popular literature.

There is a tendency to classify cult beliefs under an all-encompassing cognitive umbrella. However, we should not assume that these beliefs come out of the same giant cultural grab bag. All are primarily based on unsubstantiated or distorted claims, but they can be classified into several categories based on different attributes. The typology below forms a basis for testing the assumption that the cult claims in the survey are part of a native belief system shared by most members of the society as measured by the levels of respondents' belief in the questions. The typology can also be used to determine if some questions or categories of questions are not part of general knowledge among college students as measured by the percentage of never heard of it responses from the survey. In addition, regional differences in world view can be determined by measuring different levels of belief between categories or by region.

Seven categories of cult beliefs were generated from the survey items based on the following attributes.

Type 1: UFOs and Aliens. These deal with beliefs that aliens from outer space either have visited or are observing our planet.

Type 2: Speculative Fact. These questions deal with future possibilities and probabilities (for example, time travel) based on still unknown "laws" or otherwise yet to be discovered data.

Type 3: Unexplained Mysteries. These relate to those claims that there are mysterious beings, creatures, and places, the evidence for which is based on unsupported or elusive data. They provide the fodder for many popular pseudoscience books in which the authors, through use of hearsay and distortion of facts, perpetuate a "mystery," whether or not it has already been solved. They include the Bermuda Triangle (Kusche 1981), Atlantis (Krupp 1981), and Bigfoot and the Loch Ness monster (Cohen 1981).

Type 4: Beyond the Pale, and *Type 5: Occult and Magic.* These two categories are usually merged into one—the occult. However, the term *occult* has contradictory definitions and encompasses various attributes (Truzzi 1971:244). For this study two categories were used based on the following definitions.

Beyond the Pale. The belief in occurrences "beyond the range of ordinary knowledge; mysterious" (Truzzi 1971:243), including beliefs in spirits and ESP.

Occult and Magic. Those practices "of or pertaining to magic, astrology, and other alleged sciences claiming use or knowledge of the secret, mysterious or supernatural" (Truzzi 1971:243).

Type 6: Religious Cult. The questions in this category are somewhat ambiguous in that they could easily fit into two or three others, such as Unexplained Mysteries or possibly Occult and Magic. They also might fit

TABLE 1. Belief Types

Type 1: UFOs and Aliens
* 61 Extraterrestrials built ancient monuments
  65 UFOs are alien spacecraft
  82 Extraterrestrials visited earth in past
  87 Government is hiding UFO information

Type 2: Speculative Fact
  67 Intelligent life elsewhere in universe
  69 Time travel possible

Type 3: Unexplained Mysteries
* 63 King Tut's curse
  64 Loch Ness monster
  72 Bigfoot (Sasquatch)
  79 Bermuda Triangle
  80 Lost continent of Atlantis

Type 4: Beyond the Pale
  74 Reincarnation
  77 Communication with the dead
  78 Psychic prediction of future (prescience)
  92 Psychic mind reading (ESP)
101 Ghosts

Type 5: Occult and Magic
  76 Black magic
  89 Astrology predicts the future
100 Astrology predicts personality

Type 6: Religious Cult
* 97 Shroud of Turin is Christ's burial shroud
* 99 Noah's Ark found on Mt. Ararat

Type 7: Diffusion
* 62 Pre-Viking European visitors to America
* 83 New World civilizations founded by Egyptians
* 95 American Indians are Ten Lost Tribes of Israel
* 88 Human evolution in North America, not Old World

Type 8: Evolution
  60 World is 4–5 billion years old
* 75 Modern man goes back about 40,000 years
  81 Evolution theory explains history of life
103 Scientists believe evolution is valid theory
104 Evolution should be taught in public schools

Type 9: Creationism
  66 Human evolution controlled by God
  68 Adam and Eve created by God
  70 Plenty of scientific evidence for creationism

* 84   Dinosaurs and humans were contemporaries
  85   Bible is literally true
  91   God created man within last 10,000 years
  94   Noah's Flood really happened
105   Creationism should be taught in public schools

Note: For items marked with an asterisk, the NHI response (never heard of it/don't know enough to have an opinion) was 10 percent or greater in all three subsamples. Item numbers refer to the full questionnaire in the appendix.

into Creationism (see Type 9); but the Shroud of Turin is usually associated with Catholicism. The existence of Noah's Ark, although connected with the Flood, is also more of a mystery. The attribute "religious" thus places them into their own category.

Type 7: Diffusion. The questions in this category deal with distortions of facts and misleading evidence on unsubstantiated claims that there were contacts between the Old and New Worlds before the Vikings and, in some cases, as far back as Neanderthal Man (Goodman 1982). They are included in this survey because often these claims are used to "explain" some of the Unexplained Mysteries (Gardner 1957: 164).

Table 1 lists two additional categories, Evolution and Creationism, which are not directly dealt with in this paper. One of the goals of the survey was to determine if beliefs in evolution and claims by creationists tended to be mutually exclusive.[2] That is, if there is a high level of belief in one category, there should tend to be a low level of belief in the other category. Questions relating to creationist beliefs, as well as those on beliefs in various aspects of evolution, were placed into two separate categories on the assumption that there would be a negative correlation between levels of agreement in these two areas (Harrold and Eve, this volume).

Another hypothesis formulated by Harrold, Eve, and myself was that there would be no correlation between responses to the creationism questions and the cult questions, except where a cult belief item conflicted directly with a religious dogma. Eve and Harrold (1986) had explored this area in a prior study. Their results suggested that creationist religious groups often have rigorous systems of belief control placed on their members. Thus some cult-type beliefs (for example, astrology) might be excluded from this system. Their findings were that the two systems (creationism and cult) functioned independently of one another. If one scored high on one creationism question, then one would tend to score high on others in that category, but this would not allow us to predict the respondent's score for any cult belief.

In this chapter we can test hypotheses on widely held assumptions about our students' levels of belief in any particular item or category of items. If, for example, the assumption that students have equal awareness or knowledge about all types of cult beliefs is not validated, then this could have significance for future teaching, both in methods and subject matter, as well as research. One of the most predictable results of the survey is that the more we find out about beliefs, the less we know how and why they were initially adopted.

Prior surveys of these attitudes and beliefs among college populations have mostly sampled one particular college or region. For purposes of this study each state in the survey represents a different region of the United States: the Northeast (Connecticut), the West (California), and the Southwest (Texas). Because responses were from different regions we were interested in examining the assumption that there would be regional differences in attitudes and beliefs because of differences in values, ethnicity, religion, and so on.

The working hypothesis was that noticeable regional differences in levels of cult beliefs exist because of differences in attitudes and values due to regionally different modes of socialization. If this is true, then the responses to questions and/or categories of questions should differ among the three states. In the absence of previously available data, this hypothesis should be seen as an exploratory one.

Cult Belief Patterns

Variation by Region: One Man's Poison Is Another Man's Pie The bar graphs in Figures 1–10 compare responses by region for selected questions. They show the percentage of respondents who agree (strongly or somewhat), disagree (strongly or somewhat), are undecided, or have never heard of the claims.

The most general pattern noted is that responses to a particular question are usually quite similar among the three states. For example, in Figure 2, about 70 percent of the respondents disagree with the allegation that aliens from outer space built ancient monuments. In Figure 9, 19 to 27 percent of the respondents disagree that the Shroud of Turin is authentic. The range of variation in response to any particular item is seldom greater than 10 percent among the three states.

The original hypothesis, that there are interregional differences, does not appear to be validated. A possible explanation is that there are similar influences affecting the level of belief in cult items across all three states, with the result that regionalism is a minimal causal factor in what people tend to believe or not believe. This might be a result of the "democratization" of viewing and reading habits in American households whereby

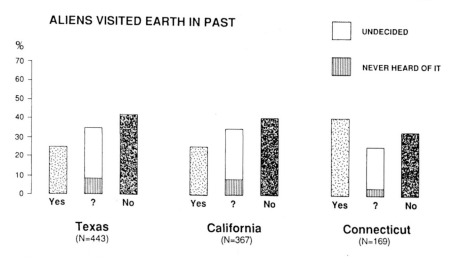

FIGURE 1. Student responses (in percentages) by state in which each sample was drawn to the assertion that "aliens from other worlds visited Earth in the past."

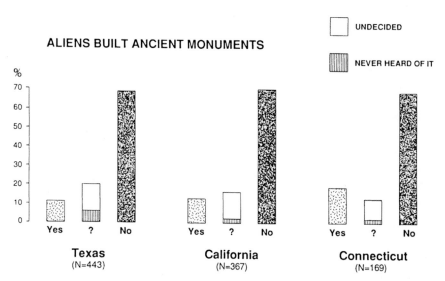

FIGURE 2. Student responses (in percentages) by state in which each sample was drawn to the assertion that "aliens from other worlds are responsible for ancient monuments like the pyramids, which primitive people could not have built."

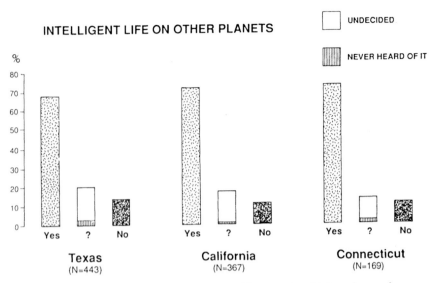

FIGURE 3. Student responses (in percentages) by state in which each sample was drawn to the assertion that "there is intelligent life somewhere out there in the universe."

the whole society is exposed to basically the same information through television, daily newspapers, and magazines such as *Time* and *Newsweek*. From the survey, the percentage of students who watch TV news and read the papers and/or newsmagazines is relatively consistent from state to state.

There are, however, some differences in belief levels. Interestingly, Connecticut has higher agreement levels for all of the cult belief categories (Types 1–7) represented in Figures 1, 4, and 9. But for Type 9, beliefs relating to creationism, Connecticut and California are lower than Texas. In this volume, Harrold and Eve found that higher levels of creationism correlated more with Protestantism than with Roman Catholicism. Connecticut has a much higher percentage of Roman Catholic respondents than do Texas and California. The difference in agreement levels might therefore reflect the tendency for creationism and cult beliefs to be somewhat mutually exclusive. It should be noted that the normal range of difference on a question between Connecticut and the other two states is within 10 percent except for two questions: belief in reincarnation (Figure 7) is 12 percent higher in Connecticut than elsewhere, and belief in aliens from outer space having visited earth in the past (Figure 1) is a whopping 22 percent higher.

One definite statement that can be made is that those respondents with

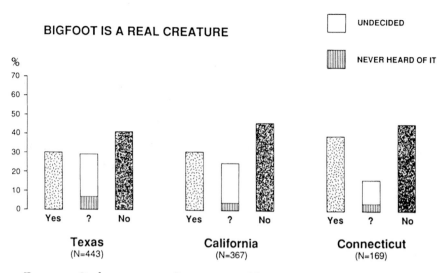

FIGURE 4. Student responses (in percentages) by state in which each sample was drawn to the assertion that "Bigfoot (Sasquatch) is a real creature roaming the woods in the American Northwest."

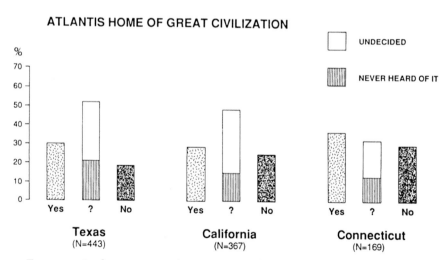

FIGURE 5. Student responses (in percentages) by state in which each sample was drawn to the assertion that "the lost continent of Atlantis was the home of a great civilization."

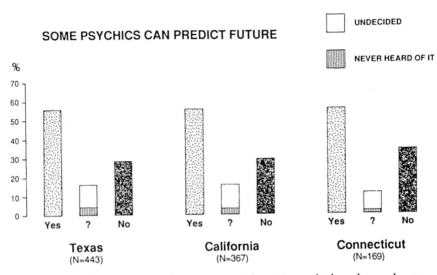

FIGURE 6. Student responses (in percentages) by state in which each sample was drawn to the assertion that "some people can predict future events by psychic power."

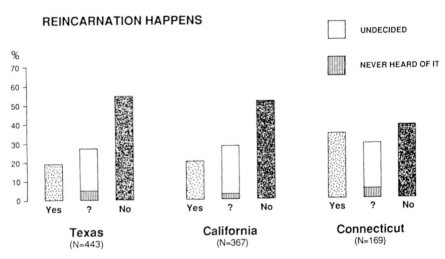

FIGURE 7. Student responses (in percentages) by state in which each sample was drawn to the assertion that "reincarnation really happens."

high levels of cult beliefs do not appear to be from the "flaky" Southern California area as one would suppose (that is, if one were not from Southern California). I found that where there is variation in the range of agreement, the California subsample is usually on the low end of belief in cult items. For example, depending on the state, 30 to 40 percent of the students believe in the existence of Bigfoot (Figure 4), and Connecticut is at the high end. This is also true with the reincarnation responses (Figure 7), which range from 18 to 33 percent. California students, though, are usually on the high end when it comes to the undecided responses. The California answers appear to indicate a wait and see attitude about the validity of the cult items.

Levels of Belief: The Good News and the Bad News The good news is that there is only one item in which agreement levels far exceed the other responses. This is the assertion that intelligent life exists on other planets (Figure 3). This is possibly due to the publication of serious books and articles by credible scientists speculating on the possibility of life in outer space (for example, Sagan 1973:195; Morrison et al. 1977:2) and is the question in Types 1 through 7 which has been given the most backing by the scientific community. To the lay public this assertion has been taken out of the arena of speculation into that of probable or even definite fact. One interesting observation is that students have a higher agreement with this question than with any of those in Type 8 (Evolution), a category which does have a sound scientific basis.

The bad news is that for about half the questions, one-third or more of the respondents believe in the claim. Even in the other cases where beliefs are lower, there is usually one state where over one-third of them agree. This trend worsens, at least by scientific standards, when the undecided responses are added in. In over two-thirds of the questions, more than half the respondents either agree with the claim or at the very least are not willing to dispute it. Undecided responses reflect the willingness of the public to wait for more information or to give some credence to the claim. These types of responses reinforce the need to carry out surveys of this kind, not only among college students but among other types of respondents as well in order to evaluate the level of public belief in the unsubstantiated.

Variation by Category: What's In and What's Out The seven cult belief categories are represented in Figures 1 through 10. As discussed in the prior section, regional differences are usually minimal. It should also be reiterated that this is an exploratory typology and represents an attempt to determine which beliefs or categories of beliefs are widely held. There

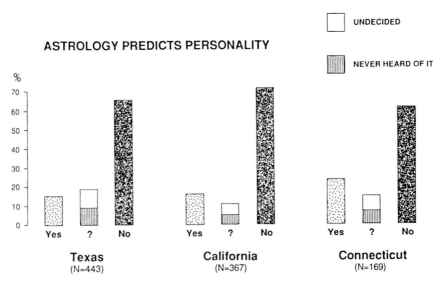

FIGURE 8. Student responses (in percentages) by state in which each sample was drawn to the assertion that "astrology is an accurate predictor of future events."

is a wide range of variation among individual questions ranging from 70 percent agreeing that there is a possibility that intelligent life exists on other planets (Figure 3) to only 9 percent agreeing that Egyptians or the lost tribes of Israel were in the New World before Columbus. The only Type 7 (Diffusion) question in which agreement levels are fairly high is for claims of pre-Viking explorations of America by Europeans (Figure 10).

Types 3 (Unexplained Mysteries) and 4 (Beyond the Pale) have a relatively strong following in that between 30 and 45 percent of the students agree with their claims (see Figures 4 and 5). In the case of the ability to predict the future (Figure 6), agreement is at 55 percent.

Agreement levels are mixed for Type 1 (UFOs and Aliens). Connecticut belief levels are higher than the other states as indicated in the prior section. It appears that more people, regardless of which region they are from, are willing to believe or at least think about the possibility that aliens from outer space have visited the planet (Figure 1) than are willing to accept the statement that these same aliens built many of our ancient monuments. This could reflect the waning influence of von Däniken–type literature, which proposes that ancient astronauts were responsible for everything from the development of the human species to the pyramids (Story 1975:2, 90).

The belief in astrology and its predictive powers appears also to be on the wane (Figure 8). People are more likely to believe in black magic, the

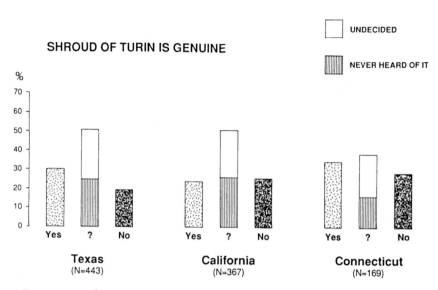

FIGURE 9. Student responses (in percentages) by state in which each sample was drawn to the assertion that "the Shroud of Turin has been proved to be the burial shroud of Christ."

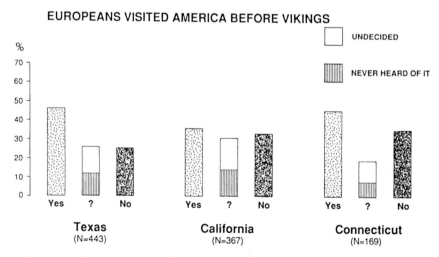

FIGURE 10. Student responses (in percentages) by state in which each sample was drawn to the assertion that "America was visited by Europeans long before either Columbus or the Vikings got here."

only Type 5 belief that has moderately high agreement levels, and Type 4 (Beyond the Pale) claims. This might be because of work done by scientists and social scientists on the psychological effects of black magic, including so-called voodoo death (Lewis 1977), and the fact that reputable institutions and scientists are looking into the possible physics of ESP and the validity of life-after-death claims (Gardner 1981; Siegel 1981).

Belief in the validity of Type 6 (Religious Cult) claims of verified mystical religious artifacts (Figure 9) is held by at least one-third of the students. When the undecided responses are added this figure is much higher. This might reflect student acceptance of information in articles published in reputable journals on scientific work attempting to authenticate the age and, by inference, the legitimacy of the Shroud of Turin (Burden 1981).

Certain categories tend to be more highly believed in than others. Type 3 (Unexplained Mysteries), Type 4 (Beyond the Pale), and, to a lesser extent, Type 6 (Religious Cult) attract higher levels of beliefs than diffusion, occult and magic, and some alien and UFO claims. What we can't predict at this point is whether a high agreement in one category would necessarily indicate high agreement in another category. A preliminary analysis has not shown any consistent associations.

Within categories there is also some variation in levels of belief between questions. There are two possible reasons. First, not all of the questions in the category are valid for that type. More work does need to be done to refine those attributes which define a category. Also, we need more input from our survey respondents as to which beliefs they think belong together in their native taxonomies. In addition, some questions might have to be rephrased because they are too ambiguous. For example, the question on psychic archaeology (#86) could be rewritten to emphasize the psychic aspect more than the archaeological aspect. Second, there might also be different sources of information for a particular claim which affect the belief level. As I have indicated, there are some serious scientific studies being conducted in certain of these areas. For these questions the simple fact that a claim is being studied by the scientific community could tend to have people consider it to be more valid than others within the same category. Also, as I will discuss in the next section, there are areas about which the public does not have much information. This too could create different levels of acceptance of claims within a category.

"I Never Heard That One" For some questions there was a large percentage of students who checked the response indicating that they did not know enough about an item to have an opinion or had never heard of it

(NHI). In prior surveys of this sort, respondents were not usually given the opportunity to say that they had no idea what the question meant or had never heard of the claim. The only alternatives were to mark "undecided" or not answer the questions.

On those questions for which there was a high NHI, the pattern of responses was consistent among regions; that is, if one state had a high NHI, then the other two usually did also. There are thirteen items in Table 1 marked with an asterisk. For these items there was an NHI response of at least 10 percent, ranging up to about 40 percent.[3] There was a low NHI for Connecticut in two cases, but the NHI for the other two states was high enough to warrant including these variables in the analysis.

This group of questions includes all four of the Type 7 items (Diffusion) as well as both of those in Type 6 (Religious Cult). Two of the Type 3 (Unexplained Mysteries) items are also unexplained mysteries to the students. The Occult, Beyond the Pale, and all but one of the UFOs and Aliens categories are not in this group. Thus it appears that students are well informed about alien encounters, the occult and the supernatural, but some beliefs are not fashionable at this time. This tends to invalidate the assumption that all of these claims are known to our society. The data also suggest that there are interregional similarities as to which claims people, or at least college-age students, have or have not heard about.

Cult Scale Analysis

One of the goals of the survey was to determine if there were any variables that might be related to cult belief. In order to examine this question a Cult Scale, used as a measure of general cult belief, was constructed in much the same way as the Creationism Scale devised by Harrold and Eve (this volume).[4]

Using the Cult Scale as a dependent variable, it was crosstabulated against socioeconomic and cultural variables in order to determine if there were any associations. There were very few associations found when crosstabulating the Cult Scale against variables such as sex, religion, ethnicity, parents' education, rural versus urban upbringings, number of books read, etc. Only California has a weak association (Cramer's $V = .18$; $p < .05$) between sex and the Cult Scale. Males might tend to be more caught up in cult beliefs than females, who are more undecided. At first glance, this California result seems inconsistent with that of Gray (this volume), who found females higher overall in cult beliefs than males. However, he also found that males had higher levels of belief in UFOs, and two of the four items in our Cult Scale are UFO related (see above).

Some Speculations and Very Few Conclusions

In their article on occult beliefs Singer and Benassi (1981) discuss four sources of pseudoscientific or occult beliefs. These sources are cognitive biases, poor science education, sensationalistic and uncritical media coverage, and sociocultural variables (see Harrold and Eve, this volume, for further discussion). Our survey instrument did not gather data in any detail which were relevant to the first two factors.

However, I was able to look for relationships between the third factor, media coverage, via comparing the students' reading and viewing habits and the Cult Scale. In addition, I also tried to correlate reading and viewing habits and the NHI levels. In those few cases where there was any correlation, the association was minimal.[5] Students' self-reported viewing of television shows like "In Search Of" and reading of weekly papers such as the *National Enquirer* did correlate weakly with the Cult Scale, as one would expect. But in just as many cases there was a weak association with use of programs like "Nova," scientific journals like *Nature*, or books by science writers like Carl Sagan.[6] Thus there is not strong support in the data for the claim that uncritical and sensationalistic media coverage is causing cult beliefs any more than are the more serious scientific publications and programs. Apparently our respondents with high cult scores do not hold their beliefs simply because they are exposed to sensationalistic media coverage and not responsible reportage. If irresponsible media play a role in adoption of these beliefs by many students, we still do not know why exposure to responsible media does not seem to have a counteracting effect, or why, of those students exposed to "gee whiz" coverage of pseudoscientific claims, some accept these beliefs, while others do not. Furthermore, the Cult Scale did not show significant patterns of correlation with Singer and Benassi's fourth factor, sociocultural variables such as age, religion, sex, etc. This is in distinct contrast to the findings by Harrold and Eve in this volume concerning creationist beliefs and a further indication that we still have much to learn about cult beliefs.

One other area that Singer and Benassi did not take into consideration is educational input by the scientific community which is neither poor nor wrong. As I stated, just seeing information published in a serious journal could be enough to validate a claim. Why? Because people are not necessarily critically evaluating the substance of the claim and the article.

The results of the analysis of the NHI category also give us food for thought. We who are teachers must be sure what the current pseudoscientific beliefs are, or we put ourselves in the position of building up our own myths about what we think people believe. These "mythologies" may then permeate our teaching and influence the world views of students in ways we had not expected. In our attempt to dispel these claims we might actually be making students aware of ones that many don't know about or might never have heard about. We are caught up in something that we analyze all the time—culture change, especially ideological change. We need to know what is believed now and teach to that. In fact, we might actually be informing students about claims that are not part of their cultural "baggage" without necessarily influencing their ability to evaluate the validity of evidence. We cannot be stagnant and teach in the mode of the 1970s. Anthropology has to be a responsive discipline and it is studies such as this that allow it to be so.

As L. Sprague de Camp (1986:217) in his essay in the tenth anniversary issue of the *Skeptical Inquirer* states: "We must continue to combat the more destructive irrationalities." A study such as this indicates to us what they are and where they are coming from. As long as a psychic can sue a doctor for taking away her psychic powers and win the suit (*Los Angeles Times*, March 29, 1986, section 1, p. 3), then we must always be combative. As de Camp put it, "The scientific debunker's job may be compared to that of the trash collector. The fact that the garbage truck goes by today does not mean that there will not be another load tomorrow. But if the garbage were not collected at all, the results would be much worse, as some cities found when the sanitation workers went on strike" (de Camp 1986:217). So, let's keep on trucking.

Notes

Note: This is a revised version of a paper co-authored by myself and Bernard K. Means titled "East Is East and West Is West? Regional Comparison of Cult Belief Patterns," presented at the fifty-first annual meeting of the Society for American Archaeology in New Orleans, April 1986.

1. The term *Yuppies* refers to young upwardly mobile professionals. These are people in their twenties and thirties who are economically well off and are the target audience for advertising and marketing campaigns.

2. For purposes of this paper definitional and social characteristics of creationism and creationists will follow Harrold and Eve's discussion in this volume. Thus, creationism is both religious and cultural—a particular way of interpreting the Bible as well as a life-style and world view.

3. Those cult questions in which, for at least one subsample (for example, Texas), 20 percent or more of the respondents stated that they had never heard of the subject include Tut's curse (#63), Atlantis (#80), Egypt colonizing the New World (#83), the Ten Lost Tribes (#95), the Shroud of Turin (#97), Noah's Ark on Mount Ararat (#99), and the belief that the government is withholding information on UFOs (#87).

4. All questions which could be used as indicators of cult belief were identified. A factor analysis was carried out on these items. The result showed a clear one-factor solution; that is, all items were sufficiently interrelated to constitute a single empirical domain. Those items with factor loadings greater than .5 for each of the three samples (California, Texas, and Connecticut) were then used to construct the scale. (The Chronbach's Alpha reliability

coefficient for this scale was .70 for the Texas data, .78 for the California data, and .73 for the Connecticut data.) Seven variables were identified for California, nine for Texas, and nine for Connecticut, all of which had a loading of .5 or more, but there were only four with loadings of .5 or greater for all three samples. These four items were then used to construct the Cult Scale in order to have as much comparability across the regions as possible. They are:

a. UFOs are actual spacecraft from other planets. (#65)
b. Bigfoot (Sasquatch) is a real creature roaming in the woods in the Pacific Northwest. (#72)
c. Aliens from other worlds visited earth in the past. (#82)
d. Ghosts really exist. (#101)

Items listed in Table 1 were used as cult belief indicators. Because some questions were asked in a negative way (for example, #79, which states that claims of a mysterious force in the Bermuda Triangle are *not* true), the answers were reversed for factor analysis and percentage comparisons to make them comparable with other items.

5. For the number of books read, Pearson's r was used. It ranged from .12 to .25. The criterion for a significant relationship was the .05 level.

6. References are made to the *National Enquirer*, "Nova," "In Search Of," and Carl Sagan–type books in an attempt to categorize the reading and viewing habits of the student population, and this should be interpreted as referring to a category of books, journals, or programs.

References

Abell, George O., and Barry Singer, eds.
1981 *Science and the Paranormal: Probing the Existence of the Supernatural.* New York: Scribner's.
Burden, Annette
1981 Shroud of mystery. *Science 81* (November):77–83.
Bainbridge, William Sims
1978 Chariots of the gullible. *The Skeptical Inquirer* 3(2):33–48.
Cohen, Daniel
1981 Monsters. In George O. Abell and Barry Singer, eds., *Science and the Paranormal*, pp. 24–39. New York: Scribner's.
de Camp, L. Sprague
1986 The uses of credulity. *The Skeptical Inquirer* 10(3):215–217.
Eve, Raymond A., and Francis B. Harrold
1986 Creationism, cult archaeology, and other pseudoscientific beliefs: A study of college students. *Youth and Society* 17(4):396–421.
Feder, Kenneth L.
1984 Irrationality and popular archaeology. *American Antiquity* 49(3):525–541.
Gardner, Martin
1957 *Fads and Fallacies in the Name of Science.* New York: Dover.
1981 Parapsychology and quantum mechanics. In George O. Abell and Barry Singer, eds., *Science and the Paranormal*, pp. 56–89. New York: Scribner's.
Goodman, Jeffrey
1982 *American Genesis.* New York: Berkley Books.
Krupp, E. C.
1981 Recasting the past: Powerful pyramids, lost continents, and ancient astronauts. In George O. Abell and Barry Singer, eds., *Science and the Paranormal*, pp. 253–295. New York: Scribner's.

Kusche, Larry
1981 The Bermuda Triangle. In George O. Abell and Barry Singer, eds., *Science and the Paranormal*, pp. 296–309. New York: Scribner's.
Lewis, G. A.
1977 Fear of sorcery and the problem of death by suggestion. In J. Blacking, ed., *The Anthropology of the Body*, pp. 111–143. ASA Monograph 15. London: Academic Press.
Los Angeles Times
1986 Woman claims CAT scan ended her psychic powers. March 29, section 1, p. 3.
Means, Bernard K.
1985 A study of pseudoscientific beliefs at Occidental College. Term paper, Occidental College, Los Angeles.
Morrison, Philip, et al.
1977 *The Search for Extraterrestrial Intelligence*. New York: Dover.
Sagan, Carl
1973 *The Cosmic Connection: An Extraterrestrial Perspective*. New York: Anchor Press.
Sheaffer, Robert
1986 Psychic vibrations. *The Skeptical Inquirer* 10(3):208–210.
Siegel, Ronald K.
1981 Life after death. In George O. Abell and Barry Singer, eds., *Science and the Paranormal*, pp. 159–184. New York: Scribner's.
Singer, Barry, and V. A. Benassi
1981 Occult beliefs. *American Scientist* 69:49–55.
Story, Ronald D.
1975 *The von Däniken Affair*. Tucson: Omen Communications.
Truzzi, Marcello
1971 Definition and dimensions of the occult: Towards a sociological perspective. *Journal of Popular Culture* 5(3):635–646.

6.

Patterns of Creationist Belief among College Students

Francis B. Harrold and Raymond A. Eve

We report in this chapter on a study of creationist beliefs among the three samples of college students described by Feder in this volume. We were interested in learning about both how much belief in creationism there was among these students and what factors underlay their acceptance of its scientifically unjustifiable claims. We were also interested to see whether important differences in patterns of belief existed among our three geographically diverse samples.

People may hold creationist beliefs for various reasons; here we follow Singer and Benassi (1981a), who have suggested four main factors which may encourage the acceptance of pseudoscientific beliefs.

1. Cognitive biases, or natural errors in human reasoning. These include the perception of patterns in random data or the failure to consider alternative hypotheses to explain an occurrence when an emotionally attractive one is already available. Consider, for instance, some people's readiness to conclude that strange lights in the night sky represent alien spaceships without really considering other possible explanations.

2. Heavy and uncritical media coverage of pseudoscientific claims which lends a spurious respectability to them. We are all aware, for example, of the enthusiastic press and television coverage given to stories about UFOs or Bigfoot.

3. Inadequate science education, which leaves many people unable to evaluate the validity of such notions as scientific creationism, or ignorant of possible natural explanations for UFOs.

4. Sociocultural factors affecting the availability and attractiveness of such beliefs. Some people hold pseudoscientific beliefs because they find them more satisfying than alternatives. They may, for instance, find belief in ancient astronauts exciting, or creationism spiritually comforting, or their life-styles may reward acceptance of these beliefs and fail to make alternatives readily available.

The first factor above, cognitive biases, involves an area which we did not investigate in this project (however, see Gray's discussion in Chapter 3). We collected information relevant to the other three factors using the survey form described by Feder (Chapter 4) and contained in the appendix.

We examined factor 2, media coverage, by gathering data on students' usage and trust of a dozen media sources, ranging from scientific journals to the *National Enquirer*. We expected that creationist students would tend to use creationist literature and to consider it reliable to a greater extent than other students, and also that they would use and trust conventional sources of information on evolution less than others.

Factor 3, poor science education, could not be extensively studied in the framework of our project, but we gathered some pertinent data and will discuss them below.

Finally, as our main topic, we have enlarged upon our previous study, done among Texas college students, of factor 4, sociocultural variables (Eve and Harrold 1986; Harrold and Eve 1986). Briefly, that study concluded that creationist belief was associated with (and partly explained by) what sociologists have called "cultural fundamentalism" (Page and Clelland 1978), a life-style and world view which is socially, religiously, and politically conservative. Cultural fundamentalists oppose evolution, not simply as an incorrect account of origins, but as an element of secular humanism, which they see as an atheistic philosophy responsible for most of today's moral and social problems. Evolution, especially when taught in public schools, is for them part of a campaign to subvert religion and morality (for example, Morris 1974a:161–168, 178–194). Creationist belief—certainly modern scientific creationism—is thus part of a larger social movement, one which can be described in anthropological terminology as a revitalization or nativistic movement, in which a threatened way of life is defended against imposed change (Wallace 1966; for further discussion, see Kehoe in Chapter 2).

We expected to find the same basic relationships between creationism and other variables in this study as in our prior one; for instance, that creationism in all three samples of students would be positively related to religious conservatism. Because Texas is more conservative, religiously and politically, than California or Connecticut, we expected that creationist belief would be strongest among Texas students.

Summary of Key Findings

A full analysis of the masses of data we collected is beyond the scope of this chapter, but the more important results include the following.

Response-Frequency Findings   We will first look at the levels of response to some of our questionnaire items—at how many students in our samples gave differing responses to selected items.

1. Media exposure. In reviewing the data on students' media exposure, we found that students in all three groups responded similarly when asked about creationist literature (for example, books advocating creationism such as Morris 1974a, 1974b). They invariably ranked it last in usage among a dozen media categories. It fared slightly better in their assessment of its reliability, ranking eighth or ninth, ahead of the *National Enquirer* and books on UFOs, but well behind science-oriented publications and television shows as well as general-interest media like newspapers. At least by their own reports, few students read creationist literature or regard it as a reliable source of information.

2. Exposure to evolution in school. To turn to an issue relevant to factor 3 above, science education, we were interested in students' exposure to the subject of evolution in high school and college. In view of the controversy over the teaching of evolution and creation in the schools, just how common is it for students to be instructed in the subject of evolution?

We asked students whether they had been taught about evolution in high school (see Figure 1 and Feder, this volume) and learned that a majority in each sample had indeed encountered it. However, most of the California students had been taught creationism along with evolution, due to educational policies adopted in that state under creationist political influence. In no sample had a majority of students, while in high school, learned about evolution unaccompanied by creationism. In Texas and Connecticut, over one-fifth reported no instruction in evolution at all. The creationists who want equal time for their beliefs in public schools have reason for satisfaction with these results, especially since, even in schools where evolution is taught, it is often de-emphasized by textbook publishers, administrators, and even teachers for fear of arousing controversy.

For students' college careers, we had no such direct measure of ex-

Were you taught evolution in high school?

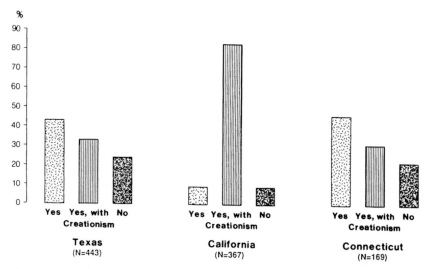

FIGURE 1. Student responses (in percentages) by state in which each sample was drawn when they were asked if they were taught evolution, evolution and creationism, or neither while they were in high school.

posure to evolution, but we did ask them whether they had taken courses in various subject fields. Sizeable majorities in all samples (63 percent to 71 percent) reported having taken at least one course from among the fields of anthropology, biology, or geology. These are fields in which at least some aspects of evolution would be hard to avoid in most courses; thus it seems reasonable to infer that most of our subjects have been exposed to evolution at the college as well as the high school level.

However, as we review their responses to several propositions about evolution and creation, it becomes clear that there is cause to doubt the effectiveness of this exposure in teaching students much about evolution or the evidence for it.

3. Student knowledge and opinions about evolution. In the first place, many students seem to be unclear about what evolution refers to. In an item adapted from biologist Paul Fuerst's (1984) study of over two thousand college biology students, we asked respondents to select the one of four statements best agreeing with their conception of the modern theory of evolution. Some 10 percent in Texas and Connecticut and 5 percent in California chose the most accurate answer, involving evolution as change in populations due to differential reproduction by differing organisms.

The most popular answer (chosen by 36 to 44 percent, depending on the sample) was the least correct in modern scientific perspective—a vitalistic characterization of evolution as a steady march of progress from microbes to man. These results are consistent with Fuerst's findings and with his general conclusion that science education, at least regarding evolution, leaves much to be desired. Thus it seems that many of our subjects, on both sides of the creationism issue, have a hazy or outright erroneous notion of what they are for or against.

We also looked at students' attitudes toward evolution, using again some items modified from Fuerst (1984). Asked whether the modern theory of evolution has a valid scientific foundation (scientific creationists, of course, claim that it does not), a majority of all three samples agreed that it does. In this and other questions, Texas students, as expected, showed consistently more negative attitudes toward evolution than others; here, 58 percent of them agreed with the proposition, compared to 74 percent in California and 79 percent in Connecticut.

Interestingly, from 21 to 26 percent of respondents (depending on the sample) agreed that evolution has a valid scientific foundation but thought that it is untestable, leading us to wonder what their conception of a scientific theory is! Since testability in some form is generally held to be a characteristic of scientific theories, we infer that many of our respondents hold to a common folk conception of the term *theory*—that it is just a notion or guess, not as sure (or as desirable) as a fact, which is something known with certainty (Cavanaugh 1985).

Perhaps most strikingly, 16 percent of the Texas students (along with 8 percent in California and 3 percent in Connecticut) denied evolutionary theory's scientific validity, not on grounds that it is untestable or speculative (other available responses), but because it contradicts their convictions. It is important not to dismiss this finding lightly. It seems to indicate that for many of our antievolutionary respondents, truth—even the validity of a scientific theory—is to be judged on the basis of faith and authority, rather than scientific investigation of the empirical world. (In this connection, see Kehoe's discussion [Chapter 2] of the creationist view of the relationship between Scripture and science.)

The proposition that the theory of evolution correctly explains the history of life on earth was also accepted by a majority of respondents, except in Texas (see Figure 2). No group, though, overwhelmingly accepted it; at least 19 percent in all groups disagreed, and "don't know" responses ranged from 14 to 23 percent.

Let us turn from general evolutionary concepts to some specific claims of scientific creationists. How popular is their message with our respondents?

One item is instructive in its own way. We asked students whether they believed that humans and dinosaurs were once contemporaries. Texas

Evolution Explains History of Life

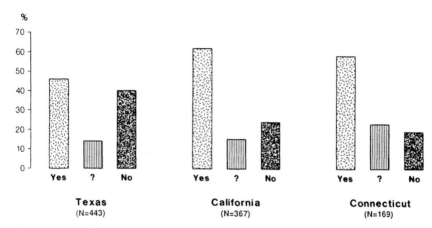

FIGURE 2. Student responses (in percentages) by state in which each sample was drawn when they were asked to indicate their agreement with the assertion that "the theory of evolution correctly explains the history of life on earth." ("?" = "Don't know" and "Never heard of it" answers.)

subjects again stood out, with more accepting than rejecting this notion (see Figure 3). The Texas students are more likely than others to be familiar with the Paluxy River (Texas) "man tracks," claimed by some creationists to be human footprints geologically associated with dinosaur footprints (for example, Morris 1980; see Cole and Godfrey 1985 for refutation). It is most remarkable that nowhere do as many as half the respondents reject this groundless claim; at least 28 percent in each group accept it, and at least 24 percent say they don't know. Though most of these students have apparently received some instruction in evolution and the history of life, many are unaware of the extremely elementary fact that dinosaurs died out many millions of years before humans appeared. We suspect that these results reflect a disturbing level of student ignorance as well as creationist belief.

Next, students were asked about the proposition that there is plenty of scientific evidence against evolution and in favor of special creation. Though simply untrue, this is the principal claim of many creationist authors (for example, Morris 1974b). In Texas, 42 percent of respondents accepted this assertion (see Figure 4); at least a quarter of the other groups did, too, and about one-fifth of each sample didn't know. One could choose to regard this glass as half empty or half full, but nowhere did over 55 percent of respondents reject the "scientific" in scientific creationism.

The item most succinctly stating the classic creationist position says,

Dinosaurs and Man Contemporary

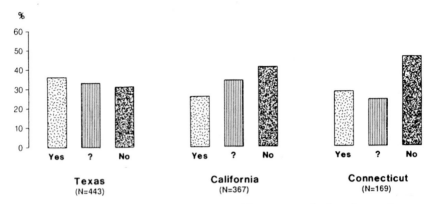

FIGURE 3. Student responses (in percentages) by state in which each sample was drawn when they were asked to indicate agreement with the assertion that "dinosaurs and humans lived at the same time, as is shown by finds of their footprints together." ("?" = "Don't know" and "Never heard of it" answers.)

There is Plenty of Scientific Evidence for Creationism

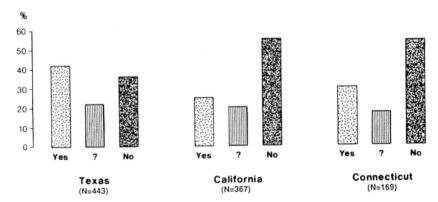

FIGURE 4. Student responses (in percentages) by state in which each sample was drawn when they were asked to indicate agreement with the assertion that "there is a good deal of scientific evidence against evolution and in favor of the Bible's account of Creation." ("?" = "Don't know" and "Never heard of it" answers.)

"God created humanity pretty much in its present form within the last 10,000 years or so." In a 1981 Gallup poll, 44 percent of a national sample of adults agreed with this statement (Moore 1983). Our response levels were not so high, but, nevertheless, 28 percent of the Texas group, and 19 percent of both others, agreed (see Figure 5). Another 23 to 31 percent said they didn't know whether man had been so created or not.

In light of these results, it should come as no surprise that a creationist position with very real political and educational consequences receives strong support in our samples; namely, that creationism should be taught in public schools as an account of origins (see Figure 6). This notion is accepted by a majority (57 percent) in Texas and a plurality elsewhere.

Indeed, when crosstabulating answers to this item with those to another about the teaching of evolution in schools, we found that no fewer than 19 percent of Texas respondents want creationism taught, and evolution excluded, in public schools. The alternative supported by most scientists and educators and upheld in federal courts—to teach evolution but not the religious doctrine of special creation—is supported by at most 31 percent among the three samples. The most popular choice (36 percent to 38 percent agreement) is to teach both evolution and creationism. This option, by the way, was favored by 76 percent of the general public in a 1981 Gallup poll (Moore 1983).

These results indicate real success for the creationist equal-time argu-

Man Created ~ 10,000 years ago

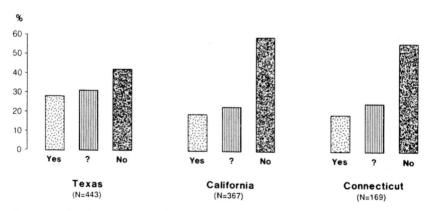

FIGURE 5. Student responses (in percentages) by state in which each sample was drawn when they were asked to indicate agreement with the assertion that "God created man pretty much in his present form within the last 10,000 years or so." ("?" = "Don't know" and "Never heard of it" answers.)

Creationism Should be Taught in Public Schools

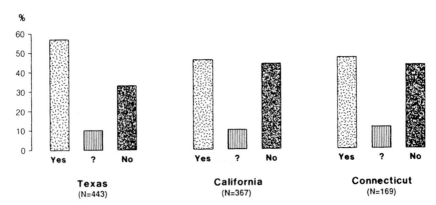

FIGURE 6. Student responses (in percentages) by state in which each sample was drawn when they were asked to indicate agreement with the assertion that "the Bible's account of creation should be taught in public schools as an explanation of origins." ("?" = "Don't know" and "Never heard of it" answers.)

ment. Scientific creationists have given many people the impression that there is a scientific case to be made for creationism. What could be fairer, they now ask, than to teach both points of view, allowing students to make up their own minds? After meeting with little success in the area of state equal-time laws, some creationist activists are concentrating efforts on the politically sensitive level of local schools and boards of education. Given our students' acceptance of the "science" in creationism and of the "fairness" tactic, we may expect continued success for creationists in having their beliefs inserted into school science curricula.

In sum, despite the prior exposure for most respondents to evolution in school, students in our three samples showed disturbingly high levels of creationist belief and of ignorance of evolution. These results, found among a relatively highly educated segment of our population, provide support for the growing perception that Americans' "scientific literacy" (Miller 1983) is low and that our system of science education is less effective than it should be.

We will next consider how creationist belief is related to several background variables about which we gathered data in an attempt to understand better who holds these beliefs and why.

Factors Associated with Creationist Belief

The Creationist Belief Scale In order to investigate the social correlates of creationist belief, we developed a scale measuring the level of such belief among our respondents. This scale could then be easily compared to independent variables related to the backgrounds of our subjects.

The first step in constructing the scale involved the statistical procedure known as factor analysis, which was performed on the total set of responses to the belief items in our questionnaire (independently for each sample).[1] Results indicated two independent underlying statistical tendencies (factors) behind the observed distribution of responses. These were associated respectively with creationism-related items and with all other pseudoscientific beliefs. Thus, as in our prior study, creationism and cult archaeology sorted into two statistically distinct domains in analysis; that is, beliefs tend not to be intercorrelated between the two domains. For a discussion of the noncreationist items, see Hudson's chapter.

We next selected five opinion items (for example, "Everything written in the Bible is literally true"; for the others, see the appendix) which were highly correlated with each other (factor loadings of .5 or higher) and thus formed the creationist belief factor just identified in all three samples. These five items were the basis of the creationist belief scale. Each student's responses to the items were summed to obtain a scale score ranging from 5 (disagreeing strongly with the creationist view on all five items) to 25 (agreeing strongly with that view on all items). Since the scale was comprised of the same five items in all three samples, there is reasonably good comparability of scores across samples, assuming equal measurement accuracy for each sample.[2]

We examined students' scores on this scale for their relationships to demographic, educational, and ideological background characteristics (see Feder, this volume). We then compared analyses of each of the three samples of students to determine the consistency across samples of the relationships found.[3]

In the following discussion, all relationships between variables are statistically significant at the .05 level (at least) unless otherwise specified. We will present in order the results related to three of the elements discussed earlier which contribute to pseudoscientific belief: media exposure, science education background, and sociocultural variables.

Creationism and Media Exposure In exploring the relationships between students' creationist belief scores and their exposure to and trust in various media, we found that creationism tended to be far more strongly related to their degree of exposure to differing media than to their judgment of the reliability of these media as sources of information.

Interestingly, frequency of use of most media types was essentially unrelated to creationism, as in the cases of TV news and daily newspapers, programs like "In Search Of" and "That's Incredible," weekly newsmagazines, books on UFOs or ancient astronauts, and science fiction.

Let us look at those cases where we did find significant relationships between media use and creationism. Frequency of use of professional science journals like *Nature* was negatively correlated with creationism scores, though only in Texas (Pearson's $r = -.26$); that is, the more subjects in Texas read such journals, the lower their creationism scores tended to be. Reading of creationist literature was positively correlated with higher creationism only in Connecticut ($r = .22$); that is, the more students read such literature, the higher their creationism scores. Reading popular science magazines like *Discover* was negatively related to creationism in Texas and Connecticut ($r = -.24$ and $-.19$), and, more weakly, in California ($r = -.10$; see Figure 7). The work of science writers like Carl Sagan showed a fairly strong inverse relationship with creationism in Texas and, to a lesser extent, California ($r = -.29$ and $-.16$, respectively).

We further found that students who reported reading the *National Enquirer* and similar papers had a modest but consistent tendency to be more creationist in all samples ($r = .15$ in Texas, $.19$ in California, and $.24$ in Connecticut; see Figure 7). (Hereafter, statistics for the three samples will always be listed in this order—Texas, California, Connecticut—unless otherwise noted.)

It was also interesting that the strongest and most consistent relationship found across all samples was that those who often watch TV science programs on PBS like "Nova" tend to be less creationist ($r = -.39$ in Texas and $-.28$ elsewhere; see Figure 7). Note that the strongest consistent relationship found here involved exposure to television programs rather than any print medium. This may be significant in the context of the rise of television as the primary source of information for more and more people. However, longitudinal research would be required to determine reliably the direction of causality in this relationship (or the others mentioned above). Whether watching these programs accounts for lower creationism or initial belief levels determine exposure to the programs remains to be learned.

In contrast to the foregoing, we found no strong or consistent relationships between creationism and students' judgment of media reliability, except that creationist students in all groups tended to rate creationist literature as highly reliable, even though they rarely read it (see Figure 7).

CORRELATIONS (Pearson's r) WITH THE CREATIONISM SCALE

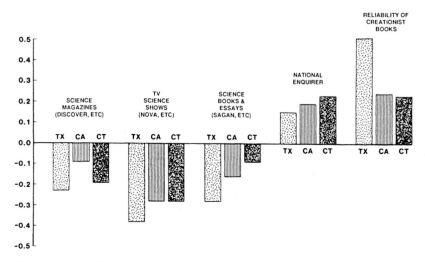

FIGURE 7. Correlations (using Pearson's correlation coefficients) between types of media used by students and their scores on the creationism scale (with an added item on the right which asked if they believed that creationist books are a reliable source of information).

Evidently, at least in the context of this study, what people read or watch is much more important than how reliable they judge it to be. Furthermore, it is interesting to note that most types of media, including newspapers and TV news, do not appear to be related one way or the other to creationism.

Creationism and Educational Background   As in our prior study, we examined relationships between creationism scores and several aspects of students' educational and intellectual experiences.

1. Grade-point average. In our prior study (Eve and Harrold 1986), we found that the overall college grade point averages (or GPAs) of creationist students tended to be lower than those of other students, presumably because they resisted learning subjects, such as evolution, which were contrary to their beliefs (remember the students mentioned above who rejected evolution as a valid scientific theory because it contradicts their convictions).

CORRELATIONS (Pearson's r) WITH THE CREATIONISM SCALE

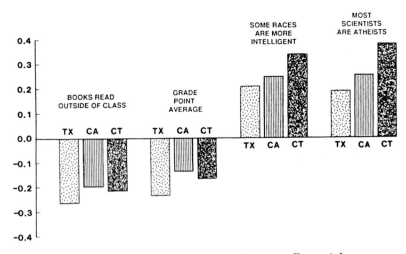

FIGURE 8. Correlations (using Pearson's correlation coefficients) between students' scores on the creationism scale and number of books read outside of class assignments, their grade point averages, and the assertions that "some races are more intelligent than others" and "most scientists are atheists."

We found similar results in this study, especially among the Texas subjects, where there is a negative correlation (r = -.21) between creationism scale scores and GPA; that is, a moderate tendency for more creationist students to have lower grades (see Figure 8). The same relationship is found, though a bit more weakly, in the other two samples (r = -.14 and -.15, respectively).

2. Choice of academic major. There is also some relationship between creationism and choice of academic major (Cramer's V = .21, .22, and .29). Anthropology majors are found relatively infrequently among those in the most creationist one-third of our students, except in California, where about a third of such majors fell into each of the three creationism-score groups. On the other hand, in all three samples business majors were highly creationist distinctly more often than other students; 47 percent of business majors were highly creationist in Texas, 56 percent in California, and 52 percent in Connecticut. We think it is no coincidence that so many creationist students tend to cluster in a major field which has fewer potentially threatening intellectual implications than most other fields.

3. Books read outside class. Again, as in the past, we found that those students who reported reading fewer books outside assigned course readings tended to have higher creationism scores (see Figure 8). In Texas the correlation between creationism and books read was -.26; elsewhere it was -.19 and -.21.

4. Exposure to evolution in school. Our findings were inconsistent regarding high school exposure to evolution and its relationship to creationism. In Texas and Connecticut, results were what might be intuitively expected: students exposed to evolution alone in high school had lower creationism scores than those who had also been taught creationism. However, in the California sample, this trend was reversed; of those exposed to both views of origins, 32 percent were highly creationist, but of those exposed to evolution only, 57 percent were highly creationist.

If high school exposure to evolution is inconsistently related to creationism, are college courses more clearly related to it? Here again, there was no neat pattern. Courses in history, logic, and (interestingly) geology were consistently unrelated to creationism across the three samples, while archaeology courses were consistently negatively related to it. Of students who had taken archaeology in California, none were highly creationist; the proportions in Texas and Connecticut were 4 percent and 19 percent, respectively.

For several other subjects, including psychology, astronomy, biology,[4] chemistry, physics, and religious studies, relationships with creationism scores varied widely between samples. Astronomy courses, for example, were unrelated to creationism in our California sample, negatively related in Connecticut, and positively related in Texas.

Perhaps the only conclusion we can draw here is that classroom instruction in evolution and/or scientific method cannot be expected to straightforwardly reduce creationist belief. The relationships we found are complex, sometimes counterintuitive, and often variable across samples; they probably interact in complex ways with situational variables, such as student lack of interest or resistance to learning some material, ineffective teaching methods, and avoidance or minimization by instructors of "controversial" topics like evolution. More research will be needed to produce any consistent explanation for these findings.

In sum, creationist students tended significantly across all three samples to have lower grades, to read fewer books, and to major in business more often than others. These relationships are probably explicable in terms of avoidance by creationist students of threatening ideas. However, as noted above in the case of media exposure, the direction of causality cannot be assumed. It seems likely that learning success (Lawson 1983), reading patterns, and choice of major among creationist students are powerfully influenced by prior beliefs; however, it may be at least partly true that learning success and the other factors also help shape such beliefs. Finally, it should come as a matter of concern to science educators that among our students, as among those in our prior study and those of Bainbridge (1978) and Feder (1984), college instruction in relevant courses did not consistently reduce creationist belief.

Creationism and Attitudes toward Science   We were able to devote relatively little attention to the relationship between students' creationism and their understanding of scientific concepts and methods, often cited as a contributing factor toward such belief. As noted above, though, we did find indications of poor understanding of evolution and other scientific concepts among our subjects.

We did, however, gather data on a closely related issue: student attitudes toward science and the relationship of these attitudes to creationism. These data were relevant to the dispute between two differing interpretations of creationism; one camp sees creationism as irrational antiscience, while the other views it as flawed but not irrational science. In the former view (for example, Norelli and Proulx 1982), creationism is another manifestation of anti-intellectualism and irrationalism in American culture, as seen before in the antievolutionism of the 1920s or, in a more recent form, in the rejection of scientific rationalism by the counterculture of the late 1960s. In the latter view, creationists, especially scientific creationists, acknowledge the high status of science by arguing that a literal reading of the Book of Genesis is scientifically valid, though they use an outmoded view of what constitutes scientific method and explanation (Cavanaugh 1983, 1985; Marsden 1984).

We reasoned that negative attitudes toward science on the part of creationists would be consistent with the first, antiscience explanation mentioned above, while positive creationist attitudes toward science would be consistent with the second. We asked respondents several questions regarding their attitudes toward science.

Despite some erosion in recent years (Walsh 1982), the American public has a generally high opinion of science and scientists (Etzioni and Nunn 1974). Our subjects were typical in this regard: they agreed overwhelmingly (70 to 78 percent) that "science has done more good than bad for the world" and that science education is a top priority for our schools (66 to 83 percent). Smaller majorities (51 percent in each case) disagreed with the negative proposition that "science makes our lives change too fast."

When we crosstabulated the responses to such items with creationism scores, few consistent associations emerged. There was a general tendency for creationists, especially in Connecticut, to think that "most scientists are atheists" (r = .19, .26, and .39, respectively; see Figure 8). Otherwise, however, the only sample with results supporting the irrational antiscience model is the Texas one. Among those students, while creationism is unrelated to the "science has done more good than bad" item, it is moderately related (r = .18) to agreement that science makes life change too fast and negatively related (r = -.11) to agreement that science education is a top priority. In the other groups, no patterned relationships were found, thus indicating that a student's attitude toward science is not a crucial factor in predicting creationism. Certainly, no overall tendency was found for creationists to be especially antiscience or pro-science. In short, neither competing view of creationism is solidly supported by these findings. We suspect that both are partly true. Like most Americans, creationists tend for the most part to favor science, though without much understanding of it (Miller 1983) and with some misgivings.

Creationist Belief and Demographic Background Characteristics A significant relationship between age and creationist belief was found only in Texas, where older students tended to be less creationist (r = -.20); however, only in Texas were there significant numbers of students older than twenty-two; that is, beyond the usual college age range. Sex, too, was related to creationist belief only in Texas, where (more traditional?) female students were slightly more creationist (r = .12). Thus, neither sex nor age could be shown in our samples to be consistently related to creationism.

Intriguingly, however, racial background was significantly related to creationism in all three samples (Cramer's V = .19 in Texas, .17 in California, and .19 in Connecticut, where there were few minorities and the relationship was significant only at the .06 level). Black, Hispanic, and Asian students tended to score significantly higher in creationist belief than whites. This finding is somewhat surprising; prominent creationists, from Duane Gish to Jerry Falwell, are invariably conservative or fundamentalist white Protestants, and it is from this sector of the populace that creationism is generally perceived to draw its support.

Based on experience in our previous study and on common racial differences in religious identification, we again compared creationism and race, this time controlling for religion. We wondered whether apparent racial differences in creationism might really be due to differing religious preferences among racial groups. However, this turned out generally not to be the case. In several important cases, there were differences in creationism between coreligionists of different races.

Black Protestants in Texas, for instance, are somewhat more likely to be highly creationist than white Protestants (V = .166, p = .067); similar re-sults were found for Hispanic Catholics (versus white Catholics) in Texas (V = .24); nonreligious Asians in Connecticut (V = .58) and California (V = .49); and, among Protestants, black Baptists in Texas (V = .30) and Asian Baptists in California (V = .78).

Thus, minority group members tend broadly to be more creationist than whites. Perhaps the theory of evolution has been sufficiently abused in the past to support racist attitudes (see Stocking 1982a, 1982b) that many nonwhites have come to be suspicious of the whole concept. Or per-haps most minority-group members are simply too concerned with other issues to consider evolution an important public problem calling for their participation. In any case, this unexpected relationship deserves further research.

Not so unexpected was the strong relationship found between cre-ationism and geographical region. Texas students had higher creationism scores than those from the other groups; the Texas mean score was 16.0 (on a scale from 5 to 25), compared to 12.9 for California and 13.3 for Con-necticut. As expected, the Texans showed the highest levels; however, be-lief levels elsewhere were certainly not low.

The level of education attained by students' parents, one indicator of socioeconomic class, was unrelated to creationism in our samples. This had been expected on the basis of both our last study's findings and the lack of a dominant class element in cultural fundamentalism (Page and Clelland 1978).

In short, we found creationism among our students to be related strongly to race but not to age, sex, or parents' education.

Creationism and Ideology   As in our prior study, we found a notable rela-tionship between political and religious conservatism and creationism. When students were asked to identify themselves as politically conser-vative, moderate, liberal, or radical, fairly strong correlations were found between creationism and conservatism in all samples (r = .26, .15, and .20, respectively; see Figure 9).

A still stronger relationship obtained in all groups when we asked stu-dents to identify their religious orientation as fundamentalist, conser-vative, moderate, liberal, or nonreligious. Here we found very strong cor-relations of, respectively, r = .48, .47, and .46 (see Figure 9) between creationism and religious conservatism. Respondents' creationism scores were also highly correlated with their self-reports of the importance of religion in their lives (r = .50, .45, and .28; see Figure 9).

Protestants tended to be the most highly creationist in all samples, fol-

CORRELATIONS (Pearson's r) WITH THE CREATIONISM SCALE

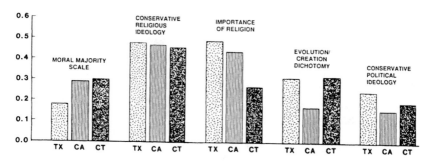

FIGURE 9. Correlations (using Pearson's correlation coefficients) between students' scores on the creationism scale and their responses favorable to the Moral Majority, their self-definition as political conservatives and religious conservatives, their self-reports of the importance of religion in their lives, and agreement with the assertion that "one can believe in the Bible and creation, or atheistic evolution; there is really no middle ground."

lowed in order by Catholics, Jews, and those professing no religion. Among Protestant denominations there was some variation across the three samples, but generally, conservative denominations like the Baptists and Churches of Christ tended unsurprisingly to be more creationist than more liberal groups such as the Episcopalians.

Creationism was also positively correlated with a tendency to polarize the concepts of creation and evolution, as denoted by agreement with the statement that one must accept either the biblical account of creation or atheistic evolution, with no middle ground possible (see Figure 9). This position is advocated primarily by fundamentalist groups and opposed by mainline denominations (for example, see Frye 1983).

As a general measure of politicoreligious conservatism, we utilized a scale adapted from Shupe and Stacey (1982) to measure students' adherence to positions advocated by the Moral Majority, specifically involving prayer in public schools, abortion, and the Equal Rights Amendment. Not surprisingly, creationism was correlated with scores on this Moral Majority scale at a level of r = .19 in Texas and .30 elsewhere (see Figure 9).

Finally, we were surprised to find that creationism was positively correlated (r = .21, .25, and .35, respectively) with agreement with the statement, "Some races of people are more intelligent than others" (see Figure 8). Not only was this relationship significant outside the southern state of Texas, it was actually stronger in the other two states. We provisionally attribute this association between creationism and such a racist assertion to the overall conservatism correlated with racism; certainly in the context of U.S. history the attitudes of earlier generations of whites tended to be more overtly racist than they are today. Furthermore, the association of creationism with both a racist claim and the assertion (noted above) that most scientists are atheists seems indicative of a tendency toward stereotypical thinking and distrust of outgroups reminiscent of the "authoritarian personality" described by Adorno et al. (1950). Clearly, this set of associations deserves further research.

Conclusion

Creationist belief, as expected, was clearly highest in our Texas sample but widespread in both other groups. On the basis of results from our three varied samples, college instructors who deal with evolution may reasonably expect that a fifth or more of their students will be creationists who think that the earth and humanity were directly created a few thousand years ago and who may be very resistant to learning any differently. This is not a cheerful finding for higher education in one of the world's most scientifically advanced societies.

Creationist belief among college students (and, indeed, generally) is a complex phenomenon, not susceptible of simple explanation. It appears that each of the four causal factors discussed above contributes to some extent to such belief. Regarding factor 1 (cognitive biases), see Gray in this volume. Our findings concerning the other factors may be briefly recapitulated.

For the most part, we found no significant relationship between creationism and what students read and watched or how reliable they thought this material to be. Where significant relationships were found, the quantity of exposure to various types of media rather than their perceived quality is what seems to be crucial (this is something television advertisers have long believed). The strongest relationship found was a negative one between creationism and television science programs. Perhaps the depiction of scientific procedures in these programs, though simplified for a mass audience, offsets the superficial and uncritical coverage of science and pseudoscience in most media; however, this is a subject for future research.

We could not thoroughly investigate the area of science education in the present study, but our data are consistent with the suggestions of others that poor science education contributes significantly to pseudoscientific belief. Students unfamiliar with scientific knowledge (for example, the relative ages of dinosaurs and man) or with scientific procedures and concepts (for example, "theory") are badly equipped to evaluate scientific creationism. Regarding attitudes toward science, students tended broadly to regard it positively, whether or not they were creationist.

As expected, our findings in the area of sociocultural factors were consistent with the proposition that cultural fundamentalism is a major factor contributing toward creationism. Texas students were distinctly more creationist than others, but the expected relationships of creationism with educational and ideological background tended to be found in all three samples. Unexpected findings meriting further study include the persistent tendency of minority-group members to be more creationist than whites and, paradoxically, the association between creationism and agreement with a racist assertion.

Can something be done about the discouraging levels of creationist belief among students like those in our study? We believe that the answer is a qualified "yes." Much has already been accomplished, especially in the response of the scientific community to demonstrate, in debates and publications, the intellectual bankruptcy of scientific creationism (for example, Godfrey 1983; Montagu 1984). Refutation, however, is not enough when so many students and others are unprepared to evaluate the rational adequacy of pseudoscientific claims. We think that the best long-term antidote to creationism within the power of the scientific and educational communities is improved education in science—not as an authoritative collection of facts to be memorized, but as a rational and reliable set of methods for learning about the world. Educators who have dealt with pseudoscience in college courses by using it as a tool to teach critical thinking and scientific method rather than ignoring it as beneath notice or too controversial have reported significant successes in reducing such beliefs (see Gray, this volume and 1984; Saladin 1986; Thwaites 1986). If such approaches became routine parts of primary and secondary schooling as well as college curricula, we suspect that creationist belief would decrease.

However, as we have seen, powerful subcultural forces encourage creationism. Deeply held beliefs are not always susceptible to change. Some who have reported reduction of pseudoscientific beliefs in the classes mentioned above are struck less by the reduction than by the level of belief remaining after "dehoaxing" (see Singer and Benassi 1981b; Gray, this volume). Whether or not science education is improved or creationism gets equal time in public schools, some level of such belief will long be with us.

Notes

1. Factor analysis statistically analyzes the intercorrelations among responses to a large number of questions in order to detect *factors*, underlying forces which operate in such a way as to cause certain items to intercorrelate highly. The technique is often used to see whether all items in a pool can be treated as if they are measuring the same underlying phenomenon (for example, creationist belief) or whether more than one underlying dimension causes multiple distinct clusters of items. We used a principle-factors analysis to determine the number of factors present in our data as represented by a plot of the eigenvalues, and then used the number of factors found to conduct a principle-components analysis to create the scales. The two factors found led to two scales, one for creationism and one for other pseudoscientific belief (discussed by Hudson in Chapter 5).

2. Furthermore, statistical measures of scale reliability were acceptable for all three samples. The Chronbach's Alpha reliability coefficient (a commonly used measure of scale reliability) for this scale was .72 for the Texas sample, .68 for California, and .60 for Connecticut.

3. Where possible, we used Pearson's correlation coefficient (r) to measure the relationship between two variables in a sample (for example, between scale scores and students' age). Sometimes, however, the independent variable of interest was nominal (in other words, it could not be ranged on a scale of high to low values, as with region of origin or religious denomination). In those cases, we assessed the significance of the relationship using the chi-square statistic and its strength using Cramer's V statistic. To allow this, each sample was broken into three groups on the basis of creationist belief scores; that is, the approximately one-third of students with the highest scores were in one group, the third with middle-range scores in the second, and the third with the lowest scores in the third group. For convenience, we will refer to these subgroups of each sample as those high, moderate, and low in creationist belief.

We suggest caution in comparing the exact magnitude of Pearson's r across the three samples. Measures of association like r may be affected by various factors, such as the somewhat differing validity and reliability of particular items across samples, and even the statistical variances of items. Nonetheless, while this caution is in order, large differences across samples will be described and discussed, because the probability of their being fairly accurate is high.

4. Fuerst (1984) found that acceptance of evolution was positively related to the number of biology courses taken by students, indicating that either more study increases acceptance, or nonaccepting students avoid further biology courses (or, to some degree, both). Our instrument did not measure number of courses taken; but, comparing those who had taken a biology course or courses to those who had not, we found no relationship between instruction in biology and creationism in Texas, a negative relationship in Connecticut, and a positive relationship in California.

References

Adorno, T. W., et al.
1950 *The Authoritarian Personality.* New York: Harper.
Bainbridge, William S.
1978 Chariots of the gullible. *The Skeptical Inquirer* 3(2):33–48.
Cavanaugh, Michael A.
1983 A sociological account of scientific creationism: Science, true science, pseudoscience. Ph.D. dissertation, University of Pittsburgh. Ann Arbor: University Microfilms International.

1985 Scientific creationism and rationality. *Nature* 315:185–89.
Cole, John R., and Laurie R. Godfrey, eds.
1985 The Paluxy River footprint mystery—solved. Special issue of *Creation/Evolution* 5(1).
Etzioni, Amitai, and Clyde Nunn
1974 The public appreciation of science in contemporary America. *Daedalus* 103:191–205.
Eve, Raymond A., and Francis B. Harrold
1986 Creationism, cult archaeology, and other pseudoscientific beliefs: A study of college students. *Youth and Society* 17(4):396–421.
Feder, Kenneth L.
1984 Irrationality and popular archaeology. *American Antiquity* 49(3):525–541.
Frye, Roland M., ed.
1983 *Is God a Creationist?* New York: Scribner's.
Fuerst, Paul A.
1984 University student understanding of evolutionary biology's place in the creation/evolution controversy. *Ohio Journal of Science* 84:218–228.
Godfrey, Laurie R., ed.
1983 *Scientists Confront Creationism*. New York: Norton.
Gray, Thomas
1984 University course reduces belief in paranormal. *The Skeptical Inquirer* 8:247–251.
Harrold, Francis B., and Raymond A. Eve
1986 Noah's Ark and ancient astronauts: Pseudoscientific beliefs about the past among a sample of college students. *The Skeptical Inquirer* 11(1):61–75.
Lawson, A. F.
1983 Predicting science achievement: The role of developmental level, disembedding ability, mental capacity, prior knowledge, and beliefs. *Journal of Research in Science Teaching* 20:117–129.
Marsden, George M.
1984 Understanding fundamentalist views of science. In Ashley Montagu, ed., *Science and Creationism*, pp. 95–116. New York: Oxford University Press.
Miller, Jon D.
1983 Scientific literacy: A conceptual and empirical review. *Daedalus* 112:29–48.
Montagu, Ashley, ed.
1984 *Science and Creationism*. New York: Oxford.
Moore, John A.
1983 Why are there creationists? *Journal of Geological Education* 31:95–104.
Morris, Henry M.
1974a *The Troubled Waters of Evolution*. San Diego: Creation-Life Publishers.
1974b *Scientific Creationism*. San Diego: Creation-Life Publishers.
Morris, John D.
1980 *Tracking Those Incredible Dinosaurs . . . and the People Who Knew Them*. San Diego: Creation-Life Publishers.
Norelli, Richard J., and Robert R. Proulx
1982 Anti-science as a component in the growing popularity of creationism. In Stephen Pasteur and William Haviland, eds., *Confronting the Creationists*, pp. 4–11. Northeastern Anthropological Association, Occasional Proceedings, no. 1.
Page, Anne L., and Donald A. Clelland
1978 The Kanawha County textbook controversy: A study of the politics of life style concern. *Social Forces* 57:265–281.
Saladin, Kenneth S.
1986 Educational approaches to creationist politics in Georgia. In R. W. Hanson, ed., *Science and Creation: Geological, Theological, and Educational Perspectives*, pp. 104–127. New York: Macmillan.

Shupe, Anson, and William A. Stacey
1982 *Born-Again Politics and the Moral Majority: What Social Surveys Really Show.* New York: Edwin Mellen.
Singer, Barry, and Victor A. Benassi
1981a Occult beliefs. *American Scientist* 69:49–55.
1981b Fooling some of the people all of the time. *The Skeptical Inquirer* 5(2):17–24.
Stocking, George W., Jr.
1982a The persistence of polygenist thought in post-Darwinian anthropology. In George W. Stocking, Jr., *Race, Culture, and Evolution,* pp. 42–68. Chicago: University of Chicago Press.
1982b The dark-skinned savage: The image of primitive man in evolutionary anthropology. In George W. Stocking, Jr., *Race, Culture, and Evolution,* pp. 110–132. Chicago: University of Chicago Press.
Thwaites, William M.
1986 A two-model creation versus evolution course. In R. W. Hanson, ed., *Science and Creation: Geological, Theological, and Educational Perspectives,* pp. 92–103. New York: Macmillan.
Wallace, Anthony F. C.
1966 *Religion: An Anthropological View.* New York: Random House.
Walsh, John
1982 Public attitude toward science is yes, but—. *Science* 215:270–72.

7.

ETs, Rafts, and Runestones: Confronting Pseudoarchaeology in the Classroom

Suzanne Knudson Engler

One reads a great deal about myths and mysteries, attitudes and beliefs these days. And I must admit that in the 1970s, when my colleague Luanne Hudson and I began to present classes on topics concerning pseudoscientific beliefs, I had no idea of the extent and depth of student interest in such matters. The beginning point of our work in this area was our first team-taught class, "Apes, Astronauts, and Androids," in which we attempted to teach anthropology through the use of science fiction. We decided to include the subject of ancient astronauts and extraterrestrial contacts almost as an afterthought. Erich von Däniken's work was extremely popular at that time, and the interest that our students expressed in the topic convinced us that pseudoscience literature needed to be dealt with in a formal class setting.

The reaction of that first class was so enthusiastic that we began to seriously consider the possibility of offering a class that dealt with nothing but monsters and mysteries, again with the overall aim of providing the student with a general introduction to anthropology and archaeology. Thus was born "Myths, Monsters, and Mysteries," a class that covered virtually everything from the Loch Ness monster to pyramid power and the Nazca lines. This was quickly followed by "Shamans, Sorcerers, and Soul-catchers: Anthropological Studies of Paranormal Phenomena," "ETs, Poltergeists, and Things that Go Bump in the Night," "The Anthropology of Fear," "Maps, Monks, and Runestones: Pre-Columbian Voyages of Exploration" and "The Culture Bearers: Travelers on the Pan American Trail" (two classes that dealt extensively with transoceanic contact theories), and a couple of others that were essentially variations on the same themes.

At this point there are probably two questions the reader might ask; namely, how did you get approval from curriculum control bodies for teaching all those "off-the-wall" classes, and why would you want to anyway? The "how" was actually simple—we started our program under the watchful eye of the College of Continuing Education (CCE) at the University of Southern California, which was at that time anxious to expand its programs and develop more innovative classes to reach outside the university. Needless to say, our classes were popular with lay public and students alike. Our own anthropology department colleagues were amused but essentially tolerant, so we got away with it—though not before we earned something of a reputation for being creative (if somewhat eccentric).

The "why" of the matter is of course much more pertinent. We began our classes for most of the usual reasons, reasons that other instructors have perhaps used to justify presenting courses of a similar nature. We found our students to be understandably intrigued with the von Däniken books and all their sequels and imitations. Atlantis had once again floated to the surface and—shades of Jules Verne—the earth was hollowed out! The New World was pictured as a virtual Grand Central Station of the ancient world, with everyone from the Phoenicians to the Celts trekking back and forth across the Atlantic at regular intervals.

Additionally, we had the unique opportunity to present programs for both credit and noncredit audiences, involving not only our regular students but the public as well. Admittedly, we were doing some marketing here—CCE programs must have high enough enrollments to pay for themselves or they are cancelled. None of ours ever were cancelled, a fact I believe reflects the tremendous interest that people continue to have in pseudoscientific ideas.

More important, we both felt it was time to take a direct approach to the whole matter of pseudoanthropology, pseudoarchaeology, and pseudoscience in general. As anthropologists we really are, as Chambers (1985) suggested in his book on applied anthropology, in the business of knowledge and information transfer. We felt that it was not enough to pay lip service to odds and ends of the pseudoscientific literature within the context of an ordinary introductory archaeology class. What was really needed was a class devoted totally to dealing with such issues and claims. And so the Popular Archaeology and Anthropology Program came into being.

Although the content of each class differed considerably we took the same basic approach to each. Our primary goal was the teaching of anthropology and archaeology, which of course is what we were hired to do. But the anthropological facts were presented in a format that provided us with the opportunity to evaluate objectively the various theories (or monsters) proposed by pseudoscientists. We always began with a thorough discussion of the scientific method: what a hypothesis is, how you devise one, how and why you test one, what constitutes adequacy, etc. This led to the evaluation of the logic involved in creating and testing a hypothesis and thus into specific discussions of the logic used (or misused) by the writers we were evaluating. We discussed the use of evidence and what happens when one takes it out of context. And we essentially tried to provide the students with enough data to formulate their own evaluations of pseudoscientific theories. One thing we conscientiously avoided was the temptation to condemn the various pseudoscientific ideas and their proponents (admittedly difficult when it comes to someone like Erich von Däniken). Rather, we attempted to provide students with the context and information base so often ignored by such writers and let them come to their own conclusions.

From the outset we realized that it would be impossible for us to take the time necessary to deal with all the literature of this kind that we would like to have presented. Anyone who has tried to examine and counter a particular pseudoscientific argument knows that covering everything is usually far too time-consuming to be practical. There is just too much of it, and by the time you have finished with one book, the author comes up with another and you must begin all over again. However, many archaeologists have taken the time to refute some theory or another that is directly pertinent to their own area of specialization.

Our approach, therefore, was to invite experts from various fields to deal with specialized aspects of the class; for example, the Bermuda Triangle, Bigfoot, and so on. For example, Edwin Krupp, director of the Griffith Park Observatory and a well-known scholar in the field of archaeoastronomy, is also a keen student of UFO and ancient astronaut literature. His theatrical lecture style, combined with his professional scientific insight and appreciation of archaeological principles, yielded lectures that were both thought-provoking and entertaining to student and layperson.

As the instructors of record in the class, our job was to provide the basics of archaeological background, an introduction to scientific method and research design, and the all-important thread of continuity that helped tie the diverse lecturers and their discussion materials to the course focus, whether it was an examination of the paranormal or an evaluation of the various theories of transatlantic contact. We also provided supervision of student research, which usually consisted of in-depth studies of related arguments, myths, or monsters covered marginally or not at all in the body of the course. And of course we administered exams designed to test both students' comprehension of the archaeological principles and their ability to critically evaluate pseudoscientific ideas.

In creating, organizing, and presenting our programs Hudson and I encountered both pleasures and pitfalls. The opportunity we had to invite lecturers from all over the country was something many of our colleagues have found enviable (and we ourselves enjoyed immensely). Varying the menu with people whom your students have heard about but never seen before was in itself an important addition to the academic value of the classes. We invited experts from sociology, history, psychology, anthropology, archaeology, astronomy, marine biology, and many other fields. And we also included a few somewhat more controversial characters.

Now, inviting a "psychic archaeologist" to lecture to one of your classes is not something that we "legitimate archaeologists" would ordinarily consider doing. However, we felt that since we were dealing directly with such matters anyway, we ought to give the opposition some time to present its viewpoint. Needless to say, deciding whom to invite can become a very serious consideration. Even within the ranks of pseudo-archaeology there are good scholars and not-so-good—and a number of downright terrible ones! So, for instance, when we were faced with the question of which individual to invite to discuss psychic archaeology we passed over Maxine Asher, director of the poorly conceived and ill-fated Atlantis expedition to Spain, and chose instead Stephen Schwartz, then-director of the Philosophical Research Society in Los Angeles.

Schwartz was a fairly respected scholar, documentary filmmaker, and self-styled psychic researcher (Schwartz 1978) working at the time at a reputable research facility on Eastern religions, and we calculated that he would be a bit safer than someone like Asher. Unfortunately, Schwartz committed some of the very logical errors we dealt with in the class. He turned out to belong to the class of researchers that use classic, scientific "If A, then B" logic, but somewhere along the line seem to forget or overlook the "If, then" part. His lecture basically revolved around the theme of "what do you want to believe of the data?"

This kind of event was actually something we had prepared ourselves for, and in later classes we were able to turn Schwartz's presentation into a good teaching exercise by asking the students themselves to critically evaluate his ideas and the methods he had used to present them. We found that the class, originally very impressed with his presentation, profited from discussing the more egregious flaws in argument and logic. In short, we used the chance to teach them better critical thinking.

Schwartz served well to convince them that just because someone is teaching a class he or she is not necessarily scientifically or logically correct in his or her arguments.

A pitfall which we had not anticipated surfaced on another occasion when a lecturer blatantly used his lecture in our program as an excuse to claim affiliation with a major university in the promotional materials for his pseudoscientific "research." We have lost our naiveté on the "affiliated-with-a-major-university" ploy and are now much more careful to weigh the possible implications of this kind of uninvited association. One's university publicity department can get rather testy about these things if they go too far, but we have been fortunate and have not experienced any serious repercussions. Perhaps more important, one must also consider the reactions of one's own colleagues, who often think that this kind of class is not academically credible anyway. So we have, wisely I think, limited the number and kind of controversial lecturers we invite to participate but have not eliminated them entirely.

Although one can anticipate problems with some guest lecturers in a class on pseudoscience, it is often those whom you least suspect who turn out to be problems. In fact, we received some of our biggest surprises from our colleagues in anthropology. On one occasion, one of the anthropologists who participated in our classes on the paranormal brought a *curandera* (a curer who uses traditional folk techniques) from the local Hispanic community. The *curandera* was just one of a number of such women our friend was engaged in studying at the time. The *curandera* carried out a healing ceremony in the classroom that evening and the students were fascinated. What was most fascinating to us, however, was the lack of objectivity displayed by our colleague in the class summation following the ceremony. As it turned out, the colleague was one of the *curandera's* patients. The colleague had come from the same cultural background as the curer and was obviously still wrapped tightly in the same belief system. I think this is a very good example of how one's own ideas tend to remain "real" or "true"—a warning that we need to be consciously aware of our cultural ideas and how they influence our perceptions of others as well as ourselves.

In still another instance we had the shock of realizing that a colleague had, in essence, "gone native" in the classroom. In this case it was very obvious that the colleague's study of paranormal phenomena had become a belief system for that individual. Perhaps this is not as blatant a case as Carlos Castaneda's, but like the *curandera* incident it immediately makes it necessary for the instructors to regroup and help lead the students to a more critical analysis of the content and intent of the lecture.

We generally assume that our colleagues are scientifically reasonable, even if our hypotheses or approaches don't always see eye to eye. What happens when they are not? Students unfortunately tend to be less critical than they should or could be. They generally believe what they read and, especially, what they hear an "expert" say in a classroom situation. If you are not there to mitigate the information transmitted by such lecturers (to point out, as we did, the glossing over of alternate hypotheses and subsequent overemphasis given to the notion of UFOs as extraterrestrial anthropologists) you will find that your students come away believing in all manner of pseudoscientific nonsense. We have learned to use these run-ins to our advantage. In follow-up lectures these incidents can be used to help the students practice evaluation of faulty arguments, and they may lead to fruitful discussions on many levels, from data collection to hypothesis formation. But there is yet another forum from which students learn that is not so easy for us to deal with in a classroom situation.

Every year one can attend professional meetings like those of the Society for American Archaeology, the Society for Historical Archaeology, the Southwestern Anthropological Association, and the American Anthropological Association and hear pseudoscientific nonsense about transatlantic contact theory being dispensed by otherwise respectable archaeologists or anthropologists. The membership and guests of our society meetings are regularly treated to organized symposia dealing with extrasensory ecology, transpersonal anthropology, and workshops in what might be called the Harner method (how to be your own shaman in three easy lessons) (Harner 1980). Indeed, there has been so much of this type of material that it is beginning to look as though some anthropologists are coming up with their own pseudoanthropology. One might well ask, who needs Erich von Däniken?

I am not trying to take potshots at those legitimate scholars who choose to do research in areas that many of their colleagues consider kooky. No aspect of the human endeavor should be ignored by anthropology—that is what we are here to explore, after all. In our classes, Hudson and I have had the opportunity to examine the work of a number of anthropologists whose research into the paranormal has been presented. In method and research design many of them do exemplary work. What I seriously object to are the scholars who use poor research methods in their attempts to establish flawed hypotheses through poor science and/or misuse of data. When we allow our pet theories to become our belief system we have indeed "gone native."

If our meetings were attended only by professionals in our discipline, this matter would probably be less important; however, each symposium is a public forum attended by interested students and lay people, too. It is most unfortunate that this kind of "poisoned chocolate" (as Glyn Daniel

[1977] so elegantly put it in his review of Barry Fell's work) is dispensed in the context of a professional forum where uninformed people tend to accept it, giving it a sort of legitimacy by association. One can only guess what these anthropologists are teaching their students in the classroom.

Obviously we cannot walk into the classrooms of our colleagues and start berating them in front of their students. And yet I think it is important for students to be given the opportunity to have equal time with someone who can give them the means by which to critically evaluate an argument—any argument—in a logical, scientific manner. This problem makes classes like the one we offer at USC a vital part of the academic structure, not just some frivolous, peripheral offering. It is sad to think that the most important role of our classes may be to help counter the faulty logic and misuse of facts of someone who should definitely know better.

One must of course address at some point the efficacy of one's efforts at debunking pseudoscientific myths. The best way to accomplish this would naturally be to administer the survey outlined by Feder in this volume before giving such a class. A follow-up survey should ideally be given at the end of the course and at some future time, too—perhaps a year later. This process has not yet been attempted at USC. In the meantime, Hudson and I have had to rely on test results and the random bits of feedback that we occasionally get from our students.

Test results seem to point to an improvement in students' ability to ferret the flaws out of pseudoscientific arguments; however, some continue to be susceptible to the stuff until you directly counter each individual bit of nonsense. Since we teach a number of different classes, not all of which are focused on pseudoscience, we often encounter students who have taken one or more of our courses previously. The feedback from these students—in the form of their comments and the mere fact that they have come back for more anthropology—has been very positive and encouraging.

It is also very encouraging to know that there are so many more people in anthropology and other disciplines who are beginning to teach serious classes that deal with pseudoanthropological issues and topics. In the eight years since beginning our program, Hudson and I have been gratified to see the publication of a number of good texts in this area. Abell and Singer (1981), as well as Cazeau and Scott (1979), are two texts we have found particularly useful in our courses. The publication of these texts reflects, I believe, an increasing awareness of the need for such classes. Perhaps one day we will see general education classes in debunking pseudoscience as a regular part of college curricula.

8.

A Century after Darwin: Scientific Creationism and Academe

Laurie Godfrey and John Cole

> "I weep for you," the Walrus said:
>   "I deeply sympathize."
> With sobs and tears he sorted out
>   Those of the largest size,
> Holding his pocket-handkerchief
>   Before his streaming eyes.
> —Lewis Carroll, *Through the Looking-Glass*

In Charles Dodgson's (Lewis Carroll's) masterful portrayal of social para-dox, seven-year-old Alice puzzles over the seemingly endless contra-dictions between social action and the spoken word. Never short of in-tellectual curiosity, she sets for herself the task of deciding whom she should dislike the most—the calculating Walrus, who at least feigns sor-row for the poor oysters as he methodically devours them, holding his handkerchief over his face to hide his enormous greed, or the callous Car-penter, who shows not a shred of remorse for the gullible creatures but who is not nearly so greedy as his deceitful accomplice. Along with her empathic young readers, Alice learns to approach her world analytically but not literally.

Alice in Wonderland and *Through the Looking-Glass* first appeared in the decade following the publication of Charles Darwin's *On the Origin of Species*. Darwin, like Alice, confronted a world that didn't fit prevailing explanations. Even before he wrote his *Origin*, scientific discoveries had led increasing numbers of individuals to reject a literal reading of the Bible; biblical literalism simply did not work. Darwin studied variation in form and distribution of organisms and devised what he thought was the best explanation for their geographical and morphological diversity: evolution via descent with modification by natural selection. In the 128 years since the *Origin*, evolutionary biology has grown and changed dramatically. It is still growing, still changing. But in the Western world today, just as in the world of Charles Dodgson and Charles Darwin, large numbers of college-educated individuals still cling to a literal reading of the Bible to explain the history of life on earth. To many theologians as well as nontheologians this is harder to fathom than all of the curiosities in Alice's Looking-Glass House taken together.

Of course, the social paradoxes of the 1980s are no less striking than those of the 1860s, so it is perhaps not astounding that some of the most irrational claims about the history of life on earth are occasionally taken seriously by modern school teachers, book publishers, legislators, and even some professional scientists. These include claims that the earth's geological formations were formed catastrophically during a single global flood; that the earth and all living organisms were created only a few thousand years ago; that humans and apes do not share common ancestry. Paradoxically, so-called scientific creationists espousing such claims are ostensibly rationalists, not anti-intellectuals (Cavanaugh 1985). Paradoxically, scientific creationism is gaining support through an appeal to educational pluralism and fair play, although its hard-core Christian defenders will admit, when pressed, that they find the idea of evolution abhorrent precisely because, in their fixed world of a single God-given truth, flux, change, and explanatory pluralism exist only as notions invented by Satan to deceive the unfaithful (Kehoe 1983, 1985, n.d., and in this volume).

In general, though, the claims of scientific creationism are not taken seriously by educators and academics; even people sympathetic to the notion of equal time often find the specific claims of scientific creationism repugnant on scientific or religious grounds. And, despite claims to the contrary by creationists themselves, it is not at all clear that the general public favors the creationists' educational "reforms," since equal time has received little support from popular (as well as academic) presses. Fairness has popular appeal, but limited research on the issue implies that while the equal time argument is attractive, only a minority support the complete scientific creationist agenda in detail (compare Cole 1983a; Eve and Harrold 1986). Most academics view equal time for creation science as a dead issue; have not two equal time laws (in Arkansas and Louisiana) been ruled unconstitutional? Judge William Overton's Arkansas Federal Court decision, a century after Darwin's death in 1882, is widely hailed by scientists as a brilliant summary of constitutional and substantive reasons why creationism should not be taught in public schools (see Overton 1982, 1983).

And creationists have suffered some rather major embarrassments in the past few years: their few empirically testable claims have not held up under scrutiny. For example, their "best" case (see Morris 1980)—the claim that the Cretaceous rocks along the Paluxy Creek of Central Texas contain human as well as dinosaur footprints, proof that all creatures lived together until Noah's Flood—has been shown to be unequivocally wrong (Milne and Schafersman 1983; Cole 1984, 1985; Cole and Godfrey 1985; Hastings 1985, 1986; Kuban 1986a, 1986b, 1986c; Godfrey and Cole 1986). Some of the most ardent mantrack supporters are issuing reluctant retractions couched in qualifying phrases (Morris 1986a, 1986b, 1986c; Taylor 1985; Bible-Science Association 1986). In effect, weathering of bipedal dinosaur footprints has accentuated some tracks' reptilian characteristics, transforming the "best" of the so-called giant human trails into obvious dinosaur trackways that should fool a layman no more easily than an anatomist. And those Paluxy mantracks that are neither carved frauds nor genuine dinosaur tracks have been shown to be erosion marks, burrow casts, and other natural features.

And, it seems, God hath wrought other disasters upon the creationists. Two of the largest states of the Union, California and Texas, employ statewide textbook adoption approval procedures, making them prime targets for creationist textbook censors (Nelkin 1977, 1982). But recently the California Committee of Correspondence countered the inroads of creationist textbook critics and, with state Superintendent of Education Bill Honig, forced publishers to improve their texts' coverage of evolution. Similar proscience pressures are now at work in Texas.

Scientists' efforts seem to have succeeded. Since 1980 scientists and academics in other fields have responded to equal time for creation science demands with dozens of books for the layperson exploring creationist political, pedagogical, empirical, legal, and religious arguments (for example, Eldredge 1983; Frye 1983; Futuyma 1983; Godfrey 1983; Kitcher 1982; La Follette 1983; Montagu 1984; Newell 1982). Some have pursued legal and political tactics to counter creationist attacks on science education by joining the nationwide network, the Committees of Correspondence (now incorporated into the National Center for Science Education); others have worked with the American Civil Liberties Union, People for the American Way, Americans for Religious Liberty, and other civic, legal, religious, and scientific groups. A small but effective quarterly, *Creation/Evolution*, was founded in 1980 as a resource for teachers, students, and scholars to explore and answer specific antievolutionist arguments. And journals with large secondary school teacher readership (for example, *Phi Delta Kappan, Journal of Geological Education, Physics Today, Educational Leadership, American Biology Teacher*) began focusing much attention on the issue.

A sense of complacency has returned to the scientific community, along with a bit of self-congratulatory pride. Niles Eldredge, an invertebrate paleontologist who entered the fray when he found his ideas on the tempo and mode of evolutionary change (see Eldredge and Gould 1972) misrepresented by creationists as evidence for sudden (and presumably simultaneous) creation of independent "kinds," recently declared the creationist challenge virtually dead. He had been one of a number of prominent scientists who worked hard to counter the creationist lobby: he wrote a popular book on evolution and creationism (1983), became New York State liaison for the Committees of Correspondence, and was a key witness at the Arkansas creationism trial. As discussant for a symposium on creationism at the annual meeting of the American Anthropological Association in 1985, Eldredge suggested that the time had come for scientists to cease discussing scientific creationism; in effect, the scientific community had met the challenge and won. For the first time since the late nineteenth century, when some Fundamentalist churches under the leadership of people like Ellen White and Uriah Smith railed against evolution as "unscientific" (and not merely un-Christian) (Numbers 1975, 1982), the scientific community had created a resource base for nonscientists that answered numerous recurrent creationist arguments. Now that such resources were available for all to see, scientific creationism would die an inevitable, quiet death.

But has the scientific community won? If so, just what has it won? Have academics been sensitive to real changes in the perceptions of school teachers, book publishers, and politicians? How have nonacademics responded to the pressures of equal time advocates? What issues are being addressed by members of different academic disciplines? How sensitive have they been to the social and political bases of the modern creationist movement?

Eldredge is certainly justified in feeling pride in the accomplishments of the scientific community over the past few years. It requires an enormous (and generally thankless) commitment for scientists to leave academically "worthy" pursuits in order to write for local newspapers and address public meetings, school boards, schoolteachers, and church groups about a politically and religiously sensitive issue. Colleagues may regard such endeavors with disdain; the public may regard the less eloquent academic defenders of evolution as intellectual snobs or blind dogmatists. But pride in the success of the academic response must be tempered by some less sanguine observations.

1. Antievolutionism is still quite strong in America, and the seductive rhetoric of equal time continues to be persuasive to some judges and many laypersons and politicians. Textbook publishers have not buckled under the counter-pressure of California's new textbook adoption rulings—anyone who has read a sampling of the "improved" versions of middle-school science books must be surprised by the continuing deficiencies in their treatment of evolution. Wording is oblique and apparently designed to placate possible creationist critics (for example, "Many scientists believe that dinosaurs once lived on earth"). On the other hand, some publishers have announced their intention to work with scientists in developing the next generation of books, so perhaps the recently publicized "victory" will bear fruit after all.

Meanwhile, a market research survey of science teachers (Austin Analytical Consulting 1986) suggests that forthcoming textbooks may still be geared to consensus opinions, not scientific rigor.[1] This "Opinion Poll for Biology Teachers" begins with the statement, "Your answers to the following opinion questions are very important to writers and publishers in preparing the best educational materials possible." There follows a series of questions for teachers concerning their views on life origins, evolution, creationism, and so forth. Perhaps votes for evolution will win—perhaps not. But the survey is clearly designed to help publishers produce the least objectionable texts, regardless of current scientific knowledge. Scientists often forget that publishing is a business, not a social service.

Recently the United States Court of Appeals (Southern District) narrowly defeated creationist efforts to reinstate the Louisiana equal time law. The vote was 8 to 7, and the seven judges sympathetic to the creationist case wrote a strong and well-publicized dissent, claiming that no one had questioned the scientific validity of the creationist model ("there are sworn statements in the . . . record, statements executed by scientists of impeccable credentials, which establish for the purposes of the summary judgement proceedings that creationism is a valid scientific theory or group of theories, supported by respected, secular evidence" [Gee 1986]). The issue, the minority maintained, is not whether creationism is scientifically valid but whether the state could require that it be taught. The state of Louisiana and the Creation Science Legal Defense Fund filed an appeal, accepted by the Supreme Court, maintaining (as had the seven-judge appeals court minority) that equal time "does not infringe the Constitution" but simply requires that "the truth be taught," including "scientific evidence supporting either view." The argument thus claims that "truth" should somehow be taught without endorsing any existing scientific, religious, or philosophical views. Creationists are confident that future court appointees, by Reagan or his successor, will tip the balance in federal courts in their direction (see Bird 1986).

The Supreme Court appeal heard in December 1986 was a narrow one: should the lower court of appeals have agreed to hear the case fully, including new arguments as well as reviews of lower court records to be judged summarily? The case could drag on for several years without any actual ruling on the basic question of the legality of requiring equal time for scientific creationism whenever evolution is taught in public schools, although the Supreme Court may choose to issue a sweeping opinion. In any case, the ruling will not deal with underlying legal, scientific and pedagogical issues: Is scientific creationism science? Is it pseudoscience? Is it religion? Is it simply an equal but opposite world view? Whatever the courts' rulings, these questions will continue to confront teachers and scientists. Is scientific creationism something like driver's education, which a state may require to be taught (or not) without infringing on the constitutional separation of church and state?

2. The academic response to the resurgence of antievolutionism has been surprisingly weak in some areas, notably in sociological and anthropological analyses of the nature of the cultural movement. In fact, in our survey of computerized data bases (see below), sociological and anthropological analyses represented a very small percentage of published work on the creation/evolution controversy. As creationism is one of the more remarkable and influential social movements of the past three decades, it is curious that so few of the volumes of material written on the subject since 1977 have focused on this aspect of the phenomenon.

Many academics seem to assume that modern antievolutionism reflects a last gasp of the Scopes era, a passing fad, despite some striking changes in creationist political rhetoric which are often overlooked. Modern antievolutionism is surely linked with that of the agrarian Populist tradition, but it is equally certainly not equivalent. William Jennings Bryan may have leaped into the Spanish-American War with enthusiasm, but by the mid-teens he resigned as secretary of state to protest President Wilson's growing inclinations to enter into the World War. He had become a pacifist who found Darwinian competition ("nature red in tooth and claw") repulsive; he blamed evolutionary theory for America's increasing jingoism, actively denouncing "American colonialism" in the Philippines. In contrast, today's antievolutionists tend to be among America's most jingoistic political leaders. Jerry Falwell embraced Ferdinand Marcos as a "friend" of America and anti-Communist hero only days before he was toppled, and he staunchly supports the South African regime. Many in the religious Right see in nuclear weapons a vehicle for the realization of the Book of Revelation, Armageddon, and salvation. Some welcome nuclear proliferation as the duty of the faithful preparing for their preordained conflict with Russia, tool of the Devil (for example, Lindsay and Carlson 1976). Old-time Populists were often racists, and their political theory was perhaps ad hoc, but they tended to favor economic "leveling"—progressive income taxes, state-owned utilities, government aid to farmers, Social Security, and much of the subsequent New Deal program. Today's antievolutionists may be less racist than their Populist forebears, but modern antievolutionists are almost universally resolute defenders of middle-class "privilege" and the rights of big business, not the unemployed refugee from capitalism.

Why have sociologists and anthropologists virtually ignored these issues? Why, also, given the creationists' fundamental philosophical rejection of explanatory pluralism, have so many people been duped into accepting literally the creationists' plea for educational pluralism under the guise of "equal time for creation science"?

One might argue that anthropologists are not numerous but counterargue that, aside from biologists, they are the most frequent victims of creationist wrath and misquotation. And what of sociologists, a cadre of scholars vastly outnumbering anthropologists who specialize in contemporary Western cultural ideas, movements, and perturbations? Their relative silence is perhaps even more baffling.

Academics are sometimes accused of being impulsive or trendy, but our experience suggests otherwise; at least the reputation is exaggerated. Academia in general and social science in particular constitute a sort of ghetto wherein misfits can speak fairly freely, advocating unpopular causes harmlessly. But despite exceptions, most academics are careerists, and topics such as creationism and similar popular foibles are minor tempests in tiny teapots to many scholars. Dealing with popular issues in general can be disdained by peers as silly diversions from "real" research and simply irrelevant. The head-in-the-sand position is widely popular, despite the target it presents to critics.

The reticence of social scientists to address the issue may also be influenced by the marketplace. Commercial publishers seem wary of publishing social or political analyses of modern antievolutionism, apparently regarding such books as too sensitive. Books countering specific creationist claims (but generally avoiding analysis of the social movement per se) seem to have saturated the limited market for critiques. Yet there is a booming market for popular books vaguely supporting creationism and attacking evolution, at least by dealing naively with theoretical controversies: books such as Denton's *Evolution: A Theory in Crisis*, Hitching's *The Neck of the Giraffe*, Macbeth's *Darwin Retried*, Goodman's *American Genesis* and *The Genesis Mystery*, Fix's *The Bone Peddlers*, Litvak and Senzee's *Toward a New Brain*, and Rifkin's *Algeny*. The latter, for example, quotes generously from Duane Gish of the Institute for Creation Research while building a case against modern-day Merlins' tinkering with genetics; they apparently "got that way" by reading too much Darwin.

Unsurprisingly, creationists view these books as a boon to their cause. The Bible-Science Association, for example, recently published a list of books which demolish evolution but are "acceptable" for libraries and schools because they are not "creationist" in origin (Bergman 1986).[2] Many (though not all) of these books profess to be "proevolution"; however, most express disdain for "so-called experts" who can't recognize a dead paradigm even when they fall into it head first. Some spout creationist rhetoric more influentially (and with more sophistication) than do creationists themselves.

In addition to such books, journalistic attacks on evolutionism and secular humanism may well be the legacy of modern antievolutionism. Tom Bethell, Joseph Sobran, M. Stanton Evans, John Lofton, and other influential conservative political columnists have embraced creationist rhetoric in this form. Titles such as "Reagan's 'Evolution' Comment Was Correct" and "Triumph for the God of Humanism" (Evans) and "Proletarian Evolution" (Bethell) are telling. Sobran has written, "Nature didn't make men out of monkeys. The naturalists have made monkeys out of men." And White House policy advisor Rachel Flick wrote in the winter 1985 issue of *Policy Review* that natural selection is tautological and therefore evolutionary theory's fatal flaw. While she acknowledges that evolution seems to have happened somehow, she strongly implies that creationism might be good for the schools, balancing rigid Darwinian dogma. Scientific creationists may lose political influence, but this mass of "unbiased" writing, featured in science book clubs and the secular press, not insular creationist circles, will probably remain with us for decades to come.

Ironically, Darwinism has long been confounded with Spencerism and the "Doctrine of Progress" (Godfrey 1985) and as such has been defended and maligned by both the Left and Right.[3] Himmelfarb (1968), Barzun (1958), and Koestler (1978) critiqued Darwinism as justifying the Marxism they opposed; and Marx and Engels embraced Darwinism for the same reason. White (1949) also considered Darwinism a basic element of Marxism, but the Victorian robber barons saw Darwinism as justification for their rapaciousness.

3. Antievolutionists may be winning a war of attrition. Academics have been slow to respond to creationist political moves, and they have been

YEARLY TRENDS
THREE DATA BASES

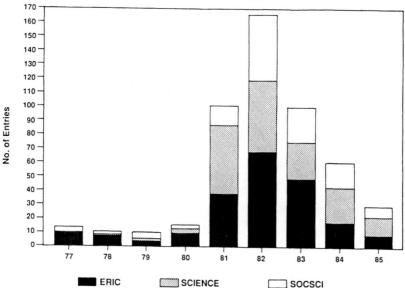

FIGURE 1. Yearly trends in the three academic data bases yielding the greatest number of items on the creation/evolution controversy. The increase in interest in the early 1980s and subsequent decline are paralleled by all academic data bases examined by us (see text). Note that entries for 1985 are incomplete, since our survey was conducted in November 1985. However, it is highly unlikely that they would have reached 1984 levels by the year's end.

quick to withdraw after winning the first major battle—the Arkansas decision. Retreat has not been universal, but it has been dramatic—well documentable in the changing themes and frequencies of journal, magazine, and book commentaries on the movement over the past decade (Figures 1 and 2). In the mid 1970s, despite the many pressures on public schoolteachers and school boards by small but disciplined groups of parents opposed to the teaching of evolution, the issue was all but ignored in print. The academic community became concerned only as the legal threat formalized, and a formidable academic effort was indeed mounted for the Arkansas trial.

In the midst of largely undocumented assertions from various sources about the current status of creationist theory among scholars and writers, we sought an empirical test of the nature of creationism among intellectuals. While computerized data are less than complete (there is no truly

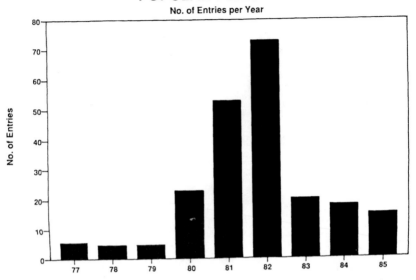

FIGURE 2. Items on the creation/evolution controversy indexed in the *Popular Periodicals Index, Readers' Guide to Periodical Literature,* and Dialog's *Magazine Index* show a secular trend similar to that exhibited by academic data bases. Interest peaked in 1981 and 1982 (at the time of the Arkansas equal time trial), then fell dramatically. Popular periodicals were surveyed from 1977 to November 1985. The total number of entries compiled was 218.

national newspaper index, for example), there are extensive electronic data bases and a few print sources which permit a quantitative examination of the subject.

We searched six on-line data bases (Figure 3) for entries on "creationis(m, t, ts)" after determining that terms such as "antievolution" and "anti-Darwinis(m, t)" were duplicative of and much less productive than other key words. We also compiled simple tallies of articles on the so-called creationist controversy indexed in such sources as the *Popular Periodicals Index, Reader's Guide to Periodical Literature,* and Dialog's *Magazine Index.* After determining that few references existed prior to 1977 (one data base, *SciSearch,* for instance, yielded only a handful of references for the period from 1974 to 1977), we decided to begin our systematic survey with 1977. Conducted in late 1985, our survey thus sampled the period from 1977 to November 1985. Not all data bases were complete for that period; the *Arts and Humanities Index,* for example, only began in 1980.

Such a computer-based survey will have obvious holes, missing appro-

ENTRIES IN DATA BASES

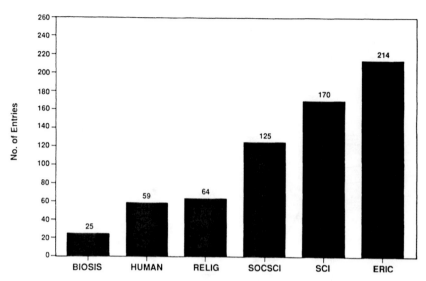

FIGURE 3. These academic data bases yielded 657 entries on the creation/evolution controversy when computer searched using keywords described in the text. There was some (but surprisingly little) overlap of entries selected by the different data bases; each is sampling a fundamentally different periodical universe. Over 80 percent of the entries compiled were from professional journals; other entries were books, microfiche, and semipopular or popular magazines (for example, *Natural History*). *Biosis* (*BioAbstracts*) sampled letters, editorials, and articles in such journals as *American Zoologist, American Journal of Physical Anthropology,* and *Evolution.* Other science journals (including some less technical biological journals) were not sampled by *Biosis* but were sampled by *SciSearch* (for example, *American Biology Teacher, Geotimes, Physics Today,* etc.). It should also be noted that professional indexing services have different policies on sampling letters to the editor and editorials; some omit them entirely.

priate references that happen to lack selected key words in their titles or abstracts. References known to us that were missed by our survey technique were not added to our tabulation; rather, we preferred to treat this tabulation as a sample of the available literature on the creation/evolution controversy, noting its limitations but also the consistency of our selection procedure. Each entry was checked for appropriateness; those that dealt with religion and not the creationist controversy were manually excluded from our tabulation.

Both the topical pattern of items and their disciplinary distribution

ERIC

FIELD OF AUTHORS

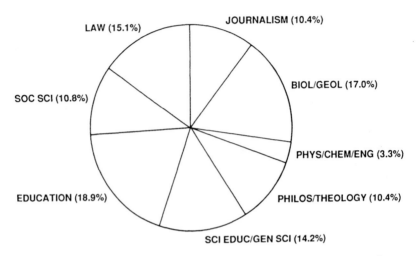

JOURNALISM (10.4%)

LAW (15.1%)

BIOL/GEOL (17.0%)

SOC SCI (10.8%)

PHYS/CHEM/ENG (3.3%)

EDUCATION (18.9%)

PHILOS/THEOLOGY (10.4%)

SCI EDUC/GEN SCI (14.2%)

FIGURE 4. ERIC was the most productive data base, yielding 214 entries on the creation/evolution controversy for the period sampled. Each data base can be characterized by the fields of authors of sampled entries as well as by the primary focus of those entries. Unsurprisingly, such profiles demonstrated the independence of the data bases: in the case of ERIC, many entries were written by people in the fields of education (18.9 percent) or science education and general science (14.2 percent). Biologists and geologists contributed significantly to all academic data bases (compare Figures 5 and 6).

were examined. The more narrowly academic scientific data bases and the nonscientific (arts and humanities, religion) data bases showed little interest in scientific creationism. The greatest number of entries on the subject occurred in the ERIC data base (education resources compiled by the U.S. Department of Education and probably teachers' most widely available and used data base in print, microfiche, and computer formats) (Figure 3). In descending order of "productivity," measured in absolute numbers of entries on creationism, were *SciSearch* (general science) and *SocSciSearch* (social science), followed by the *Religion Index, Arts and Humanities Index,* and, finally, *Biosis* (*BioAbstracts* citations; that is, typically specialized, technical journal publications). Despite some overlap, these data bases sampled different periodical universes. This was documented by coding each item by author and title, type of publication (for example, journal item, conference paper, popular article, news item,

SCI SEARCH

FIELD OF AUTHORS

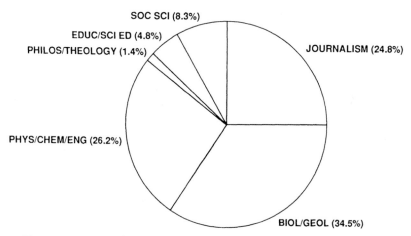

FIGURE 5. *SciSearch* (general science) was the second most productive data base, yielding 170 entries on the creation/evolution controversy. Entries here were written primarily by biologists and geologists, closely followed by physicists, chemists and engineers, and journalists.

SOC SCI SEARCH

FIELD OF AUTHORS

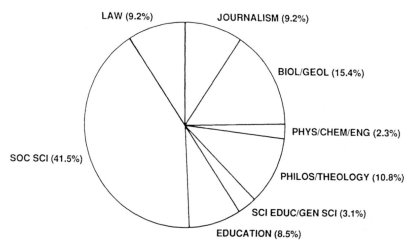

FIGURE 6. The third most productive data base was *SocSciSearch* (social science), which yielded 125 entries for the period sampled. Unsurprisingly, the largest percentage of entries (41.5 percent) in this data base were written by social scientists.

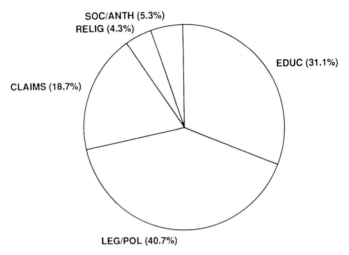

ERIC

FOCUS

SOC/ANTH (5.3%)
RELIG (4.3%)

EDUC (31.1%)

CLAIMS (18.7%)

LEG/POL (40.7%)

FIGURE 7. If we examine the focus of entries rather than the fields of the authors, we can assess the primary concerns of the authors writing for different periodical universes. Here we see that authors writing in education journals focused primarily on legal, political, and pedagogical issues. (Note that, when an entry had several foci, we coded only its primary concern.)

etc.), viewpoint (pro-creationism, anti, mixed, neutral), focus (legal, historical, theological, pedagogical, and social issues, specific claims, etc.), and the field of the author when known. Summary statistics were then calculated and pie charts drawn (Figures 4–10).

We expected to see a major contrast between academic and popular periodical responses to creationism; this we did not find (Figure 11). Despite polls which show 70 percent, 80 percent, or more of Americans favoring equal time for creationism in schools, the popular media showed only 20 percent of articles or letters sympathetic to equal time. It had already been shown that the leading proponents of scientific creationism do not publish their views in scientific media (Cole and Scott 1982; Scott and Cole 1985); we found that they do not publish in indexed popular magazines either (although their politically right-wing journalistic sympathizers do, occasionally). However, contrary to creationist cries of censorship (Bergman 1986), there was no apparent bias against publishing items favorable to equal time; indeed, items sympathetic to creationism

SCI SEARCH

FOCUS

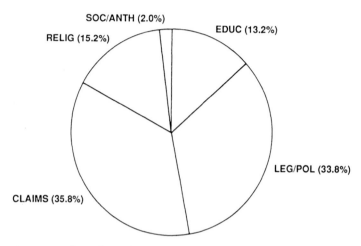

FIGURE 8. *SciSearch* authors focused primarily on specific creationist claims (young earth, creationist interpretations of the fossil record, biostratigraphy, thermodynamics, probability, etc.). Legal and political issues were a close second concern. Note the small percentage of articles focusing on sociological and anthropological issues. (Discussions of creationist treatments of the human or primate fossil record were coded by us as dealing with "specific claims.")

comprised a surprising 18 to 20 percent of our sample in all data bases, with the exception of *Biosis* (academic as well as popular; scientific as well as religious) (Figures 11 and 12).[4] But with few exceptions these were fairly minor items—letters to the editor, "alternative views," and the like. Despite their numbers they do not rival in content the articles, books, editorials, and news stories critical of equal time.

This of course does not mean that there is no constituency for scientific creationism; there is, but it is not manifested in normal publication routes. Creationists publish their own literature. *Acts and Facts, Bible-Science Newsletter, Creation Research Society Quarterly*, and dozens of smaller publications represent forms of witnessing, an activity which aims at public proselytizing, playing upon the emotions and scientific illiteracy of the public at large. They also serve as ritual reassurance for people who seem to demand materialistic evidentiary justification for their religious faith.

Creationists' failure to publish in popular magazines is nevertheless

SOC SCI
FOCUS

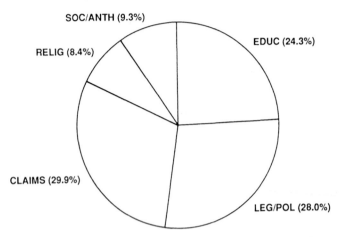

FIGURE 9. The social science index also showed major concern with specific creationist claims and with legal, political, and pedagogical issues. Note the small percentage of authors focusing on sociological and anthropological issues, despite the high percentage of authors in the field of social science (compare Figure 6).

RELIGION INDEX
FOCUS

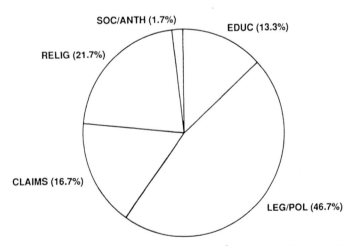

FIGURE 10. Entries in this data base focused primarily on legal and political issues, followed by religious issues. Sociological and anthropological analyses represent a minuscule percentage of entries in this data base.

POPULAR AND ACADEMIC DATA BASES

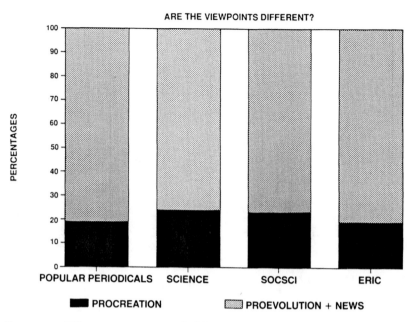

FIGURE 11. When entries were coded by viewpoint (procreationism, proevolution, and neutral news reports), items sympathetic to equal time (expressing either overt approval or mixed approval) comprised around 20 percent of entries in academic as well as popular data bases. It is clear that the popular and educational data bases do not show the highest approval ratings for scientific creationism. (In this pictorial representation, news reports were lumped with proevolution entries; in fact, most journalists clearly disapproved of creation science, although their style of reporting tended to be neutral. Journalistic items advocating equal time were, of course, coded as procreationism.)

surprising, given the popularity of the issue and the apparent general willingness of editors to cater to popular interests at least to some extent. Despite their public posturing, creationists have not really tried to present a secular case. And despite this fact, they continue to enjoy a fair amount of support from judges and legislators who are convinced that they have demonstrated the scientific legitimacy of their claims.

We also did not expect to see the relative dearth of sociological and anthropological analyses of the modern antievolutionist movement (see especially Figures 7, 8, 9, and 10). Even in the social science data base (*SocSciSearch*), entries focusing on sociological and anthropological issues constituted little more than 9 percent of the total, while in ERIC and *SciSearch* they constituted 5.3 and 2 percent, respectively. Biologists and

VIEWPOINTS, FOUR DATA BASES

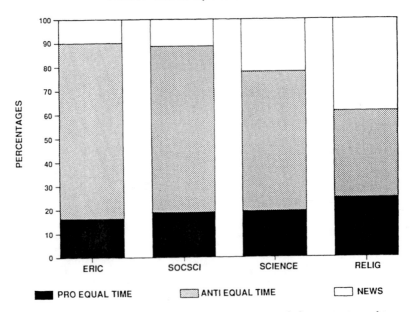

FIGURE 12. Here neutral news reports were separated from entries taking a stance (pro or anti equal time) to show relative percentages of straight reporting versus advocacy in the four largest academic data bases. Note that the education data base contained the smallest percentage of neutral news items and the largest percentage of entries critical of equal time. The religion data base showed relatively the most news reports and the fewest items critical of equal time, but even here, entries opposing equal time far outnumbered those favoring it, and total items favoring equal time barely exceeded 20 percent. (Note that *Biosis* does not compile news items even for journals with regular science news columns such as *Science* or *Nature*; all *Biosis* entries were articles or conference presentations that opposed equal time.)

geologists have confronted biological and geological issues raised by scientific creationists better than anthropologists have confronted what ought to be their domain—the cultural, political, and economic bases of modern antievolutionism. While there have been some exceptions (see Cavanaugh 1985; Cole 1983b; Eve and Harrold 1986; Feder 1984; Gieryn, Bevins, and Zehr 1985; Gray and Wolfe 1982; Kehoe 1983, 1985, n.d.; McIver 1986; Nelkin 1982), social scientists have tended to focus on specific creationist claims or on legal and pedagogical issues. Physical anthropologists and archaeologists especially have attempted public outreach through grass roots political networks, publications in such lay journals as

Natural History, Creation/Evolution, and *American Biology Teacher,* or public confrontation (debates and the like).

In our sample, of all groups of scientists, physicists and engineers were the most sympathetic to scientific creationism, although they, too, overwhelmingly oppose it. Of entries favorable to equal time in the *SciSearch* data base, a full 67 percent were written by physicists or engineers. Other data bases did not exhibit the same lopsided pattern; fewer than 20 percent of ERIC and *SocSciSearch* entries favorable to equal time were written by physicists or engineers. Rather, they tended to be written by people with careers in law, education, or diverse academic disciplines; some were signed by people without stated fields or affiliations, possibly laymen. The total frequencies in each discipline were generally too small to calculate meaningful percentages.

Some disciplines have had little to say about creationism. Psychologists seem to have virtually ignored the controversy, as have economists and most historians, despite creationist claims upon the subject matter of these disciplines. Humanities scholars have been rather silent, with the exception of a few philosophers and science historians; reactions from religion scholars in religion-oriented periodicals have been numerous, but in the other data bases we searched scientists and other nontheologians were a large source of items focusing on religion (Figure 13). Political science attention was largely subsumed by the news and current events and legal issues categories. A few such entries argued for equal time; most endorsed an ACLU-like position on church-state separation.

In sum, the academic response to antievolutionism a century after Darwin has been strong in some areas and weak in others. Academics have crossed disciplinary lines, contributing to journals outside their normal disciplinary specializations; biologists have discussed legal, pedagogical, and religious issues, and news reporters and theologians have discussed the specific pseudoscientific claims of the scientific creationists. Meanwhile, the ground swell of support for creationism has manifested itself outside normal publication routes, encouraging speculations about the general anti-intellectual nature of the movement.

While academicians have dutifully responded to specific religious, legal, and scientific claims of scientific creationists, they have been relatively insensitive to issues surrounding the broader threat of creationism, perhaps trusting the problem to go away once the facts are brought to bear on the subject. But anthropologists especially should realize that one cannot merely issue rational pronouncements and expect a movement of this nature to evaporate. Despite the continued, undaunted efforts of the Creation Science Legal Defense Fund to win both legal and political victories, academic interest in the problem has dwindled to nearly pre-

FOCUS, THREE DATA BASES

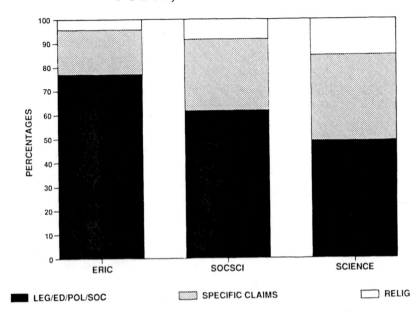

FIGURE 13. For the purposes of this pictorial representation, specific creationist claims were divided into religious and nonreligious (general scientific or empirical) categories and then entries were grouped according to their primary focus on (1) religious claims, (2) other specific claims, or (3) other aspects of the creation/evolution controversy (legal, educational, political, historical, social issues). Note the relatively strong religion interest among authors writing for the general science data base. Specific claims were of greater concern to *SciSearch* authors than to *SocSciSearch* authors; legal, political, and educational issues were of greatest concern to educators.

Arkansas levels of noninvolvement. The academic community can take pride in the fact that specific answers to many creationist arguments are now available to the general public in nontechnical jargon. But this alone does not guarantee their use by educators, judges, parents, and politicians.

In fact, creationists are working tirelessly through newsletters, radio emissions, and creationist press books to teach the public lessons of "true" science. In many quarters, their messages are still enthusiastically received. Academe must not, therefore, abandon its concern for this threat to the scientific literacy of the general public. As Stanley Weinberg, founder of the Committees of Correspondence, has noted repeatedly, this is a political and public relations battle, not simply a dispute over facts (Weinberg 1980). The Scopes trial is a useful analogy here: in that famous victory for reason and evolution, John Scopes was actually convicted of having violated the law by teaching evolution, the Monkey Law stayed on the books in Tennessee until 1967, and evolution was systematically dropped from the pages of secondary school textbooks until *Sputnik* shook American educators into attempting some dramatic improvements in secondary school science education (Grabinger and Miller 1974; Nelkin 1977, 1982; Cole 1983b). Just as the Carpenter and Walrus's empathy for the fate of the oysters was illusory, scientific rationality was not the true victor of the Scopes Monkey Trial.

There is still work to be done.

Notes

1. This consulting firm has the same P.O. box number and address as a creationist think tank called the Foundation for Thought and Ethics.

2. Bergman (1986:1–2) recommends the following books for creationists to insinuate into libraries. While some of these books are by no means antievolutionary (for instance, Broad and Wade is merely a demonstration of historic cases of fraud in science), many feed overtly into the hands of creationists. Some were actually written by creationists, despite Bergman's claims to the contrary. (See bibliography for complete references): Sunderland (1985); Taylor (1983); Fix (1984); Taylor (1984); Gale (1982); Leith (1982); Hitching (1982); Hedtke (1983); Grasse (1982); Allford (1978); Monsma (1966); Eads (1982); Moorhead and Kaplan (1967); Kerkut (1960); Willis (1940); Broad and Wade (1982); Thaxton, Bradley, and Olsen (1984); Drlica (1985); Chittick (1985).

3. While Darwin came to adopt Spencer's phrase "survival of the fittest," he never endorsed the vectorial progressionism that many Victorians thought it implied. To Darwin, "fitness" could only be understood as adaptation to particular local environments; in their own worlds, barnacles, parasites, and earthworms are as "perfect" as horses, falcons, and people. Darwin was a product of his times, but he and his theory transcended them to remain useful today. Meanwhile, the Spencerian notion that northern European human biology and culture represent the pinnacle of evolution is ignored as racist ethnocentricity by biologists and students of culture.

4. *Biosis* was the only data base that yielded no entries sympathetic to scientific creationism, but the total number of entries on the subject in this data base was small.

References

Allford, D.
1978 *Instant Creation—Not Evolution.* New York: Stein and Day.
Austin Analytical Consulting
1986 Opinion poll for biology teachers. Richardson, Tex.: Austin Analytical Consulting.
Barzun, J.
1958 *Darwin, Marx, Wagner.* Garden City, N.Y.: Doubleday. (revised second edition).
Bergman, J.
1986 Recommendations of books on creationism and evolution for public libraries. *Bible-Science Newsletter* 24(5):1–2.
Bible-Science Association
1986 BSA issues statement on the Paluxy footprints. *Bible-Science Newsletter* (March).

Bird, W.
1986 February 21 fund drive letter for Creation Science Legal Defense Fund.
Broad, W., and N. Wade
1982 *Betrayers of the Truth*. New York: Simon and Schuster.
Cavanaugh, M.
1985 Scientific creationism and rationality. *Nature* 315: 185–189.
Chittick, D.
1985 *The Controversy: Roots of the Creation-Evolution Conflict*. Multonomah Press.
Cole, H., and E. Scott
1982 Creation science and scientific research. *Phi Delta Kappan* 63(8): 557ff.
Cole, J.
1983a Facts, artifacts, and aren'tifacts. Symposium paper presented at Society for American Archaeology annual meeting, Pittsburgh.
1983b Scopes and beyond: Antievolutionism and American culture. In L. Godfrey, ed., *Scientists Confront Creationism*, pp. 13–32. New York: W. W. Norton.
1984 *The Case of the Texas Footprints* (executive producer), video. Philadelphia: ISHI Films.
1985 Did humans and dinosaurs live together in Texas?—NO! *Origins Research* 8(2): 6–7.
Cole, J., and L. Godfrey, eds.
1985 *The Paluxy River Footprint Mystery—Solved*. Special issue of *Creation/Evolution* 5(1).
Denton, M.
1985 *Evolution: A Theory in Crisis*. Hagerstown, Md.: Adler and Adler (with Harper and Row).
Drlica, K.
1985 *Understanding DNA and Gene Cloning*. New York: John Wiley.
Eads, B.
1982 *Let the Evidence Speak*. Atlanta: Peachtree Press.
Eldredge, N.
1983 *The Monkey Business*. New York: Washington Square Press.
1985 Discussant for symposium Scientific creationism, now, more than ever, annual meeting of the American Anthropological Association, Washington, D.C., December 4.
Eldredge, N., and S. J. Gould
1972 Punctuated equilibria: An alternative to phyletic gradualism. In T. J. M. Schopf, ed., *Models in Paleobiology*, pp. 82–115. San Francisco: Freeman, Cooper and Co.
Eve, R., and F. Harrold
1986 Creationism, cult archaeology, and other pseudoscientific beliefs: A study of college students. *Youth and Society* 17(4): 396–421.
Feder, K.
1984 Irrationality and popular archaeology. *American Antiquity* 49: 525–541.
Fix, W.
1984 *The Bone Peddlers*. New York: Macmillan.
Flick, R.
1985 In the beginning . . . *Policy Review* (Heritage Foundation) 31: 58–61.
Frye, R. M., ed.
1983 *Is God a Creationist?* New York: Scribner's.
Futuyma, D.
1983 *Science on Trial*. New York: Pantheon Books.
Gale, B.
1982 *Evolution without Evidence*. Albuquerque: University of New Mexico Press.
Gee, T. G.

1986 Judge Gee on the dissent in creationism ruling. *The Times-Picayune/The States-Item* (New Orleans), p. A18, January 23.

Gieryn, T., G. Bevins, and S. Zehr

1985 Professionalization of American scientists: Public science in the creation/evolution trials. *American Sociological Review* 50:392–409.

Godfrey, L.

1983 *Scientists Confront Creationism*. New York: W. W. Norton.

1985 Darwinian, Spencerian, and modern perspectives on progress in biological evolution. In L. Godfrey, ed., *What Darwin Began*, pp. 40–60. Boston: Allyn and Bacon.

Godfrey, L., and J. Cole

1986 Blunder in their footsteps. *Natural History* 95(8):4, 6, 8, 10–12.

Goodman, J.

1981 *American Genesis*. New York: Summit Books.

1983 *The Genesis Mystery: A Startling New Theory of Outside Intervention in the Development of Modern Man*. New York: Times Books.

Grabinger, J., and P. Miller

1974 Effects of the Scopes Trial: Was it a victory for evolutionists? *Science* 185:832–837.

Grasse, P.-P.

1982 *Evolution of Living Organisms*. New York: Academic Press.

Gray, J., and L. Wolfe

1982 Sociobiology and creationism: Two ethnosociologies of American culture. *American Anthropologist* 84:580–594.

Hastings, R.

1985 Tracking those incredible creationists. In J. Cole and L. Godfrey, eds., *The Paluxy River Footprint Mystery*, pp. 5–15.

1986 Tracking those incredible creationists—The trail continues. *Creation/Evolution* 6(1), issue 17:19–27.

Hedtke, R.

1983 *The Secret of the Sixth Edition*. New York: Vantage.

Himmelfarb, G.

1968 *Darwin and the Darwinian Revolution*. New York: W. W. Norton.

Hitching, F.

1982 *The Neck of the Giraffe—Where Darwin Went Wrong*. New York: Ticknor and Fields.

Kehoe, A.

1983 The Word of God. In L. Godfrey, ed., *Scientists Confront Creationism*, pp. 1–12. New York: W. W. Norton.

1985 Modern antievolutionism: The scientific creationists. In L. Godfrey, ed., *What Darwin Began*. Boston: Allyn and Bacon.

n.d. *The Paradox of the Western World*. Ms.

Kerkut, G.

1960 *Implications of Evolution*. New York: Pergamon Press.

Kitcher, P.

1982 *Abusing Science: The Case against Creationism*. Cambridge, Mass.: MIT Press.

Koestler, A.

1978 *Janus: A Summing Up*. London: Hutchinson.

Kuban, G.

1986a The Taylor site "man tracks." *Origins Research* 9(1):1, 6–8.

1986b Review of ICR impact article 151. *Origins Research* 9(1):11–14.

1986c *The Texas "Man Track" Controversy*. Brunswick, Ohio (self-published).

La Follette, M., ed.

1983 *Creationism, Science, and the Law: The Arkansas Case.* Cambridge, Mass.: MIT Press.

Leith, B.
1982 *The Descent of Darwin.* London: Collins.

Lindsay, H., and C. Carlson
1976 *The Late Great Planet Earth.* Grand Rapids, Mich.: Zondervan.

Litvak, S., and A. Senzee
1986 *Toward a New Brain.* Englewood Cliffs, N.J.: Prentice-Hall.

Macbeth, N.
1971 *Darwin Retried.* New York: Dell Publishing Co.

McIver, T.
1986 Ancient tales and space-age myths of creationist evangelism. *The Skeptical Inquirer* 10:258–276.

Milne, D. and S. Schafersman
1983 Dinosaur tracks, erosion marks, and midnight chisel work (but no human footprints) in the Cretaceous limestone of the Paluxy River bed, Texas. *Journal of Geological Education* 31:111–123.

Monsma, J., ed.
1966 *Behind the Dim Unknown.* New York: Putnam's.

Montagu, A., ed.
1984 *Science and Creationism.* Oxford: Oxford University Press.

Moorhead, P., and M. Kaplan
1967 *Mathematical Challenges to the Neo-Darwinian Interpretation of Evolution.* Philadelphia: Winston Press.

Morris, J. T.
1980 *Tracking Those Incredible Dinosaurs and the People Who Knew Them.* San Diego: Creation-Life Publishers.
1986a The Paluxy mystery. *Impact* 151 (January).
1986b The Paluxy River mystery. *Nature* 321:722.
1986c Identification of ichnofossils in the Glen Rose Limestone, Central Texas. *Proceedings of the First International Conference on Creationism,* vol. 1, pp. 89–91. Pittsburgh: Creation Science Fellowship.

Nelkin, D.
1977 *Science Textbook Controversies and the Politics of Equal Time.* Cambridge, Mass.: MIT Press.
1982 *The Creationism Controversy: Science or Scripture in the Schools.* New York: W. W. Norton.

Newell, N.
1982 *Creation and Evolution: Myth or Reality?* New York: Columbia University Press.

Numbers, R.
1975 Science falsely so-called: Evolution and adventists in the nineteenth century. *Journal of the American Scientific Affiliation* 27:18–23.
1982 Creationism in twentieth century America. *Science* 218:538–544.

Overton, W.
1982 Creationism in the schools: The decision in McLean v. Arkansas Board of Education. *Science* 215:934–943.
1983 McLean vs. Arkansas. Opinion. [529 F.Supp. 1255 (Eastern District, Arkansas, 1982)]. In M. La Follette, ed., *Creationism, Science, and the Law: The Arkansas Case,* pp. 45–73. Cambridge, Mass.: MIT Press.

Rifkin, J.
1983 *Algeny.* New York: Viking.

Scott, E., and H. Cole
1985 The elusive scientific basis of creation "science." *Quarterly Review of Biology* 60(1):21–30.
Sunderland, L.
1984 *Darwin's Enigma: Fossils and Other Problems.* San Diego: Master Book Publishers.
Taylor, G.
1983 *The Great Evolution Mystery.* New York: Harper and Row.
Taylor, I.
1984 *In the Minds of Men: Darwin and the New World Order.* Toronto: T. S. E. Publishers.
Taylor, P.
1985 Notice regarding the motion picture *Footprints in Stone.* Form N-6, dated December 4, rev. December 5. Mesa, Ariz.: Films for Christ Association (2 pp.).
Thaxton, C., W. Bradley, and R. Olsen
1984 *The Mystery of Life's Origin: Reassessing Current Theories.* New York: Philosophical Library.
Weinberg, S.
1980 Reactions to creationism in Iowa. *Creation/Evolution* 2:1–8.
White, L.
1949 *The Science of Culture, a Study of Man and Civilization.* New York: Farrar, Straus.
Willis, J.
1940 *The Course of Evolution.* Cambridge: Cambridge University Press.

9.

Fantastic Archaeology: What Should We Do about It?

Stephen Williams

This volume has dealt with the important topic of pseudoscience in archaeology and anthropology. I am focusing on what I term *fantastic archaeology*, but, call it *fringe* or *cult* or *alternative archaeology* (Daniel 1979), it is essentially the same beast. What we are concerned with is the fringe of the field versus the central place of generally accepted data and the interpretations thereof. As in all studies of pseudoscience, we must be aware that some ideas on the fringe may eventually move toward the center: unfortunately, there is no example that I can think of in archaeology that compares with the changing views in geology on continental drift and its eventual acceptance. Indeed, just the reverse has been the case, as with the Piltdown man fraud which held, for many, a position in center stage which it was later forced to relinquish. I use the term *fantastic archaeology* because it gives me a bit more latitude than some others.

Whatever we choose to call it, this pseudoarchaeology has been around for a very long time. It is definitely not a new phenomenon, although there are special characteristics that can be used to distinguish various time periods, such as the advent of astronauts. I feel that one can indeed trace aspects of fantastic archaeology back to the very earliest debate on the origin of the American Indians, wherein between 1580 and 1610 the Spanish Jesuit fathers Acosta and García forcefully argued the question

(Huddleston 1967). Acosta critically evaluated the numerous views on the subject and correctly tossed out the solutions that we would today call "fantastic," such as solitary ships lost at sea or immigrants from Atlantis. On the other side García took the easy way out: all eleven hypotheses, good and bad, were given equal weight. He gave no critical testing to them at all. It was not a happy beginning.

One answer to the question "What to do about fantastic archaeology?" is surely to discuss it. When in 1856 Samuel Haven wrote his pace-setting *Archaeology of the United States*, he dealt with the history of the field in great detail and also critically categorized the literature. His "vagaries," including the works of Josiah Priest and others, were what today I term fantastic archaeology. He was very straightforward in his critical appraisal of these early sensational and best-selling precursors of Barry Fell. Would that the profession had remained this vocally committed to setting the record straight.

There were other defenders of the truth as they perceived it, especially at the Smithsonian in the latter part of the nineteenth century. The Davenport (Iowa) Tablets, nineteenth-century forgeries claimed to bear hieroglyphic inscriptions, drew the scorn of Henry Henshaw (1883); later Cyrus Thomas (1894) attacked them too, as well as a number of other purported Moundbuilder inscriptions. Charles Whittlesey (1872, 1876) of Ohio wrote several comprehensive papers on archaeological frauds such as the Grave Creek tablet and the Newark Holy Stones. Justin Winsor, a Harvard librarian, included a lot of useful commentary on problematic archaeological finds such as "Viking" rune stones and the Newport Tower (a stone tower in Rhode Island supposedly medieval but actually of Colonial age) in his 1894 *Narrative and Critical History of America*. The only professional journal of the time, *American Anthropologist*, also published at the turn of the century several articles denouncing archaeological frauds (Jenks [1900] on some fake chipped artifacts and Kelsey [1908] on the Michigan Relics), but then it fell strangely silent.

The nineteenth century was a busy time for writers in the fantastic field: Ignatius Donnelly (1882) would imprint Atlantis forever in the minds of all seekers into the past, and the Maya area was full of exotics like Le Plongeon and Brasseur de Bourbourg (Wauchope 1962). Even some famous archaeologists were touched by it: Boucher de Perthes would be hoaxed by the Moulin Quignon jaw (a modern human jaw supposedly found in ancient deposits) and some fake hand axes, and even Heinrich Schliemann has recently been accused of tampering with his data.

The early twentieth century was not much better, and two Harvard professors would join the club: Eben Horsford (1890), a chemist, would find Vikings all over the Charles River Basin; and Leo Wiener (1922,

1926), a Slavic linguist, would see strong ties between Africa and America, especially with the Maya. Other transoceanic ties would be forged in 1926 by James Churchward and his Land of Mu in the Pacific. What a lot of archaeological humbug it all was!

But, although individuals in the profession occasionally spoke out about a particularly glaring piece of fantasy, there really was little in the way of a structured response. Alfred Tozzer collected some fakes at the Peabody Museum and had a running file on the topic, but it seemed enough to just privately let your colleagues know what you thought. Frederic Ward Putnam was deeply involved in three serious cases: the Davenport Tablets, the Lenape Stone of Henry Mercer, and the Holly Oak gorget, yet he never published a word on any of them; we only know his true feelings from archival sources. Both Putnam (1883) and Tozzer were very moral beings, and Tozzer especially was not afraid to stand up and be counted in difficult situations.

In the early 1950s, when I was in graduate school, fantastic archaeology was certainly not seen as a serious question. At the three institutions that I knew best, Yale, Michigan, and Harvard, no one seemed to see it as a topic worth discussing formally with the graduate students.

However, the post–World War II period was surely not a quiet time in the annals of fantastic archaeology; after all, Velikovsky's *Worlds in Collision* hit the best-seller list in 1950 and all the media took off in pursuit. But in the 1960s the tide started to turn in archaeology with the first debunking book from a professional addressed to the general public: Robert Wauchope's classic *Lost Tribes and Sunken Continents*, which threw the gauntlet down in fine fashion. Other important works on pseudoscience such as Martin Gardner's significant *Fads and Fallacies in the Name of Science* (1957) and L. Sprague de Camp's comprehensive Atlantis study, *Lost Continents* (1954) served as important forerunners for workers in the decades ahead; nonsense would not be suffered gladly anymore. Even the sacred cow of water dowsing got careful scrutiny by my anthropological colleague Evon Vogt and psychologist Ray Hyman (1959).

But it was the 1970s that would be the real watershed experience on both sides of the divide. Erich von Däniken's *Chariots of the Gods* started off the decade with a bang heard round the world; the battle was joined for sure. Both von Däniken's success and the extravagance of his thesis made rebuttals necessary. Not since Velikovsky had the media been so enthralled: his challenging charisma and the blatant attack on the archaeological Establishment and their "conservative" views made silence by the profession impossible. So the rebuttals came in debates, articles, books, and even television shows.

But if the Swiss ex-innkeeper with his outrageous extraterrestrials was hard to take, what about a marine biologist, riding atop professorial credentials from Harvard, whose ability to read ancient inscriptions seemed to know no limits? Barry Fell began his Polynesian odyssey in 1973 and published *America B.C.* in 1976. North American archaeology had been "rewritten," according to the book jacket, and, strange to say, there were thousands who seemed to agree, as Fell's trilogy appeared (Fell 1976, 1980, 1982).

With all this going on in archaeology and a whole raft of operations in other paranormal fields such as ESP and UFOs (to get into the alphabet soup mode), it is not surprising that in 1976 the Committee for the Scientific Investigation of Claims of the Paranormal (CSICOP) was established in Buffalo, New York, with Professor Paul Kurtz as chairman. The committee and their journal, now called the *Skeptical Inquirer*, are a strong voice for pseudoscience debunking and have just had their tenth anniversary. The range of topics covered has included both archaeology and anthropology.

Members of the archaeological profession have not stood by the wayside. Peter White led off with his informative *The Past Is Human* (1974), though it is not too well known by many. The roll call of those who have spoken out on this topic is now quite long and naturally well represented in this volume: Cole (1980), Feder (1984), Fitzhugh (1979), McKusick (1984), Rathje (1978), Sabloff (1982), Snow (1981), Stiebing (1984), and Willey (1980). No longer is the answer to fantastic archaeology the unspoken hope of earlier decades: "If we don't talk about it, it will go away" or, conversely stated, "Talking about it will only give the crazies the publicity that they were searching for in the first place." Instead, the response is to attack. As Isaac Asimov has recently stated so well, "We must therefore present the view of reason, not out of a hope of reconstructing the deserts of ruined minds that have been rusted shut, which is all but impossible—but to educate and train new and fertile minds" (Asimov 1986). We have a cause and we must go forward.

In this new era, since the seventies, archaeologists have felt a need to explain the phenomenon of fantastic archaeology: what are the basic causes? Willey (1980), Feder (1984), McKusick (1984), Cole (1980), and Stiebing (1984) have all usefully addressed this question. I have already noted the long history of the problem; therefore, I feel that we cannot really blame current societal unrest as the basic cause. No doubt the anti-Establishment and anti-intellectual currents of the late 1960s served as a rich seedbed for the growth of some of these notions. Their intellectual ancestors were really Donnelly and others, although they were often loath to admit it, via citations and the like. Replacement of religious beliefs destroyed by post-Darwinian enlightenment certainly played a part in the nineteenth-century popularity of new sects such as the Theosophists, for whom Atlantis was a part of their mythology. However, plenty of other factors were at work; de Camp's view of the pervasive search for an earthly paradise being reflected in the Atlantis myth does truly seem quite widespread (de Camp 1954). There are many facets to the problem, some surely social and psychological; since we cannot yet affect the cause, we must face the result.

How is the profession as a whole dealing with fantastic archaeology? Feder (1984) has done an opinion poll with some success. My own review of seven introductory archaeology texts indicates that the authors are about evenly split in their response as to how to deal with the subject. Four ignore it—it doesn't exist, or at least let's not tell newly interested students about this aspect of the field. The remaining three texts, those by Fagan (1981), Rathje and Schiffer (1982), and Sharer and Ashmore (1979), all treat pseudoarchaeology as a serious problem, and they all use Atlantis and von Däniken as prime examples. Sharer and Ashmore go so far as to call it one of the two greatest challenges to contemporary archaeologists—the other is destruction of archaeological remains. They feel that "archaeology has a responsibility to prevent pseudoarchaeologists from robbing humanity of the real achievements of past cultures" (Sharer and Ashmore 1979).

Indeed, there does seem to be general concern for the problem, as exemplified especially in the 1980s by numerous articles in professional journals where publication generally reflects a broad consensus of perceived importance. Works such as those by Feder have tried to probe both the nature of professional awareness and the possibility of teaching basic concepts despite prior bias among students in favor of pseudoscientific beliefs. But are textbooks and journal articles enough? Are they the only solution?

Fortuitously, the tenth anniversary issue of the *Skeptical Inquirer* arrived as I wrote this paper with a broad overview of pseudoscience that has much to tell us in general. Archaeologists should take some comfort in the knowledge that we are not alone. There are times when our tunnel vision makes us feel that we are singled out for these bizarre attacks by "crank scientists," but that is not so, as these recent articles (1986) by Asimov, de Camp, Sagan, and Kurtz reassure us. We can and must learn from the experience of others in facing this challenge of unreason.

How should archaeology approach the task? First, a "don't." Do not use invective or sarcasm. The Smithsonian's over-strong attack on the Davenport Tablets was counterproductive; it poisoned the waters of discourse between amateur and professional archaeologist for a long time and in a very unfortunate manner. I realize that this injunction is hard to follow.

We, the debunkers, do care. The published nonsense makes us mad; my good friend and colleague, Glyn Daniel, from his *Antiquity* desk sometimes lets this outrage show. The targets are so obvious and plentiful; like shooting fish in a barrel, as they say. We must be accurate, untiring, and restrained.

L. Sprague de Camp (1986) has recently used another appropriate metaphor: "The scientific debunker's job may be compared to that of the trash collector. The fact that the garbage truck goes by today does not mean that there will not be another load tomorrow. But if the garbage were not collected at all, the results would be much worse, as some cities found when the sanitation workers went on strike." So we do have our daily task set out for us, but I reiterate that overstrong or demeaning language only strengthens the other side's hand. The attack on Velikovsky and his publisher gave astronomy a black eye (with a crimson edge) and was very counterproductive. The pseudoarchaeologists are already characterized as "the underdogs." Brutal attacks only solidify opinion against the Establishment; the perceived cruel and unjust treatment of the less fortunate becomes a strong argument to support them. Their case does not need our help.

On a positive side, I feel that our attempts to resist the spread of fantastic archaeology should continue on two levels. First, we should continue to "preach" to the profession; that is a worthy job and an important one. Does pseudoarchaeology hurt the profession? The answer is yes; it is not just an amusing joke that no one need take seriously. The effect on the profession can be seen in the recent George Carter–Jeffrey Bada–Jeffrey Goodman connection. This scenario saw unreasonable dates of 100,000 years for Paleo-Indians in America given spurious credibility by amino acid racemization dating done by Bada using some of Carter's dates, all of which was ultimately turned into favorable support for Goodman's (1981) *American Genesis*, a classic fantastic archaeology volume. Bada's (1985) graceful retraction, in December 1984, of all these dates is the only positive aspect of the whole situation.

There is a more general aspect that must be met as well, and that is the anti-intellectual thrust of much of fantastic archaeology. This mind-set, and the racism that is inherent in many of the hyperdiffusionist arguments, as pointed out by Sabloff (1982) and others, cannot be allowed to stand without confrontation. Graduate students need to learn how to look carefully at data. The lessons learned on fantastic archaeology cases can be used more broadly, a point made by Paul Kurtz (1986) recently with reference to his own teaching on paranormal investigations. As Kenneth Boulding (1980) set forth a few years ago, there is a triad of fantasy, testing, and veracity that is basic to all scientific research. With experience in testing and in discerning qualities of veracity, graduate students can learn how to question authorities in a useful fashion in all their work. The solution is thus to provide courses that do not shy away from critical testing and discussions of professional ethics.

The second front for our confrontation with the purveyors of fantastic archaeology must be in the public sector. We must expand with debunking articles in substantial journals such as *American Heritage*, as Dean Snow (1981) did with "Martians and Vikings, Madoc and Runes." We should also try to reach the public in magazines like *Smithsonian, Natural History*, and *Discover*; *Omni* is already in the other camp, I'm afraid. Here is a job that needs to be tackled by the best of our supporters, since the exposure would really have some public impact, unlike our professional journals. With regard to books, I can only raise this suggestion as a question: How do we "help" the major book publishers to evaluate critically what they are publishing as "archaeology"? How do we tell them convincingly that "psychic archaeology" is not the wave of the future, the new frontier of the field? I don't know the answer.

The art of debunking does seem to have some credibility in the television world, if Glyn Daniel's recent BBC program "Myth America" is any example. "Nova's" critical and successful show on von Däniken in 1979 was a fine example of how charisma can be met by tough investigative reporters; unfortunately, it was flawed by a tail-end segment which gave credence to claims that the Dogon of Africa gained detailed astronomical knowledge of the Sirius B star system via extraterrestrials.

A second part of the public approach must be to teach the "right stuff"; that is, real archaeology as the truly fantastic study of human development on this planet. Here we have a broader problem that our own professional society (the Society for American Archaeology) is just starting to face. We all need better public awareness of what we as archaeologists are doing; we need this to gain support both federally and locally. Our questions and answers must be known to a larger percentage of the population; therefore, newspaper and television journalists and publishers could make better informed decisions about their space, time, and dollar allocations.

How do we achieve this needed public awareness? As Brian Fagan has suggested by word and deed, we must write more good popular books and articles about the really challenging discoveries of archaeology, from Koobi Fora to Williamsburg. It is amazing to me that there is still no concise and easy-to-read volume on the archaeology of the American Southwest, surely one of the most interesting and visually exciting regions of archaeology in the whole world. Of course, articles in journals like *Archaeology* and *Scientific American* help, but the impact is relatively small due to circulation size.

For greater audiences we must go to television. I was involved with the two-season "Odyssey" series on educational networks which made some useful contributions to this sensitivity-raising problem. But that contribution was short-lived, except for the films that are still available and a few reruns. However, we can hardly expect to see a mini-series aired on national networks called "Indiana Jones Discovers the True Fantasy of Archaeology." Therefore, we must continue to hit educational television, where a combination of debunking and the right stuff might be a very sellable commodity. In my own course on "Alternative Views of the Past" I try to balance the two: debunk the Kensington Runestone and the Newport Tower, and then give students L'Anse aux Meadows in Newfoundland (the only excavated Norse site on this continent) as the real Vikings in America.

Of course, we must always discuss both sides of the debate, with proper referencing of the literature. "Nova" built its original story themes on argumentation in science, and Daniel's "Myth America" does briefly use a spokesperson from the other side. It is certainly healthy to show the pros and cons of any archaeological question, as *National Geographic* did recently regarding Maya looters, and the need is all the greater in controversies such as those surrounding fantastic archaeology.

All in all, we have a good product to sell—archaeology is a fascinating subject and is viewed as such by millions of people. We have got to make our brand as palatable as that being marketed by Erich and Barry, with their bright shadow-lettered covers and their snappy, eye-catching titles. We are facing slick writers and rogue professors, so it won't be easy. Harrison Ford, where are you when we need you? But the results will be worth it.

Acknowledgments

This paper has drawn upon researches that I am currently carrying out while writing a book on fantastic archaeology in North America. I am grateful to my colleagues Jeffrey P. Brain, Ian W. Brown, and T. R. Kidder for their helpful comments on an earlier draft of this paper.

References

Asimov, Isaac
1986 The perennial fringe. *The Skeptical Inquirer* 10(3):212–214.
Bada, Jeffrey L.
1985 Aspartic acid racemization ages of California Paleoindian skeletons. *American Antiquity* 50(3):645–647.
Boulding, Kenneth
1980 Science: Our common humanity. *Science* 207.

Churchward, James
1926 *The Lost Continent of Mu: The Motherland of Man.* New York: W. E. Rudge.
Cole, John
1980 Cult archaeology and unscientific method and theory. In Michael B. Schiffer, ed., *Advances in Archaeological Method and Theory*, vol. 3, pp. 1–33. New York: Academic Press.
Daniel, Glyn
1979 The forgotten milestones and blind alleys of the past. *Royal Anthropological Society Newsletter*, no. 33.
de Camp, L. Sprague
1954 *Lost Continents: The Atlantis Theme in History, Science, and Literature.* (Reprinted and revised, Dover Press, 1970.)
1986 The uses of credulity. *The Skeptical Inquirer* 10(3):215–216.
Donnelly, Ignatius
1882 *Atlantis: The Antediluvian World.* (Modern revised edition, 1949, New York: Harper.)
Fagan, Brian
1981 *In the Beginning: An Introduction to Archaeology.* Boston: Little, Brown.
Feder, Kenneth
1984 Irrationality and popular archaeology. *American Antiquity* 41(3):525–541.
Fell, Barry
1976 *America B.C.* New York: Times Books.
1980 *Saga America.* New York: Times Books.
1982 *Bronze Age America.* Boston: Little, Brown.
Fitzhugh, William W., with Ives Goddard
1979 A statement concerning *America B.C. Man in the Northwest* 17:166–172.
Gardner, Martin
1957 *Fads and Fallacies in the Name of Science.* New York: Dover.
Goodman, Jeffrey.
1981 *American Genesis.* New York: Berkley.
Haven, Samuel F.
1856 *Archaeology of the United States. Smithsonian Contributions to Knowledge*, no. 8.
Henshaw, Henry
1883 *Animal Carvings from the Mounds of the Mississippi Valley.* Bureau of American Ethnology, *Annual Report*, no. 2.
Horsford, Eben
1890 *The Discovery of the Ancient City of Norumbega.* Boston: Houghton, Mifflin.
Huddleston, Lee E.
1967 *Origins of the American Indians: European Concepts, 1492–1729.* Austin: University of Texas Press.
Jenks, Albert Ernest
1900 A remarkable counterfeiter. *American Anthropologist* 2(2):292–298.
Kelsey, Francis W.
1908 Some archaeological forgeries from Michigan. *American Anthropologist* 10(1).
Kurtz, Paul
1986 CSICOP after ten years: Reflections on the "Transcendental Temptation." *The Skeptical Inquirer* 10(3):229–232.
McKusick, Marshall
1984 Psychic archaeology from Atlantis to Oz. *Archaeology* 37(5):48–52.
Putnam, Frederic Ward
1883 Archaeological frauds. *Science* 1(4):99.

Rathje, William L.

1978 The ancient astronaut myth. *Archaeology* 31(1):4–7.

Rathje, William L., and Michael Schiffer

1982 *Archaeology.* New York: Harcourt Brace Jovanovich.

Sabloff, Jeremy A., ed.

1982 *Archaeology: Myth and Reality.* Readings from *Scientific American.* San Francisco: Freeman.

Sagan, Carl

1986 Night walkers and mystery mongers: Sense and nonsense at the edge of science. *The Skeptical Inquirer* 10(3):218–228.

Sharer, Robert, and Wendy Ashmore

1979 *Fundamentals of Archaeology.* Menlo Park, Calif.: Benjamin/Cummings.

Snow, Dean

1981 Martians and Vikings, Madoc and runes. *American Heritage* 32(6):102–108.

Stiebing, William H.

1984 *Ancient Astronauts, Cosmic Collisions and Other Popular Theories about Man's Past.* Buffalo, N.Y.: Prometheus Books.

Thomas, Cyrus

1894 *Report on the Mound Explorations of the Bureau of Ethnology.* Bureau of American Ethnology, Annual Report, no. 12.

Velikovsky, Immanuel

1950 *Worlds in Collision.* Garden City, N.Y.: Doubleday.

Vogt, Evon Z., and Ray Hyman

1959 *Water Witching, U.S.A.* Chicago: University of Chicago Press.

von Däniken, Erich

1970 *Chariots of the Gods.* New York: Putnam.

Wauchope, Robert

1962 *Lost Tribes and Sunken Continents.* Chicago: University of Chicago Press.

White, J. Peter

1974 *The Past Is Human.* New York: Taplinger.

Whittlesey, Charles

1872 *Archaeological Frauds.* Western Reserve and Northern Ohio Historical Society, tract no. 9.

1876 *Archaeological Frauds.* Western Reserve and Northern Ohio Historical Society, tract no. 33.

Wiener, Leo

1922 *Africa and the Discovery of America* (3 vols.). Philadelphia: Innes.

1926 *Maya and Mexican Origins.* Cambridge, Mass.: privately printed.

Willey, Gordon R.

1980 The social uses of archaeology. Murdock Lecture.

Winsor, Justin

1894 *A Narrative and Critical History of America.* Boston: Houghton, Mifflin.

10.

Multiculturalism, Cult Archaeology, and Pseudoscience

Bernard Ortiz de Montellano

A number of efforts have been made in the last few years to increase the multicultural content of public education and particularly to replace Eurocentric content with other "centrics." The best-developed and most widely diffused of these schools is Afrocentrism, and it will be my primary focus. Other ethnic groups have not developed or widely implemented their version of multiculturalism and will only be mentioned briefly. I will focus primarily on Afrocentric scientific claims and a particular example of cult archaeology because these are the claims that are most comparable to those of "scientific" creationists and of other cult archaeologists, and because scientific claims are easier to handle epistemologically than historical or literary claims. Aspects of Afrocentrism have great similarity to cult archaeology and scientific creationism as described previously in this volume. This chapter will briefly describe some Afrocentric claims and discuss why they are erroneous. It will also describe the similarity of the authors' techniques, methods, and motivations to those of "scientific" creationists and cult archaeologists and propose some reasons for why these claims persist and spread.

Claims can be analyzed in terms of myths—not in the vernacular sense of "not true" but as myths are defined in anthropology. Myths are the basis of all religions because they are "authoritative accounts of great foundational forces that generate and govern the world" (Paden 1988:69). Myths are also "mythic charters" that explain and justify the origins of the world, life on earth, and other aspects of the human experience. A key characteristic of myths is that they cannot be proved or disproved. Myths are purely a matter of belief. Thus, a biblical fundamentalist cannot conceive that the Genesis account could be disproved because that would negate the existence of God. On the other hand, a biblical fundamentalist cannot prove the literal interpretation of the Bible without referring to the Bible itself. For many years, even in the West, the world was explained primarily on a religious (mythical) basis. However, the success of science and technology in the last century has led to the primacy of science as a method for explaining the world. Because of this, there are many attempts to use the prestige of science to "prove" the validity of myths, for example, the Genesis version of creation, the biological superiority of white or of black people, or making Egypt the sole source of all civilization. Most of these attempts are pseudoscientific and rely for their acceptance on the high level of scientific illiteracy in the United States, as documented in previous chapters.

Mythic Charters

At the turn of the century, hyperdiffusionist European scholars argued that all civilization began in Egypt and diffused to the rest of the world (Churchward 1913, 1921; Massey 1907; Smith 1923; Perry 1923). These were racist authors who considered the ancient Egyptians to be Caucasians. Afrocentrists have adopted the entire concept, but they claim that the ancient Egyptians were black. Afrocentrists claim that the Greeks (and, therefore, the West) stole all their knowledge from Egypt (James 1988; Ben-Jochannan 1971) and that a black Egyptian civilization was the impetus for other civilizations such as those of the New World (Van Sertima 1976; Van Sertima, ed. 1992), India, and China (Van Sertima 1985).

I will here deal only with the claim that black Nubians came to the New World and were the crucial impetus to the Olmecs and the subsequent civilization in Mesoamerica.

Like "scientific" creationists, Afrocentrists have made vigorous efforts to introduce their beliefs into the science curriculum of the schools. Their primary vehicle has been the pseudoscientific Portland Baseline Essay, "African and African-American Contributions in Science" (Adams 1990), which is used or has been adopted by a number of large urban school districts, such as Detroit, Atlanta, and Milwaukee (Ortiz de Montellano 1991, 1992). This essay makes claims reminiscent of Russian efforts during the Cold War: that ancient Egyptians were the first to discover various modern scientific concepts, such as Darwin's theory of evolution, electroplating of gold, the philosophical aspects of quantum theory, and glider flight (Adams 1990). A much more dangerous characteristic of the essay is Adams' advocacy of religious and New Age concepts as an integral part of science: "For the ancient Egyptians as well as contemporary Africans world-wide, there is no distinction and thus no separation between science and religion" (Adams 1990:S-14). Adams (1990) argues that Egyptian science and technology surpassed modern science because the Egyptians used a superior paradigm, *Maat*, that involved the acknowledgment of a Supreme Consciousness of Creative Force (i.e., a deity) and the existence of "transmaterial causation" (i.e., supernatural causes). Further, Adams (1990:S-14) states that "many Western scientists conduct their process of science from a totally different ideological basis. One which has, as its main concern, non-ethical considerations such as cost effectiveness." It is certainly true that *Maat* is antithetical to Western science—not for Adams' reasons, but because it is an attempt to teach that religion, under the guise of "Egyptian science," is science. Moreover, Judge Overton in *McLean v. Arkansas*, the "scientific" creation case, explicitly ruled that science can only be guided and explained by reference to natural law and excludes references to the supernatural (Anonymous 1982). Adams also claims that astrology is valid and that there is a scientific basis for paranormal phenomena, such as precognition, psychokinesis, and psychoenergetics (for critiques of the Portland Science Baseline Essay, see Ortiz de Montellano [1991, 1992], Klotz [1993], and Rowe [n.d.]).

A group of Afrocentrists, whom I call melanists, proposes a "scientific" explanation for the superiority of a black Egyptian civilization. Their argument purports that melanin, the universal pigment, has extraordinary properties which make black persons with a lot of melanin biologically superior to white people (Welsing 1991a; King 1991; Barnes 1988). Melanin is supposed to absorb and interconvert all wavelengths of the electromagnetic spectrum, act as a superconductor, and be crucial to the control of human memory and mental activity. This is the "scientific" reason for Egypt's role as the sole source of civilization: ancient Egyptians were black, and their melanin endowed them with superior mental powers. According to melanists, people with a lot of melanin have paranormal abilities, are more spiritual, and have more "soul" (Barnes 1988:39, 60; King 1991:72; Welsing 1991a: 171). These theories are the underpinning for claims made in the Baseline Essays by Adams, who is also a member of the melanist group.

Melanists make even more extreme claims: that George Washington Carver's successful discovery of useful plant products happened because melanin enabled him to talk to plants (Welsing 1987); that the blood pressure in African Americans is directly correlated to the depth of skin color because their melanin detects the energy emitted by people under stress (Welsing 1991a:237); and that the Dogon of Mali and the ancient Egyptians knew of the existence of a star invisible to the naked eye, Sirius B, because their melanin functioned as an astronomical detector (Welsing 1987). Adams (1990:S-60) makes the same claim but omits melanin or any other explanation. An earlier Adams (1983) publication attributed this knowledge to the use of telescopes by the Egyptians; he claimed that Russians discovered such telescopic lenses in Egypt.

The crucial flaw in all these arguments is the use of the name "melanin" to identify two completely different compounds. Neuromelanin is the compound found in the brain; eumelanin is present in the skin. Any purported properties of "melanin" involving mental activity would involve neuromelanin, not eumelanin. The two melanins are synthesized by completely different mechanisms, and there is no correlation whatsoever between eumelanin and neuromelanin. White albinos have a normal amount of neuromelanin, and, because the amount of neuromelanin is directly proportional to age, an old albino has more neuromelanin than a black teenager. The claims made by melanists refer to neuromelanin, not to skin melanin (for a detailed critique of the melanin question see Ortiz de Montellano 1993; Graves 1993). Practically all of their assertions about neuromelanin are false; even if they were all true, all humans would have the same abilities, regardless of skin color.

Anthropologists have worked for a long time to refute the existence of biological races. We are all *Homo sapiens sapiens*. Most of the genetic diversity in humankind is due to differences between individuals belonging to the same "race" or tribe, while only 10 percent of the total diversity occurs between "racial" groups (Latter 1980; Lewontin 1972). The Afrocentric emphasis on race and melanin invokes an outmoded and useless concept (Graves 1993).

The Afrocentrists' fixation on biological races actually makes their task more difficult. The claim that Egyptian culture is African is quite supportable on its merits. No one disputes that Egypt is in Africa or that its civilization had elements in common with sub-Saharan Africa, particularly in religion. However, the Afrocentrists claim that Egyptian civilization was a "black" civilization, and this is not accurate. Even if "races" existed, the Afrocentrists' claim that Egypt was a "black" society (with the connotation that Egyptians looked like African Americans) is wrong. Genetically, Egyptians are not closely related to sub-Saharan Africans (Brace et al. 1993). Most scholars believe that ancient Egyptians looked pretty much like today's Egyptians—that is, they were brown, becoming darker as they approached the Sudan (Snowden 1970, 1992; Smedley 1993). Egypt was a multiracial society that did not discriminate internally on the basis of color but looked down on all foreigners regardless of color (Yurco 1989; Snowden 1970, 1989, 1992; Young 1992; Levine 1992; Coleman 1992; Kelly 1991; for a fuller discussion, see Ortiz de Montellano 1993).

Creationism

Pseudoscientific creationism is not unique to Afrocentrists. Some Native Americans claim that the peopling of the New World via migration through the Bering Strait is just a plot by Establishment archaeologists and a theory without evidence (Forbes 1973; see McGhee 1989). Some textbooks on multicultural education endorse the idea of teaching that "Indians . . . evolved or were created in the Americas" (Bennett 1990:287). Goodman (1981) asserts that there is archaeological evidence for the presence of modern humans in the New World 500,000 years ago, which would support Native American myths. Goodman's evidence is, however, tainted by the fact that the site excavated was chosen through psychic archaeology, while his results have not been published in the archaeological literature (Goodman 1977a, 1977b).

Argüelles (1987) maintains that the Classic Maya civilization achieved unparalleled heights because Mayans came from another world. Argüelles states that the Maya were transmitted to Earth from outside the solar system in the form of DNA code with orders to synchronize Earth and the solar system with the larger galactic community. Argüelles, an artist, seems to have derived most of his data and arguments through a series of artistic visions. He incorporates a number of New Age fads such as the Chinese I Ching into his proposals. The book is written in a complicated pseudoscientific babble resembling a word salad.

Afrocentrists blatantly distort (or ignore) modern paleontological understanding of human evolution; the following are examples. King (1991:17–19), based on Churchward (1913), claims that modern African Twa pygmies are *Homo erectus* and that all humans descend from them.[1] Both Welsing (1991a:23–24) and Finch (1990:43) state that whites are albinos who originated from the inbreeding of Negroid albinos who migrated from Africa, the place of origin of modern humans, to Europe.[2] Forbes (1992) tells a more elaborate creation story which "will demonstrate . . . that modern man arose from the deliberate manipulation of genetic material by scientists in antiquity, that an identifiable African female immortalized in sculpted works of art served as the egg donor, and that an Egyptian deity served as the first surrogate mother." Forbes' article is a selective excerpt of the theory elaborated by Zechariah Sitchin (1976). What Sitchin actually claims is that modern humans were created by biblical Nephilim, who were actually life forms that periodically visited Earth from a twelfth planet, Marduk, which circles the Sun in a 3600-year orbit. According to Sitchin (1976:340–357), modern humans were created 300,000 years ago by the artificial insemination of ova from a female *Homo erectus* with sperm from male Nephilim and with the use of numerous female Nephilim as surrogate mothers.[3]

New World Contacts

A number of Afrocentrists, led by Ivan Van Sertima, claim that the civilizations in the New World are greatly indebted to Egypt (or Nubia) for their most important accomplishments. Supposedly, black Egyptians sailed to Mexico about 700 B.C., propelled the Olmec civilization to greatness, and laid the foundation for all the civilizations of Mesoamerica. Yet, the best evidence for contact between peoples is supplied by genuine artifacts scientifically excavated by archaeologists. While the presence of Vikings around A.D. 1000 at L'Anse-aux-Meadows, Newfoundland, has been thus documented (Ingstad 1969), no genuine African or Egyptian pre-Columbian artifacts have ever been found in the New World.

The next best type of evidence for contact between cultures is the presence of domesticated plants native to another continent. Two species found in the New World, the bottle gourd (*Lagenaria siceraria*) and New World cotton, originated in Africa. However, they were present and utilized in the Americas thousands of years before they were used in Africa and were carried to the New World naturally rather than by humans (Cowan and Watson 1992).

The most striking visual evidence cited by Afrocentrists for an African presence in the New World is the massive Olmec basalt heads with flat noses and thick lips. However, Nubians, the purported carriers of Egyptian civilization to the Olmecs, are desert dwellers with thin noses and could not have been the models for those sculptures (Haslip-Viera and Ortiz de Montellano n.d.). Additionally, the Olmec heads were all carved before 900 B.C., several hundred years before the contact claimed by Van Sertima (Lowe 1989).

Similarity to "Scientific" Creationism and Cult Archaeology

Stiebing (this volume) and Cole (1980) describe a number of characteristics that Afrocentrists share with "scientific" creationists and cult archaeologists. Some general comments are in order before citing specific examples. As is the case with the creationists and cult archaeologists, most Afrocentric authors lack academic credentials in the appropriate fields and do little or no original research. Proponents of contacts with the Olmecs have not turned a spadeful of dirt in Mexico; melanists do no biochemical laboratory research; and none of them publish in the appropriate refereed disciplinary journals. As in the case of "scientific" creationists, their research consists of dredging through the scientific literature for supportive snippets. They cite other Afrocentrists or their own previous work and rely on unreliable or outdated sources, often taken out of context. They use myths as though they were historical or scientific facts. Mary Lefkowitz (1993), referring to Martin Bernal's claims of massive Egyptian influence on Greece, describes another common technique: " . . . because something is possible, it can be considered probable, or even actual, *si potest esse, est.*"[4] Many Afrocentrists are less cautious and use the following chain of reasoning: if it is conceivable, it is possible, it is probable—it is true.

Reliable scholarship characteristically makes efforts to cite the most current information available. Afrocentrists resemble creationists and cult archaeologists in the kind of sources they use and the way in which they use them. Just as creationists cite Lord Kelvin's 1866 estimate of the age of the earth as if it were a contemporaneous source (Gould 1985:126–138), Afrocentrists make much use of antiquated sources such as Churchward (1913, 1921), Massey (1907), and Budge (1904), citing them often from recent reprints without indicating their original date of publication. Forty-eight percent of Van Sertima's (1976) citations in *They Came Before Columbus* are older than 1940, and he relies massively on Wiener, who wrote in the 1920s. Similarly, 48 percent of Jackson's (1972) citations predate 1930. The sources Afrocentrists rely on to support their claim that Egypt was the world's original civilization were written before the scope and extent of Babylonian civilization were known, and before stratigraphy and radiocarbon dating greatly extended the time depth of civilizations and the reliability of the associated dates. Wiener's (1920–1922) work predates the discovery of the Olmec heartland and the explosion of knowledge about Mesoamerican civilizations that has occurred in the last fifty years.

Sources of different reliability are given equal weight. For example, Adams' (1990) bibliography includes newspapers, magazines, and publications from vanity presses along with a few refereed articles from the journal *Science*. King (1991) uses as scientific resources the eighty-year-old works of James Churchward and the theosophical works of the mystic Schwaller de Lubicz (1982). King, Welsing, Adams, and Bernal, among others, use Tompkins's (1971, 1976) fanciful and unreliable books on pyramids.

In Cole's (1980) terms, Afrocentrists have "an ambivalent antielitism." They vilify the Establishment because it does not support Afrocentric claims, or they consider it part of a conspiracy to hide the truth; yet they display an inordinate respect for and envy of it. In the past, religion was invoked to provide explanations for different events and phenomena. As stated earlier, the success of science and technology in the twentieth century has led to science replacing religion as a source of truth and explanation. Because of this, myths such as creationism or Afrocentrism are cloaked in the mantle of science; their proponents search for scientific quotations to support their contentions. Creationists misquote or partially quote Stephen Gould (Gould

1983); Afrocentrists similarly employ distorted quotations. For example, Adams (1990:vi) cites Louis de Broglie (with no bibliographic entry or page number) purportedly supporting the existence and validity of the paranormal. However, de Broglie explicitly rejects the paranormal four pages after the passage used by Adams: "I must say that the existence of most of these phenomena [the paranormal] does not seem to be scientifically established in a serious manner. . . . Further, a great number of those who write on these subjects give evidence of an insufficient general scientific education, confusing the most clearly expressed ideas and interpreting the theories of modern physics in the most fantastic manner" (de Broglie 1955:235–236). Van Sertima (1976:84) attributes to Eduard Seler statements concerning the god Quetzalcoatl's hat, which in fact are completely opposite to what Seler wrote (Seler 1963: 70). Bernal tries to discredit Otto Neugebauer, the great expert on ancient science, by claiming that Neugebauer was condescending and contemptuous toward Egypt; Palter (1993) has clearly shown that to be untrue. Melanists derive most of their scientific citations from a long speculative article by Barr (1983). Barr continually speaks of properties of melanin as if they applied to humans. In fact, the experiments referred to were carried out on rats; this is very misleading because these extrapolations are not valid. Barr deletes some of the cautionary statements made by the original investigators. Melanists, following the principle of "conceivable equals actual," delete even the few cautionary statements made by Barr and ignore his repeated injunctions that neuromelanin is unrelated to skin color and that the properties he attributes to melanin are pan-human and not racial.

Afrocentrists share with cult archaeologists what Cole (1980) calls "intimations of persecution." They allege a conspiracy by the Establishment to conceal the truth, which Afrocentrists then claim they are trying to reveal. Deborah Moore (1992) claims that the information about melanin and the pineal has been hidden for forty years. Van Sertima (1992:7, 37–38), referring to an Olmec head which is supposed to have Ethiopian braids, claims that it is "probably the best kept secret in Mesoamerican archaeology" and that the head "has never appeared, in any work on the subject, outside of Mexico."[5] Bernal (1987: ch. 4–5) claims that the "classics Establishment" has suppressed or ignored what he considers overwhelming evidence of Egyptian contributions to Greek civilization. Jordan (1992:107, n. 20) claims that he had some difficulty in obtaining a reference about the presence of Negroid skeletons in Tlatilco in the New York Museum of Natural History and that he was told that the museum had no such volume. Jordan also found it suspicious that the Anthropology Department had checked out a volume by the cult archaeologist Rafique Jairazbhoy, intimating that it was done to keep it out of circulation.

Why Has This Ideology Spread?

Given the tragic history of African Americans and the harshness of the present circumstances of many African Americans—hopelessness, high unemployment, high dropout rates, and the escalating effects of drugs and violence on the black community—the development of Afrocentrism is understandable. Projects such as the Portland Baseline Essays are misdirected efforts to use the schools to raise the self-esteem of African American children by claiming a previous racial greatness and declaring not only parity but superiority to the European oppressors. Melanist proposals are psychologically attractive because they convert pigmentation, which has been a badge of inferiority in a racist society, into the instrument for the mental, moral, and spiritual superiority of all blacks (Egyptians, Africans, and the Diaspora). Melanin, instead of being negatively correlated with intelligence, as claimed in Richard Herrnstein and Charles Murray's *The Bell Curve* (1994), is presented as positively correlated to intelligence.

However, a wrong cannot be remedied by committing another wrong. Many African American children need more self-esteem, but self-esteem is not achieved by being taught pseudoscience. Gwin (1990) points out that children acquire self-esteem by accomplishing increasingly complex tasks, by learning, and by being able to use what they have learned. Gwin also notes that one of the most important characteristics of successful people is accurate perception. A curriculum that consists primarily of assertions of black superiority with little development of critical thinking, of high expectations for performance in an effort to develop self-esteem, will ultimately be self-defeating. Stevenson, Chen, and Uttal (1990) compared black, Hispanic, and white children in Chicago and found that the self-evaluation of African American children exceeded their actual achievement scores. Stevenson's group felt that this was due to blacks not getting, or not incorporating, reliable and accurate feedback on their performance. "Teachers praise the children for modestly good performance instead of pushing them to do better" (Anonymous 1992). Stevenson points out that praising work that is substandard, often on the pretext of protecting the self-esteem of the child, does not do the child any favor, because one of the most important sources of children's self-esteem is realizing that they have mastered a challenging task (Stevenson, Chen, and Uttal 1992; Gwin 1990). Eliot Morgan (1992) made the point in an editorial that what he and other African Americans needed from schools was a rigorous curriculum emphasizing the basics and not inaccurate Afrocentrism.

African Americans are greatly underrepresented in science. African American children deserve to be taught the best science we can muster to encourage and nurture greater participation in scientific careers. It is perpetuation of a cruel hoax not to teach them the critical thinking that is so essential to success in science.[6] A problem with Afrocentric melanists is that they promote an essentialist view of race, the existence of immutable races that are recognizable by stereotypic characteristics, that these races have biological and evolutionary significance, and that some races are superior to others. This is racism, pure and simple. The essentialist concept of race is rejected by the overwhelming majority of anthropologists, biologists, and geneticists (Littlefield, Lieberman, and Reynolds 1982; Graves 1993).

Another factor influencing the spread of the melanin theory is that it provides a "scientific" justification and validation of fears that already exist in the African American community. The proposal that whites are "albinos" that can be destroyed genetically by the "melanin-dominant" genes of blacks (see note 2) provides a "scientific," and therefore supposedly true, basis for belief in the existence of a "conspiracy to destroy Black men" (Kunjufu 1989; Welsing 1991a:4, 1991b). The genetic argument provides a seemingly credible explanation for the crisis and for some of the conditions of black Americans. It provides a rationale for the epidemics that are devastating that community. Fear of "melanin dominance" explains the belief that whites manufactured AIDS in order to destroy the black community (Adams 1988; Welsing 1991a: 299–300; Strecker n.d.; Snead 1994). Melanists state that the drug epidemic in African American communities is part of the "conspiracy to destroy Black men" (Welsing 1991a:4, 1991c). Barnes (1988:75–76) involves melanin directly, claiming that it has a special affinity for illegal drugs and that melanin co-polymerizes with cocaine, thus remaining in the bodies of blacks for months. These medicalized theories have a special resonance in the African American community because of the precedent of the "Tuskegee Experiment," in which, for many years, physicians of the Public Health Service unethically withheld medical treatment against syphilis from a group of black men in order to study the natural progression of the disease (Jones 1981).

The problem with a "scientific" basis for a "conspiracy to destroy Black men" is that it exacerbates and complicates the already tense relationships between the races; it can also have harmful consequences for the health of African Americans themselves. The idea of a conspiracy has led to propaganda urging parents not to take their children to get vaccinated because white doctors will infect them with AIDS (Watson 1994). Michael Ellner (1994), with the endorsement of the host of a television program, Tony Brown, bragged of his success in getting African American women to withdraw from research efforts to diminish transmission of the HIV virus to newborns and urged other pregnant women not to participate. Ellner argued that the drug used, AZT, is a poison and that its use is part of the plot to destroy black people. However, the prophylactic use of AZT with HIV-positive pregnant women has been shown in a clinically controlled test to reduce the transmission of the virus to newborn babies by two-thirds (Connor et al. 1994). Nonparticipation in this therapy condemns black babies to death.

As other chapters in this book have detailed, an important factor contributing to the spread and persistence of these theories is the high level of scientific illiteracy in this country. African Americans are no exception; most members of the community don't know enough science to be able to ask critical questions. Furthermore, many melanists have Ph.D.s or M.D.s, and some are faculty members at universities; these credentials, even if not in the appropriate disciplines, impress their intended audience. Like other pseudoscientists, they also use what I call "newspeak," an impressive, scientific-sounding babble. A couple of examples will suffice:

. . . essence of their [hieroglyphs'] meaning eludes us. This is primarily because the ancient Egyptians' polyocular epistemology renders their written style of communication multicontextural [*sic*]. This is to say, there is a high degree of simultaneity and spontaneity, and also rhythm and symbolic logic in their thought; for example, superimposed upon a single image are many points of view and moments in time. (Adams 1990:S-30)

Therefore if you move away from that system, whether you are moving into disease, or death or entropy as opposed to negative entropy. In the context of healing we must be about moving into superhigh velocities as our ancient ancestors did. Now, the rituals that you see traditional healers go through— the meditation, the so-called incantation, the rituals, do something. They change the flow of energy within a circumscribed area. And you can put the voltometers [*sic*] in the room and you can measure the actual transfer. Traditional healers are able to tap that other realm of negative entropy—that superquantum velocity and frequency of electromagnetic energy and bring them as conduits down to our level. It's not magic, it's not mumbo jumbo. (Newton 1993)

Afrocentric pseudoscientists have found allies and theoretical support from postmodernists in academia. Postmodernists argue that science is not a body of knowledge about the "real" world and a technique for testing its accuracy but rather a form of "discourse" controlled by culture, social organization, and economics (see discussion of perspectivism in Gross and Levitt 1994:ch. 3). On this basis, Afrocentrists argue that their New Age claims for the existence of ESP, "transmaterial causation," and the psychic abilities of ancient Egyptians constitute a scientific paradigm that is superior to that of Eurocentric Western science. Based on postmodernism, they further argue that their interpretations of matters Egyptian should be "privileged" over other interpretations because their melanin gives them "ownership" of the topic. This attitude is reciprocated. Feminist philosopher Sandra Harding (1991:223–227) repeats a number of outlandish claims in Van Sertima's (1983) *Blacks in Science*, including the Dogon Sirius B myth, without a trace of skepticism or critical thinking.

The scientific establishment has itself contributed to the spread of this pseudoscience in two ways. One of the key reasons why the Portland Baseline Essays have been adopted by so many schools is that they are expanding into a vacuum. There is an enormous demand in large urban school districts for materials that will illustrate and reflect some of the science done by non-Western peoples to be used to inspire and to provide role models for minority children. As Diana Marinez and I (1983, 1993) have pointed out, if done in a scientifically accurate manner, this "culturally relevant" science can be a useful adjunct in the classroom. The scientific and science education establishment has abdicated any role in this effort. There are no reliable materials of this type available, and the highly touted science education reform of the American Association for the Advancement of Science (AAAS), Project 2061, is completely devoid of any "culturally relevant" material.

A more important factor, one which is in sharp contrast with "scientific" creationism, is the extreme reluctance of the scientific establishment to criticize any aspect of Afrocentric pseudoscience. Whereas the AAAS, the National Academy of Science (NAS), and numerous well-known scientists like Stephen Gould and Carl Sagan vigorously and openly criticize "scientific" creationism, these bodies have been pusillanimous in confronting Afrocentric pseudoscience. Several bodies within the AAAS have refused to take stands on the use of the Baseline Essay in Science when asked to do so; the Project on Science Education Standards of the NAS did not even want to hear a presentation on the topic; and the American Anthropological Association would not schedule a symposium entitled "Pseudoanthropology and Multiculturalism," which dealt with Afrocentrism, at its 1992 annual meeting, which had multiculturalism as its theme. The fear of being called racist seems to produce a paralyzing effect on consciences and on scientific integrity. This is unfortunate and shortsighted. In the future, minorities will make up an increasingly larger proportion of the work force, and simultaneously, the skills in science and mathematics needed for jobs will greatly increase (Anonymous 1988; National Center for Education Statistics 1993). It is a cruel hoax to deprive an African American child of the opportunity to learn critical thinking and to develop skills crucial to the jobs available in the future, only because those who lead the reform of science education, as well as our leading scientists, are unwilling to confront pseudoscience, whatever its color.

Notes

1. This is utterly wrong. Pygmies are modern humans (*Homo sapiens sapiens*) and not our ancestral and extinct *Homo erectus*. It is ludicrous for someone with an M.D. to cite, in 1990, as an authority on paleontology and evolution a 1910 publication by a retired colonel of the Bengal Lancers who also believed in the existence of the Lost Continent of Mu (Churchward 1932). It is also amusing that melanists are so enthused with Churchward because, according to him, the inhabitants of Mu—the ultimate source of all civilizations, including the Egyptian—were white (Wauchope 1962:42).

2. Again, this is utterly wrong. Albinos, by definition, do not synthesize eumelanin. Whites have eumelanin and are not albinos. Skin color is regulated by four to five genes. Albinism results from a recessive mutation; i.e., in order to produce the effect, both alleles must code for albinism (a, a). Persons who are homozygous normal (A, A) or heterozygous (A, a) will produce normal amounts of melanin. Thus, two albinos (a, a) could mate forever and not produce a white person (A, A or A, a).

3. Sitchin claims that Nephilim established Sumerian civilization, which was the first and only civilization and from which knowledge diffused to all others, including the Egyptian. Forbes, with no evidence or justification, shifts the entire scenario to Egypt and converts Sumerians into black Egyptians. Forbes also changes the presumed date of the origin of modern humans from 300,000 years ago to the Egyptian civilization of some 5000 years ago. It is hard to believe that this piece of science fiction was published in a reputable journal edited by the doyen of Afro-centrism, Molefi Kete Asante. I can only conclude that Asante did not read the article carefully or that his susceptibility to pseudoscience is even greater than the levels shown in his 1990 book.

4. Bernal (1987, 1991) would seem to be a special case among Afrocentrists. His book, *Black Athena*, explicitly rejects an exclusively Negroid character for ancient Egyptians. His work, al-though much better documented than that of most Afrocentric authors, still employs many of the techniques of cult archaeologists, particularly in arguments about Egyptian science. Citing Peter Tompkins, a journalist who has also written a book claiming that plants talk to people (Tompkins and Byrd 1973), Bernal argues that Newton depended on Egyptian ideas for his development of the theory of gravity (Bernal 1987:166–169). Bernal also cites such outdated works as Lockyer's *The Dawn of Astronomy* (1894), while denigrating Otto Neugebauer, the acknowledged authority on ancient astronomy, because Neugebauer did not support exagger-ated claims of Egyptian accomplishments. Barnes (1991) also points out that Bernal sees much historical value in the Atlantis myth. Although Bernal has performed a useful service by exposing the racist and anti-Semitic biases of nineteenth-century German and British scholars, his attri-bution of similar feelings to modern scholars is not accurate and places him in the same niche as other cult archaeologists. For a thorough critique of Bernal's claims for Egyptian science, see Palter (1993).

5. A full description of this head was published, as one would expect, in the reports of the archaeological expedition to the area (Clewlow et al. 1967).

6. Claims by Adams (1990:S-52–54) that Egyptians flew in full-size gliders for business and tourism in 2000 B.C. could not withstand ten minutes of critical thinking on the question of what this actually implies and how the ancient Egyptians could have done this. The Baseline Essay is replete with similar examples.

References

Adams, Hunter H.

1983 African observers of the universe: The Sirius question. In I. Van Sertima, ed., *Blacks in Science: Ancient and Modern*, pp. 27–46. New Brunswick, N.J.: Transaction.

1988 Lecture, Second Melanin Conference, San Francisco, September 16–18. Broadcast on "African World View," WDTR-FM, Detroit Public Schools Radio, September 25, 1990.

1990 [1987] African and African-American contributions in science. Portland, Ore.: Multnomah County School District.

Anonymous

1982 Creationism in schools: The decision in *McLean versus the Arkansas Board of Education*. *Science* 215:934–943.

1988 Human capital. *Business Week*, September 19, 100–121.

1992 Can U.S. math and science soar? *Research News* (University of Michigan) (Spring):1–5.

Argüelles, Jose

1987 *The Mayan Factor: Path beyond Technology*. Santa Fe; N. Mex.: Bear Co.

Asante, Molefi K.

1990 *Kemet, Afrocentricity and Knowledge*. Trenton, N.J.: Africa World Press.

Barnes, C.

1988 *Melanin: The Chemical Key to Black Greatness*. Houston: C. B. Publishers.

Barnes, J.

1991 Was civilization made in Africa? *New York Times Book Review*, August 11, pp. 12–13.

Barr, F. E.

1983 Melanin: The organizing molecule. *Medical Hypothesis* 11:1–139.

Ben-Jochannan, J.

1971 *Africa: Mother of "Western Civilization."* New York: Alkebulan Books.

Bennett, C. I.

1990 *Comprehensive Multicultural Education. Theory and Practice*. 2nd ed. Boston: Allyn & Bacon.

Bernal, Martin

1987 *Black Athena: The Afroasiatic Roots of Classical Civilization*. Vol. 1, *The Fabrication of Ancient Greece [1785–1985]*. New Brunswick, N.J.: Rutgers University Press.

1991 *Black Athena: The Afroasiatic Roots of Classical Civilization*. Vol. 2, *The Archaeological and Documentary Evidence*. New Brunswick, N.J.: Rutgers University Press.

Brace, C. Loring, et al.

1993 Clines and clusters versus "race:" A test in ancient Egypt and the case of a death on the Nile. *Yearbook of Physical Anthropology* 36:1–21.

Budge, E. A. Wallis

1904 *The Gods of the Egyptians*. 2 vols. London: Methuen.

Churchward, James

1913 [1910] *Signs and Symbols of Primordial Man*. 2d ed. London: George Allen & Unwin.

1921 [1912] *The Origin and Evolution of the Human Race*. London: George Allen & Unwin.

1932 *The Lost Continent of Mu*. New York: Ives Washburn.

Clewlow, C. W., R. A. Cowan, J. F. O'Connell, and C. Beneman

1967 *Colossal Heads of the Olmec Culture*. Contributions of the University of California Archaeological Research Facility, No. 4. Berkeley: University of California Press.

Cole, John R.

1980 Cult archaeology and unscientific method and theory. In Michael B. Schiffer, ed., *Advances in Archaeological Method and Theory*, vol. 3, pp. 1–33. New York: Academic Press.

Coleman, J. E.

1992 Did Egypt shape the glory that was Greece? *Archaeology* 45(2):49–52, 77–81.

Connor, E. M., et al.

1994 Reduction of maternal-infant transmission of Human Immunodeficiency Virus Type I with Zidovudine treatment. *New England Journal of Medicine* 331:1173–1180.

Cowan, C. Wesley, and Patty Jo Watson, eds.

1992 *The Origins of Agriculture: An International Perspective*. Washington, D.C.: Smithsonian Press.

de Broglie, Louis

1955 *Physics and Macrophysics*. M. Davidson, trans. London: Hutchinson's Scientific and Technical Publications.

Ellner, Michael

1994 Are children the victims of AIDS treatment? *Tony Brown's Journal* 1708. Broadcast on WTVS-TV, Detroit, Michigan, April 17.

Finch, C. S.

1990 *The African Background to Medical Science*. London: Karnak House.

Forbes, J. D.

1973 Teaching Native American values and cultures. In J. A. Banks, ed., *Teaching Ethnic Studies: Concepts and Strategies*, pp. 201–223. Washington, D.C.: National Council for the Social Studies.

Forbes, L.

1992 Mitochondrial Eve: Critical reflections on an African basis to science and religion. *Journal of Black Studies* 22(4):593–616.

Goodman, Jeffery

1977a Psychic archaeology: Methodology and empirical evidence from Flagstaff, Arizona. In J. K. Long, ed., *Extrasensory Ecology: Parapsychology and Anthropology*, pp. 313–329. Metuchen, N.J.: Scarecrow Press.

1977b *Psychic Archaeology: Time Machine to the Past*. New York: Berkley.

1981 *American Genesis*. New York: Summit Books.

Gould, Stephen Jay

1983 Evolution as fact and theory. In Stephen Jay Gould, *Hen's Teeth and Horse's Toes*, pp. 253–262. New York: Norton.

1985 *The Flamingo's Smile*. New York: Norton.

Graves, Joseph L., Jr.

1993 Evolutionary biology and human variation: Biological determinism and the mythology of race. *Sage Race Relations Abstracts* 18(3):4–34.

Gross, Paul R., and Norman Levitt

1994 *Higher Superstition: The Academic Left and Its Quarrels with Science*. Baltimore: Johns Hopkins University Press.

Gwin, J.

1990 Self-esteem vs. academic excellence: Are the two on a collision course? *Crisis* 97(10):16–18, 21.

Harding, Sandra

1991 *Whose Science? Whose Knowledge? Thinking from Women's Lives*. Ithaca, N.Y.: Cornell University Press.

Haslip-Viera, G., and B. R. Ortiz de Montellano

n.d. Afrocentrism and the origins of civilization in the Americas: A critique. Unpublished ms.

Herrnstein, Robert J., and Charles Murray

1994 *The Bell Curve: Intelligence and Class Structure*. New York: Free Press.

Ingstad, Helge

1969 *Westward to Vinland*. London: Jonathan Cope.

Jackson, J. G.

1972 *Man, God, and Civilization*. New Hyde Park, N.J.: University Books.

James, G. G. M.
1988 [1954] *Stolen Legacy*. San Francisco: Julian Richardson Associates.
Jones, J. H.
1981 *Bad Blood*. New York: Free Press.
Jordan, K. M.
1992 The African presence in ancient America: Evidence from physical anthropology. In Ivan Van Sertima, ed., *African Presence in Early America*. New Brunswick, N.J.: Transaction.
Kelly, D. H.
1991 Egyptians and Ethiopians: Color, race, and racism. *The Classical Outlook* (Spring): 77–82.
King, R.
1991 *African Origin of Biological Psychology*. Germantown, Tenn.: Seymour Smith.
Klotz, I. M.
1993 Multicultural perspectives in science education: One prescription for failure. *Phi Delta Kappan* (November):266–269.
Kunjufu, J.
1989 Lecture, broadcast on "African World View," WDTR-FM, Detroit Public Schools Radio, May 9.
Latter, B. D.
1980 Genetic differences within and between populations of the major human subgroups. *American Naturalist* 116:220–237.
Lefkowitz, Mary R.
1993 Ethnocentric history from Aristobulus to Bernal. *Academic Questions* 6(2):12–20.
Levine, M. M.
1992 The use and abuse of Black Athena. *American Historical Review* 97:440–464.
Lewontin, Richard C.
1972 The apportionment of human diversity. *Human Genetics* 6:381–398.
Littlefield, A., L. Lieberman, and L. Reynolds
1982 Redefining race: The potential demise of a concept in physical anthropology. *Current Anthropology* 23:641–656.
Lockyer, J. N.
1894 *The Dawn of Astronomy: A Study of Temple-Worship and Mythology of the Ancient Egyptians*. London: Cassell and Co.
Lowe, G. W.
1989 In the heartland of the Olmec: Evolution of material culture. In Robert J. Sharer and David C. Grove, eds., *Regional Perspectives on the Olmec*, pp. 33–67. New York: Cambridge University Press.
McGhee, Robert
1989 Who owns reality? The Bering land bridge dilemma. *Canadian Journal of Archaeology* 13:13–20.
Massey, G.
1907 *Ancient Egypt. The Light of the World*. London: T. Fisher Unwin.
Moore, Deborah L.
1992 Lecture, broadcast on "African World View," WDTR-FM, Detroit Public Schools Radio, January 28.
Morgan, Eliot
1992 Like other fads, Afrocentrism will only harm black youths. *Detroit Free Press*, September 28.

National Center for Education Statistics
1993 *Adult Literacy in America*. Washington, D.C.: Government Printing Office.

Newton, P.
1993 Symposium, "Healing Techniques: Ancient and Traditional," at National Medical Association (NMA) 98th Annual Convention, San Antonio, Texas, August 7–12.

Ortiz de Montellano, Bernard R.
1991 Multicultural pseudoscience: Spreading scientific illiteracy among minorities. *The Skeptical Inquirer* 16:46–50.
1992 A critique of the Portland School's Baseline Essay on African-American Science by Hunter Havelin Adams III. Presented at the Annual Meeting of the American Association for the Advancement of Science, Chicago.
1993 Melanin, Afrocentricity, and pseudoscience. *Yearbook of Physical Anthropology* 36: 33–58.

Ortiz de Montellano, Bernard R., and Diana I. Marinez
1983 Teaching culturally relevant science: A possible remedy to underrepresentation. Paper presented at Michigan Hispanic Education Conference, Dearborn, May 13–14.
1993 Multiculturalism in science: Why and how? Paper presented at Joint Meeting of the National Science Teachers Association and Asociación Mexicana de Maestros de Ciencia, Mexico City, July 24.

Paden, W. A.
1988 *Religious Worlds: Comparative Study of Religion*. Boston: Beacon.

Palter, R.
1993 Black Athena, Afro-centrism, and the history of science. *History of Science* 31:227–287.

Perry, W. J.
1923 *The Children of the Sun: A Study of the Early Study of Civilizations*. New York: E. P. Dutton.

Rowe, W. F.
n.d. School daze: A critical review of the *African-American Baseline Essays for Science and Mathematics*. Unpublished ms.

Schwaller de Lubicz, R. A.
1982 *The Temple of Man: The Secrets of Ancient Egypt*. New York: Inner Traditions International.

Seler, E.
1963 [1905] *Códice Borgia*. Vol. 1. M. Frenk, trans. Mexico: Fondo de Cultura Económica (facsim.).

Sitchin, Zechariah
1976 *The 12th Planet*. New York: Avon.

Smedley, A.
1993 *Race in North America: Origin and Evolution of a Worldview*. Boulder, Colo.: Westview Press.

Smith, Grafton Elliot
1923 *The Ancient Egyptians and the Origins of Civilization*. New York: Harper and Bros.

Snead, E.
1994 Interview, broadcast on "African World View," WDTR-FM, Detroit, Public Schools Radio, April 19.

Snowden, Frank M.
1970 *Blacks in Antiquity: Ethiopians in Greco-Roman Experience*. Cambridge: Harvard University Press.
1989 Bernal's "blacks," Herodotus, and other classical evidence. *Arethusa* (Special Issue, Fall): 83–93.

1992 Whither Afrocentrism? *Descant* (Georgetown University) (Winter):8–9.
Stevenson, H. W., C. Chen, and D. Uttal
1990 Beliefs and achievement: A study of black, white, and Hispanic children. *Child Development* 61:508–523.
Strecker, R. B.
n.d. *The Strecker Memorandum*. Eagle Rock, Calif.: The Strecker Group.
Tompkins, P.
1971 *Secrets of the Great Pyramid*. New York: Harper and Row.
1976 *Mysteries of the Mexican Pyramids*. New York: Harper and Row.
Tompkins, P., and C. Bird
1973 *The Secret Life of Plants*. New York: Harper and Row.
Van Sertima, Ivan
1976 *They Came Before Columbus*. New York: Random House.
1992 Evidence for an African presence in Pre-Columbian America. In I. Van Sertima, ed., *African Presence in Early America*, pp. 29–81. New Brunswick, N.J.: Transaction.
———, ed.
1983 *Blacks in Science, Ancient and Modern*. New Brunswick, N.J.: Transaction.
1985 *African Presence in Early Asia*. New Brunswick, N.J.: Transaction.
1992 *African Presence in Early America*. New Brunswick, N.J.: Transaction.
Watson, JoAnn A.
1994 Broadcast on "JoAnn Watson Show" WCHB-AM, Detroit, April 25.
Wauchope, Robert
1962 *Lost Tribes and Sunken Continents*. Chicago: University of Chicago Press.
Welsing, Frances C.
1987 Lecture, First Melanin Conference, San Francisco, September 16–17. Broadcast on "African World View," WDTR-FM, Detroit Public Schools Radio, September 5, 12, 1989.
1991a *The Isis Papers*. Chicago: Third World Press.
1991b Lecture, broadcast on "African World View," WDTR-FM, Detroit Public Schools Radio, June 25.
1991c Lecture, broadcast on "African World View," WDTR-FM, Detroit Public Schools Radio, July 2.
Wiener, Leo
1920–1922 *Africa and the Discovery of America*. 3 vols. Philadelphia: Innes & Sons.
Young, P. A.
1992 Was Nefertiti black? *Archaeology* 45(2):2.
Yurco, Frank Y.
1989 Were the ancient Egyptians black or white? *Biblical Archaeology Review* 15(5):24–29, 58.

11.

Cult Archaeology and Creationism in the 1990s and Beyond

*Francis B. Harrold, Raymond A. Eve,
and Geertruida C. de Goede*

In this closing chapter we will describe trends in pseudoscientific beliefs about the past since the publication of the first edition of this book. We will also discuss current thinking on the causes of the widespread acceptance of these beliefs. We will evaluate the response to these beliefs by the scientists and scholars who study the past. Finally, we will hazard some predictions about the future of creationism and cult archaeology.

Trends in Cult Archaeology and Creationism

For the most part, a tour in the mid-1990s of the pseudoscience of the past finds a similar landscape to that of the 1980s. Most of the same old claims, as poorly supported as ever, are widely repeated in books, on television, and in other media. The levels of belief in both creationism (Gallup and Bezilla 1994) and various cult archaeology claims (Feder, 1995; Eve, Harrold, and Taylor 1995) in the 1990s are very similar to those of the 1980s. Nonetheless, significant developments are visible. One is found in certain pseudoscientific aspects of Afrocentrism, discussed at length by Ortiz de Montellano in Chapter 10 (see also Graves 1992, 1993; Graves and Leigh, in press).

Setbacks for Pseudoscience At least two developments offer encouragement to opponents of fantastic archaeology. One is the near disappearance from the North American public arena of Erich von Däniken, once the epitome of the successful pseudoscience entrepreneur. The last book by von Däniken published in the United States appeared in 1984 (sales were disappointing), and his tomes are to be found today mainly in used-book stores. In our classes, most students now do not recognize his name.

If von Däniken is down, however, he is hardly out. He still has many devotees, especially the 10,000 worldwide members of the Ancient Astronaut Society (Huyghe 1994). And his popularity has never faded in Europe, where his new books continue to roll off the presses in several languages. He starred in a twenty-five-part European television series (*On the Trace of the Almighty*) in 1993 and is a popular lecturer.

Furthermore, he has succeeded in implanting his ancient astronaut thesis firmly in North American popular culture. Our students who fail to recognize his name are generally acquainted with his basic claim that extraterrestrials long ago visited earth and greatly affected the evolution (cultural and even biological) of humanity. In Feder's recent study (1995) of Connecticut college students, the ancient astronauts thesis actually found higher acceptance in 1994 than it had a decade earlier. Whatever von Däniken's personal fortunes, his ancient astronauts are alive and well.

A second important development concerned the Shroud of Turin, a cloth bearing a mysterious human image, long claimed to be the burial shroud of Christ. The Shroud, the subject of a large and contentious literature (see Nickell 1989; Gove 1990; Feder 1990a:182–188), finally underwent radiocarbon dating in the 1980s. In 1988 three of the world's top radiocarbon laboratories announced their results: the samples of linen from the Shroud had an average date of A.D. 1325, plus or minus 60 years. This time range includes the year (1353) of the earliest historical record of the Shroud's existence. For most observers, including the mainstream news media and some former believers, this result showed that the Shroud could not be genuine and that it was indeed—as had long been claimed—a medieval forgery.

However, some Shroud supporters refused to concede defeat, arguing that the radiocarbon dates must be somehow flawed or even fabricated. Books defending the Shroud's authenticity have continued to appear (e.g., Hoare 1994). Like other claims discussed in this volume, the Shroud thesis seems for some people to be invulnerable to empirical disconfirmation.

New Age Prehistory "New Age prehistory," a term coined by Feder (1990a), refers to what we might call the past tense of the "New Age." The New Age draws on the 1960s counterculture, occult beliefs and practices, mysticism, Eastern spiritualism, American Indian and other "pagan" religions, and even some strands of environmentalism and feminism (e.g., White 1990; see Gardner 1988; Basil 1988; Schultz 1989; Porterfield 1987) to fashion an exotic collection of unconventional worldviews. People adopt these beliefs and practices in search of everything from healing to personal improvement to expanded consciousness to spiritual power. One factor uniting most varieties of New Age beliefs is a rejection (or at least suspicion) of modern science as a way of gaining knowledge; New Agers often prefer instead such means as intuition, crystals, ESP, or trance channeling.

New Age prehistory replaces conventional archaeology with highly imaginative accounts of the paranormally powerful citizens of Atlantis; with purported revivals of ancient Druidic, Wiccan, or goddess religions (e.g., Luff 1990; Ringel 1994); or with Stonehenge and other sites as prehistoric powerhouses of spiritual energy (see Chippindale 1994:233–249). One popular variant of New Age prehistory is that of Jose Argüelles (1987), who "discovered" the "Harmonic Convergence." He tells us that the ancient Maya were galactic agents from the star Arcturus, sent to help humanity join the cosmic consciousness (Feder 1990a:189–190).

Despite their apparent novelty, some of these beliefs draw on a tradition going back to the books of Ignatius Donnelly and Madame Helena Blavatsky in the last century (see Williams 1992); other beliefs are modeled self-consciously by New Agers on ancient pagan cults, real or imagined. Whatever their inspiration, New Age beliefs are widespread in American culture. New Age books are often best-sellers, frequently showing up in venues (e.g., upscale bookstores or the offerings of the Quality Paperback Book Club) indicating that many well-read Americans take them seriously.

Creationism Update   The "creation vs. evolution" controversy is as hot as ever. Americans are still nearly evenly divided on whether humanity originated through organic evolution or through direct divine creation (Gallup and Bezilla 1994).[1] However, the years since 1987 have seen important developments in the struggle.

In 1987 the U.S. Supreme Court upheld a lower court's summary judgment overturning a Louisiana law that had mandated teaching creation science in public schools (Larson 1989; Eve and Harrold 1991:151–154). The court held that the law violated the constitutional separation of church and state. For the foreseeable future, this ruling has effectively ended creationists' attempts to use legislation to promote their beliefs in public schools.[2]

Creationists have responded to the setbacks of the 1980s with changes in both their message and their political strategy. Regarding the message, there are signs that a softer, less militant form of antievolutionist rhetoric is on the rise. American creationism has long been dominated by the "strict" scientific creationism advocated by Henry Morris and his colleagues at the Institute for Creation Research (e.g., Morris 1984; Gish 1985). The terms "scientific" and "strict" need some explanation in this context. "Scientific" creationists claim that—whatever the scientific community says—fossil and other scientific evidence, properly interpreted, actually show that evolution never happened, especially in the case of human beings. We have argued elsewhere (Eve and Harrold 1991:54–67, 111–117; see also Toumey 1994a,b; Numbers 1992) that scientific creationism has become popular as a way for conservative Christians living in an advanced industrialized society to defend perceived threats to their religious faith and worldview without having to reject modern science wholesale.

"Strict" creationists hew to a highly literal interpretation of the creation account in the Book of Genesis, holding that Adam and Eve and the rest of the universe were divinely created in six twenty-four-hour days only a few thousand years ago. As Numbers (1992) has recounted, strict creationism became the dominant form only in the 1960s; earlier, most creationist writers had been willing to concede that the earth and life were very ancient, that the geological and fossil records could not be explained by Noah's Flood, and sometimes even that limited forms of evolution (not involving human origins) had occurred. Strict creationists may or may not be scientific creationists, depending on whether they claim that scientific evidence supports their strict views. And scientific creationists may or may not be strict creationists, depending on whether they accept a young earth, a six-day creation week, and other literal interpretations of Genesis.

Creationist spokesmen still advocate scientific creationism, but there are signs that a softer variety is re-emerging to challenge strict creationism.[3] For example, a Dallas-area creationist organization called the Foundation for Thought and Ethics has sponsored an antievolutionist supplemental biology textbook, *Of Pandas and People* (Davis and Kenyon 1989, 1993; see Larson 1994). It does not mention God or creation but argues that scientific evidence indicates "intelligent design" of life forms and the "abrupt appearance" of new species in the fossil record. Literature of this sort does not so completely reject the findings of geology and other natural sciences as does strict creationism, perhaps making it more palatable for some believers. Henry Morris, the charismatic champion of strict scientific creationism, is approaching age eighty; his eventual departure from the struggle may open the way for soft creationism to achieve dominance.

The political activities of creationists have also seen some interesting developments. The political focal point of the creation/evolution controversy has always been the teaching of evolution in public school science classes. The creationists of the 1920s tried to ban evolution by law from the schools and partly succeeded, until a 1968 U.S. Supreme Court decision voided all such laws (Larson 1989; Eve and Harrold 1991). Since the 1960s, however, creationists have focused on attempts to ensure that creationism was taught alongside evolution in public schools—or to make the issue so controversial that evolution was de-emphasized or even omitted by teachers and local school authorities.

Having failed in these aims in courts and legislatures, creationists have turned increasingly in the 1980s and 1990s to local school boards, as well as to individual principals and teachers, as effective pressure points. Candidates favoring creationism (often as part of a religiously and politically conservative agenda) have run for, and been elected to, local school boards and influenced curriculum policy and textbook purchases (e.g., Scott 1994a; Matsumura 1994a,b). School board elections tend to have low voter turnouts, and the solid support of a few church congregations can often suffice to put a candidate over the top. Furthermore, some activists have run as "stealth" candidates on a platform of platitudes and generalities, while concealing—or at least not publicizing—their more controversial views until after the election.

A new dimension to the struggle began to emerge in the late 1980s and early 1990s, as the so-called Christian Right became increasingly powerful in the Republican party at the state and even national levels. Supported by such savvy national organizations as the Christian Coalition, conservative Christians organized to promote religiously and politically conservative positions on such issues as abortion, welfare, crime, and prayer and creationism in public schools. In Texas, for instance, George W. Bush was elected governor in 1994 on a Republican platform calling for mandatory teaching of creationism in public schools. While not supporting the creationism plank, Bush does advocate greater autonomy for local school boards in buying books with state funds and in setting curriculum policy without oversight by state educational officials. The result of such a policy would doubtless be inclusion of creationism in the curricula of many Texas school districts. Similar developments have occurred in a number of states, especially those with many conservative Protestants. Indeed, as we were writing this chapter in early 1995, members of several Dallas–Fort Worth–area school boards were calling for adoption of *Of Pandas and People* for their biology classes.

At the national level, Christian Right activists took much of the credit for the 1994 election victories that gave the Republicans control of both houses of Congress for the first time in forty years. One of the most powerful Republican Congressional leaders, House Majority Leader Dick Armey of Texas, has specifically cited creationism in public schools as an example of local communities' right to self-determination in the face of central government domination (Armey 1994). In Armey's view, the creation/evolution controversy is an issue not of church-state separation or of quality science instruction but of the right of local self-rule. Such statements indicate that, for the first time, creationists may find powerful allies in the national government.

One final observation, increasingly relevant in a multicultural nation and an interdependent world, is that some non-Christian religions are also experiencing an upsurge of what some observers (e.g., Marty and Appleby 1992; Misztal and Shupe 1992) have called fundamentalism—militant antimodernist movements likened to Christian fundamentalism because of their aims of reforming society along what they perceive as traditional religious lines. Whether or not that term accurately applies to religious militants in the Islamic world, Israel, and Hindu India, one can note that opposition to evolution is often a feature of their ideology—generally as part of opposition to much of Western thought (including science) as foreign and impious. Thus, we find such phenomena as "Krishna creationism" (Cremo and Thompson 1994; see Feder 1994; Tarzia 1994) and increasingly prominent Islamic creationism in Turkey and other Muslim nations (Edis 1994; Charfi 1994).[4]

Sources of Pseudoscientific Beliefs

Perhaps the most striking question raised by the issues discussed in this book is that of "why." Why are these beliefs, ranging from the speculative at best to the nonsensical at worst, accepted by so many people in a scientifically advanced nation? There is no simple answer to this question, though a number of partial explanations are well supported. As in 1987, we find Singer and Benassi's (1981) four-factor scheme, discussed in Chapter 6, useful for identifying several important causal factors.

Cognitive Biases   The rather heterogeneous category of cognitive biases includes the many ways in which humans tend to make mistakes in perception, reasoning, drawing conclusions, and accepting claims. Often cognitive biases follow our "common-sense" notion that reality is simply as we seem to perceive it. After all, common sense tells us that the sun rises and sets on an immovable earth or that the chair you sit on as you read this book is solid. Yet science has shown that the earth moves around the sun and that your chair is in fact mostly empty space. Such errors in our common sense seem to follow from the very way that our brains structure and interpret sensory stimuli. As Piattelli-Palmarini (1994) points out, the famous Gateway Arch in St. Louis still looks taller than it is wide, even after we learn that those dimensions are actually identical.

Many cognitive errors relevant to pseudoscience can result from our faulty "natural" intuitive sense of probability (Piattelli-Palmarini 1994). We often do not accept events as mere coincidences—requiring no extraordinary explanation—because they seem too improbable. One can note the attention given in 1994 to a New Jersey woman who won the state lottery jackpot twice in a four-month period (Kolata 1994). The odds against this occurrence were said to be 17 trillion to one. However, while the odds were indeed astronomical that that particular woman would win twice, they were around one in thirty that *someone* in the U.S. would win two jackpots in four months; the odds are better than even that someone will do so in a seven-year period. From this perspective, the double lottery win does not seem so incredible.

Piattelli-Palmarini (1994) discusses many more cognitive biases, including what he calls magical thinking. When a person is already convinced of a positive correlation between two variables (say, crime and the lack of prayer in schools), he or she may fail to recall or be impressed by contrary evidence and may find confirmation of his or her beliefs in just about any event. Furthermore, he shows that the easier it is for us to imagine a phenomenon, and the more impressive it is to us emotionally, the more we tend to think of it as objectively frequent (think of UFOs and rumors of Satanic crimes).

Further biases come into play when people perceive and interpret events in groups rather than individually. All judgments of what constitutes a "true" fact are susceptible to social influence by other humans. This is probably particularly true in the case of pseudoscientific beliefs. The reason for this is that many such claims are highly ambiguous. Under such conditions people often look to the opinions of others for confirmation of "correct" perception of the phenomena in question.

Examples of such processes abound. One can point to the findings of the famous Asch group studies (Asch 1951). These social psychological laboratory studies showed that subjects could be influenced in so simple a perceptual judgment as comparing the length of two straight lines. When other subjects were coached in advance to give unanimous but erroneous estimates of line length, new subjects were unconsciously influenced to err in the direction of agreeing with the majority. The more ambiguous the initial judgment, the greater the effect was on the test subjects.

Related to this phenomenon is the concept of "removal of situational anchorages." In Sherif's classic study, a point of light was shown on a wall in a completely darkened room (Sherif and Harvey, 1952). Subjects were asked how much the light moved over a period of minutes. In fact, the light did not move at all, but unable to see its relation to the walls, floor, etc., subjects tended to believe the light had moved significant distances. The reason it appeared to move was a lack of "situational anchors" against which to assess movement. Compare the lab reports by Asch and Sherif to a real-world group sighting of a UFO, for example. If the object is high in the sky there may be few or no reference points to judge its motion. Is the object large, far away, and moving fast, or is it nearby, small, and moving slowly? It is well known to scientific investigators of such reports that observers' answers are strongly influenced by both the ambiguity of the stimulus and the opinions of the group. If they expected to see a UFO, that is often what they will believe they have seen. In such a case, the ambiguity of the stimulus interacts with group pressure in a way that influences perceptual "reality."

Other social psychological factors likely to influence pseudoscientific beliefs abound but are largely unstudied in this relative new field of inquiry. As Markovsky and Thye (1992) have pointed out, there are at least five major categories of social psychological factors that probably influence people with regard to holding pseudoscientific beliefs. Among these categories of influence are: obedience, conformity, imitation, compliance, and persuasion. People may assign legitimacy to a pseudoscientific claim because of the authority of the claim-maker (obedience). Conformity would influence beliefs through implicit, rather than overt, pressures (as in the Asch group experiments). Compliance refers to direct requests from others and seems less central to the question at hand, as does direct behavior imitation. Persuasion, however, is highly relevant, as it refers to attempts to substantiate a claim by attempting to influence a person by argument or by selective presentation of information.

Persuasion is influenced by the source of the claim. For example, one must consider the apparent expertise of the claim-maker, as well as his or her attractiveness, apparent trustworthiness, and similarity to the target individual. Persuasion is also influenced by characteristics of the claim itself and its presentation. These include repetitiveness, the ability to gain attention, the ability to evoke positive mental associations, the likelihood of being understood, and the social and cultural acceptability of content. Overall, however, the most powerful persuasion factor appears to be personal contact with believers (more powerful, for example, than exposure to claims in the mass media).

Finally, there is a very complex set of target factors (a target being the person to be influenced). Prior knowledge of related material, personal involvement in the issue at hand, status of the target, self-esteem, and differing cognitive styles across individuals all seem implicated in one's susceptibility to claims.

What is obvious from the foregoing is that one development in the study of pseudoscientific beliefs is a growing awareness among researchers of the complexity of the issue of why people believe a claim. Far from being one aspect of the study of deviant behavior, the study of pseudoscientific beliefs is slowly revealing that many such beliefs are held for the same reasons as many other beliefs (say, for example, beliefs about what constitutes political reality). The factors listed above will be incorporated into a complex research agenda that will keep researchers busy for a long time to come.

Mass Media   Singer and Benassi (1981) have also specified the media as one source of erroneous beliefs; data presented in this volume bear out some connections between what people watch and read and what they report they believe about scientific issues.

Uncritical, even irresponsible treatment of cult archaeology and creationism in the media has become, if anything, even more notable in the 1990s than when the first edition of this book appeared. The biggest contributing factor has been the rapid growth of cable television and the resulting voracious appetite for programming. Various cable networks and the new fourth major network, Fox, have flooded the airwaves with specials and series like *Encounters: The Hidden Truth, Unsolved Mysteries,* and *The X-Files.* The latter, at least, is openly fictional, though allegedly based on "actual documented accounts." These programs advocate a potpourri of paranormal claims, including some of those discussed in this book. And they succeed, often producing high ratings (O'Connor 1994). Even the more staid "big three" networks sometimes present such programming. One egregious example was a creationist-produced special called "The Incredible Discovery of Noah's Ark," broadcast by CBS in 1992. Purporting to be a level headed documentary, it presented a highly uncritical and distorted picture of the Noah's ark issue (Cole 1993).

Though there are praiseworthy exceptions to this trend—notably the series *Archaeology* on the Learning Channel and *Nova* and other programs on PBS—they are outnumbered by sensationalistic programs, which might be expected to have a net destructive effect on the public's perception of the human past. Some evidence supports this contention. Take the famous case of claims of mysterious and deliberate livestock mutilations in the American West in the 1970s and 1980s. Individuals who reported television and radio (rather than print media) as their prime sources of information were especially likely to accept extreme claims about the cause of the mutilations. That is, they were more likely than others to attribute them to extraterrestrials or nefarious government schemes than to natural causes, such as scavenging of dead cattle by coyotes (Goode 1992:332). Goode notes that the verified patterns of cattle tissue damage were in fact just what coyote scavenging could be expected to produce, despite inaccurate reports of their bizarre and "surgical" appearance.

The extent to which the process of converting the public to a taste for pseudoscience has already proceeded seems disquieting in the case of the print media also. *Omni* magazine (published by the owner of the men's magazine *Penthouse,* Bob Guccione) has increasingly left middle-of-the-road science behind and dealt instead with sensationalistic "fringe" material, and, perhaps as a result, it has enjoyed great success.

The purveyors of the sensationalism we have discussed are, after all, in business to make money by maximizing their audience. They know that everyone loves a good story full of mystery and adventure. They furthermore know—witness the current spate of "infotainment" and "reality programming"—that most of us find a story all the more fascinating if it is presented as an actual event rather than as fiction (Goode 1992:323–334). They also know that some people resent the "disenchantment" of the world by science, apparently preferring to relish their mysteries rather than to see them explained (Gardner 1995).

Science Education We have seen in this book that many pseudoscientific claims about the past contradict the findings and methodological rules of science. One reason that such claims nonetheless persist is that many people are not aware of this fact. Their education in science has failed them. The scope of the problem is severe enough to indicate a widespread failure of science education. Since the early 1980s, a depressing series of studies has indicated that science education in the U.S.—with some sparkling exceptions, especially in higher education—generally does a poor job. American students compare unfavorably with those from most other developed nations in their knowledge of scientific findings and grasp of scientific methods (e.g., Walters 1995; IEA 1988). Furthermore, measures of the "scientific literacy" of the general public are not encouraging (e.g., Miller 1987). Various studies (see Fuerst 1984; Lawson and Weser 1990; Shankar and Skoog 1993 and references) link such scientific ignorance to creationism; among both college students and high school biology teachers, greater biological knowledge is associated with greater acceptance of evolution.

There are some bright spots. For instance, increased government support for public education seems to have helped to reverse the decline in science (and other) achievement by U.S. students, so that scores are back up to the levels of twenty years ago (Genoni 1995). However, it is still true that many Americans do not know that scientific findings contradict strict creationism and the existence of "ancient astronauts" or why scientific findings should be considered more reliable than these claims.

Sociocultural Factors We have seen throughout this volume that errors in scientific thinking can often be correlated with sociocultural background factors (particularly in the case of beliefs that have a religiously oriented content—e.g., see Chapter 6). People tend to adopt and maintain the beliefs of the society, social class, ethnic group, and family in which they are socialized. Indeed, it is the "gullibility" of children, who usually accept unquestioningly what they are told by adults, that allows humans to depend on complex, learned culture for their survival (Dawkins 1995). And values and beliefs (including those about the past) may vary greatly among such sociocultural groups in their availability, perceived importance, and the rewards and punishments for accepting them. Furthermore, one's preexisting values and attitudes will heavily influence whether one accepts a new reality claim to which one is exposed.

Thus, it should be unsurprising that, for example, medieval Europeans were creationists, living as they were in a prescientific society in which today's scientific view of earth history was unavailable. Nor should it be surprising that fundamentalist youth, having imbibed creationism in their families and congregations at an early age, tend to be antagonistic to evolution when exposed to it in science classes. Similarly, a study by Graves and Leigh (in press) has duplicated and highlighted a finding we note in Chapter 6—that racial minority group members, especially blacks, are more likely to embrace creationism than their white counterparts. Graves and Leigh cogently suggest that the evangelical Protestant background of most black Americans and the all-too-frequent appeal to evolution in support of racist ideology (e.g., Social Darwinism and the "race and IQ" issue) combine to make many blacks suspicious of evolutionary science.

As we and Hudson indicate in chapters 5 and 6, there appears to be a powerful dichotomy in the sociocultural background factors significant for the beliefs considered in this book. This dichotomy contrasts creationism on one hand with nearly all the other beliefs on the other. As we saw, several variables in our 1980s' study indicative of strong, conservative religious belief were associated with creationism.

Elsewhere (Eve and Harrold 1991:54–67, 94–119; 1992, 1993), we have advanced the thesis that creationism is a defense of a key element of cultural traditionalism (or cultural fundamentalism, as we call it in Chapter 6). Briefly put, creationists tend to be conservative Protestants who oppose evolution and related scientific findings because they perceive them as a direct threat to their religious faith. Some creationists simply reject evolution without further consideration (as a bumper sticker puts it: "God said it, I believe it, and that's that!"). Many creationists, though, are troubled by the prospect of rejecting a large and important part of modern science. Science is a powerful and widely respected force in our society; some creationists are technicians or scientists themselves. Instead of dismissing science, they resolve their conflict by accepting "scientific" creationism and arguing that their beliefs are fully consistent with scientific evidence. Creationism is an important element in cultural traditionalism, which involves the defense of a whole range of traditional values and beliefs. Whether involved in the controversy over evolution or those over abortion, prayer in schools, or sexual morality, cultural traditionalists perceive themselves as struggling for the perpetuation of their system of values and beliefs against the forces of modernism (often described by them as "secular humanism"). Thus, creationism is related primarily to basic matters of worldview, beliefs, and attitudes.

In contrast to creationism, acceptance of cult archaeology beliefs seems unrelated to religious or political conservatism. Indeed, as Hudson found in Chapter 5, there are few indications of any sociocultural background variables that systematically affect such beliefs. We can suggest several factors that promote them, though. One is the love of a good story (especially when it is conceived of as a true account or at least "based on" a true account), combined with ignorance of the human past. Few people learn much if anything in their formal education about the vast time depth of the prehistoric human past. This void is filled with stock images of "cavemen" and "primitive savages." None of this seems very interesting to most people, who are unaware, as Williams notes, of the fascinating real past. When, in place of these clichés, von Däniken offers prehistoric ETs, or Fell suggests heroic voyages of adventure, many find the prospect exciting and entertaining.

Indeed, the issue of entertainment value is probably significant in understanding cult archaeology beliefs. Largely unaware of the scientific methods that allow us to learn about the past, many people seem to think that the prehistoric past is unknowable—so why not make up or accept a past that is as exciting and entertaining as a space opera or a spear-and-sandal epic? Prehistory becomes anybody's game.

Another factor playing a significant role in at least some cult archaeology beliefs is ethnic or racial identity. Ortiz de Montellano's discussion of some variants of Afrocentrism illuminates one case, but others abound. Many Americans of Scandinavian descent accept the Kensington Runestone and other objects alleged to establish that the medieval Norse explored widely in North America long before Columbus, an Italian (Williams 1990: 189–223; Michlovic 1990). Other alleged trans-Atlantic voyagers include Saint Brendan of Ireland and Prince Madoc of Wales, supported by Celtic Americans (Feder 1990a:71–75). As several authors in this book point out, there is an unsavory whiff of racism in some cult archaeology. For some of Barry Fell's supporters, nothing of interest seems to have happened among American Indians until European and Mediterranean visitors arrived (Cole 1980). In other versions of cult archaeology, native American peoples were able to develop civilization only under the tutelage of Egyptians (whether black or white), Nubians, Chinese, or Atlanteans. And Erich von Däniken's past is full of primitive (usually dark-skinned) savages incapable of monumental constructions without the help of space aliens. Such beliefs always feed on widespread ignorance of the past (especially concerning what people are capable of building without bulldozers and cranes) but also use the past to bolster one's national or ethnic pride in the present. They give one a glorious past to be proud of and, sometimes, a past of victimization to vindicate.

Results of a 1994 student survey confirm the distinction we have drawn here between the sources of creationism on one hand and cult archaeology on the other (Eve, Harrold, and Taylor 1995). Respondents who scored high on creationism tended as well to exhibit conservative Protestant religious beliefs and cultural traditionalism. They also tended to agree that revelation and authority (as opposed to scientific study) were the most reliable sources of truth. These students further tended to reject cult archaeology claims, as well as others from the gamut of pseudoscience, such as ESP and UFO claims. In contrast, those students who accepted any one cult archaeology claim tended also to accept others, along with other pseudoscientific beliefs.

Furthermore, they tended to reject cultural traditionalism, as well as to show skepticism about the authority claims of both traditional Christianity and science. These results support our suggestion of different etiologies for the two categories of pseudoscience of the past. Creationists draw on traditional sources of belief; devotees of fantastic science are often skeptical about established sources of truth and yet gullibly believe (or perhaps try out) various suggested alternative "truths."[5]

The Response to Cult Archaeology and Creationism

Archaeologists, geologists, historians, and others who systematically study the past know how wrong cult archaeologists and creationists are. What has been their response to these claims? The response has generally taken two forms: refutation (or debunking) of pseudoscientific claims and the study of the claims and claimants themselves, in an effort to understand why ideas with such poor intellectual support nonetheless are popular.

In most cases, however, there has been no reaction at all, for understandable reasons. Most archaeologists, for instance, are very busy with research, writing, teaching, and other professional activities, with little time to spare for what may seem a hopeless and thankless task. In Chapter 5, Hudson aptly cites L. Sprague de Camp's comparison of the debunker to a garbage collector—someone with a disagreeable and never-ending job. Debunkers may wonder whether responding to nonsense merely publicizes and legitimizes it. Moreover, they often are pressured by colleagues not to waste time that could be spent doing science by responding to "fanatics" and "screwballs." However, we agree with Williams in Chapter 9 that those who study the past have an obligation not only to debunk nonsense but to help educate the public about the actual, fascinating record of humanity's past.

How have those archaeologists and scientists who have undertaken this responsibility fulfilled it? Their response has taken many forms—public debates with creationist spokesmen; lectures and courses on creationism and cult archaeology; reviewing textbooks or testifying for educational bodies; advising anti-pseudoscience organizations (like the North Texas Skeptics or the Bay Area Skeptics); writing letters to the editors of newspapers; and so on. Their most readily measured activity is the publication of articles and books. As Godfrey and Cole show in Chapter 8, the scientific community rose to the occasion, perhaps a bit tardily, in the early 1980s to respond to the threat of revitalized creationism—only to disengage rapidly after the immediate threat subsided.

In an effort to update the tracking of publication trends by Godfrey and Cole in Chapter 8, we conducted several computerized data base searches. Results are summarized graphically in Figure 1. We did not attempt to du-

YEARLY TRENDS
THREE DATA BASES

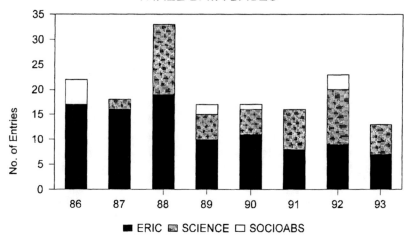

FIGURE 1. Yearly trends in three academic data bases in the number of citations with the keywords "creationism," "creationist," and/or "creationists."

plicate the total range of Godfrey and Cole's study, but we did wish to parallel the information presented in their Figure 1. That graph tracks the published response in periodicals of the educational and scientific communities to creationism between 1977 and late 1985. Cole and Godfrey compiled citations from three data bases in their Figure 1: ERIC (educational resources), *SciSearch* (the Science Citation Index on the data base vendor Dialog), and *SocSciSearch* (the Social Sciences Citation Index on Dialog). We were able to use ERIC and the Science Citation Index again, though for economic reasons we utilized *SocioAbs* (an abbreviated version of Sociological Abstracts mounted on the vendor FirstSearch, which is both less expensive and less extensive) in place of *SocSciSearch*. We thus were able to sample the same three universes, though without perfectly duplicating the earlier search. We think that the overall trends revealed can be usefully compared to those in Chapter 8.

Using the same search terms (creationist, creationists, creationism), we found far fewer citations for 1986–1993 than did Cole and Godfrey for 1977–1985 (Figure 1). Our peak year was 1988, with 33 citations, compared to their peak in 1982 of over 160. Furthermore, inspection of the 1988 citations showed that 10 were not articles but rather brief letters to the editors of two journals (*Nature* and *Physics Today*), sparked by editorials on creationism. We are confident that our lower totals are not due simply to our use of one different data base, since the most productive common data base, ERIC, provides most of both samples and shows the same patterning over the two sampling periods as the other data bases do. Clearly, the educational and scientific communities have continued the low response levels to creationism that Cole and Godfrey documented after the early 1980s.

While the response to creationism in periodicals rose and fell rapidly during the crisis of the early 1980s—never thereafter to reach a similar peak—a different pattern is manifest in books, which have a longer gestation period than articles and may have greater and longer-lasting impact. Unsurprisingly, the peak response in books occurred later than in periodicals and was more sustained. In general, debunking books tended to appear first. Thus, paleontologist Niles Eldredge's brief but effective *The Monkey Business* appeared in 1982, as did *Abusing Science* by the philosopher of science Philip Kitcher and *Darwinism Defended* by Michael Ruse, also a philosopher. In quick succession came several more primarily refutational works, like those of paleontologists Douglas Futuyma (*Science on Trial*, 1983) and Chris McGowan (*In the Beginning . . .* , 1984). Also prominent were edited volumes (often deriving from conferences), such as Laurie Godfrey's *Scientists Confront Creationism* (1983) and Ashley Montagu's *Science and Creationism* (1984)—as well as the first edition of this volume in 1987. Another early response was William Stiebing's *Ancient Astronauts, Cosmic Collisions, and Other Popular Theories about Man's Past* (1984), which mostly dealt with cult archaeology.

Books examining creationism as a historical or sociocultural phenomenon, rather than debunking it, tended to appear later, though they were led off by sociologist Dorothy Nelkin's *The Creation Controversy* (1982). Several are by contributors to this volume. Larson's *Trial and Error* (1985, 1989) is an excellent legal-historical account of anti-evolutionism, and Ronald Numbers' *The Creationists* (1992) is a history of the theological and intellectual development of scientific creationism. Eve and Harrold's *The Creationist Movement in Modern America* (1991) and Toumey's *God's Own Scientists* (1994) analyze the creationist movement from social-science perspectives. Feder's *Frauds, Myths, and Mysteries* (1990) both debunks and analyzes creationism and cult archaeology and is widely used as a college textbook. Finally, Stephen Williams's *Fantastic Archaeology* (1992) is a thorough and fascinating guide to the more outlandish claims about the North American past.

One arena of quite recent mobilization has been the opposition to the pseudoscientific aspects of Afrocentrism. Most responses from the scientific community are from the 1990s. Indeed, the response is still growing. African American biologist Joseph Graves (1992, 1993; Graves and Leigh, in press) has received funding from the National Science Foundation to organize a series of symposia, publications, and media productions for both scholarly and lay publics, with the goal of an effective and educationally constructive strategy to grapple with this problem.

Several periodicals deal consistently with the pseudoscience of the past. The best known is *The Skeptical Inquirer* (circulation over 40,000), the journal of the Committee for the Scientific Study of Claims of the Paranormal (CSICOP). This group, founded in 1976 by philosopher Paul Kurtz and such scientific luminaries as Carl Sagan and Stephen Jay Gould, opposes all manner of pseudoscientific claims. Creationism and cult archaeology appear regularly in its pages, along with ESP, astrology, UFOs, and a host of other topics. More exclusively focused on creationism is the National Center for Science Education, whose quarterly newsletter *NCSE Reports* (edited by John Cole) is the most important source of information on creationist arguments, tactics, and strategies. The journal *Creation/Evolution*, also published by NCSE and edited by Cole, runs articles refuting and analyzing creationist claims and claimants, as well as an occasional piece by a creationist.

In summing up the response by the scientific and educational communities to cult archaeology and creationism, we can make several generalizations. First, creationism has drawn the lion's share of attention, probably because of its greater direct threat to science education. Second, as measured by citations in periodical indexes, the response to creationism rose to high intensity only briefly, in answer to the creationist legislation of the early 1980s. It has been at low levels ever since. The response as measured by book publication was slower and more sustained, though it is our impression that it is tailing off in the mid-1990s. Third, the scientific reaction to this pseudoscience has always involved a good deal more refutation of beliefs than attempts to understand why they are so prevalent. This is especially so in the case of cult archaeology, whose appeal is less well understood than that of creationism.

While the response has been largely admirable, we must temper our assessment by noting that scientists have often been rhetorically less effective than their creationist counterparts (Taylor 1992; Stempien and Coleman 1985). Scientists too often address the public as if they were talking to colleagues, confusing them with unfamiliar jargon and annoying them with what is perceived as an arrogant, know-it-all attitude. Meanwhile, most creationist spokesmen communicate in a down-to-earth, folksy, rhetorically effective style.

Finally, we will note an intriguing aspect of the response we have been discussing. It might be called "anti-anti-pseudoscience" in the academic community. It is found far more often among the social sciences and humanities than among the natural sciences and ranges from the defense of

pseudoscience devotees as victims of arrogant scientists to a whole intellectual movement that deeply mistrusts conventional science.

An example of the former is found in Michlovic (1990), who in effect ap-
pealed to cultural relativism. This is the principle that, in analyzing another
culture, anthropologists should not judge it by their own standards of right
and wrong. Michlovic took several of the authors of this collection to task
for allegedly devaluing the sincere beliefs of creationists or Scandinavian-
Americans who accept the Kensington Runestone as genuine. Instead of
sneering at these people, said Michlovic, a social scientist's job is to understand them. In response, several of us (Cole 1990; Feder 1990a; Harrold and
Eve 1990; Kehoe 1990) pointed out that such analysis is just what we have
been urging and doing for years. Furthermore, we think that in our own
society, we would be irresponsible not to oppose (without condescension)
the misrepresentation presented as knowledge of the past.

There is a more profound and widespread (and to our mind, more trou-
bling) type of "anti-anti-pseudoscience," in the form of a broad intellectual
movement of recent years. Usually called postmodernism, this movement
originated mainly in the fields of literary criticism, rhetoric, and philosophy,
later spreading to the other humanities and the social sciences (e.g., see
McGowan 1991; Doherty, Graham, and Malek, 1992; see Gross and Levitt
1994 for a highly critical study).

It is impossible here to characterize adequately this multifarious intellectual trend, but we can stress its "postmodern" character, in the sense that it
rejects the "modern" worldview characteristic of most late-nineteenth- and
twentieth-century intellectuals and scientists. The modern worldview sees
science as promising an ever deeper understanding of the universe (including human behavior) and as allowing for the eventual solution of many human psychological, social, and economic problems through the application
of rationality and scientific knowledge. Postmodernists, by contrast, tend to
see the modernists' certainty of scientific knowledge as an illusion. They argue that our supposedly objective scientific knowledge is inevitably shaped
and tainted by the class, racial, and gender prejudices and interests of those
who do science. This approach has had powerful effects in such diverse areas
as the sociology of science and of knowledge (e.g., Aronowitz 1988; Longino
1990), feminist thought (e.g., Harding 1986, 1991), and archaeology (e.g.,
Shanks and Tilley 1992). While postmodernists would find little merit in the
beliefs of New Agers or creationists, they would at least agree with them that
modernism and scientific rationalism have failed us. As we have suggested
elsewhere (Eve and Harrold 1993), all of these groups are asking in effect,
"If modernism and science are so wonderful, then why aren't we all healthy,
wealthy, wise, and happy?"

The relevance of postmodernism here is in the encouragement it sometimes provides for views of the past that mainstream science and scholarship reject as unfounded. Some postmodernists promote an "epistemological relativism," in the words of anthropologist Robin Fox (1992), in which one view of the past is considered as good as another. Indeed, for some postmodern thinkers, an Afrocentric, or feminist, or Marxist prehistory is preferable to the conventional scientific view, since it is produced in the interests of victimized classes rather than those of the oppressor class of (mostly) white European males. Thus, as Ortiz de Montellano notes in Chapter 10, some postmodern authors approvingly cite Ivan van Sertima's claims of voyages to the Americas by ancient Africans, who in their alleged visits are said to have been peaceful and nonexploitative, in vivid contrast to later European conquerors (hooks 1992:25).

To condense our response to a complex set of issues, we (like most concerned with the human past) agree that biases of various kinds can and do cloud and tint the picture of reality drawn by scientists. However, we think that the best response to this problem is to identify and eliminate such biases, rather than to surrender to their inevitability. People from all backgrounds, and ideas from all corners, should be welcomed into the study of the human past. However, all ideas should be subject to the same tests of evidence and rationality. If they are not, then prehistory indeed becomes a game without rules. Despite the problems recounted here, the scientific community's response has produced a solid base of information and analysis for responding to and understanding the pseudosciences of the past.

Some Predictions

We will close by venturing a few predictions about the issues discussed in this volume. We claim no clairvoyant powers but believe that several trends can be discerned as the twenty-first century approaches.

Creationism   Because creationism is tied so closely to basic worldviews and values, the controversy over this issue will not fade away in the foreseeable future. Indeed, we expect it to intensify, as grassroots creationist groups press their cause in local school boards, aided by trends in several states toward greater local control of public school curricula and by the coalition between the Christian Right and the Republican party.

Afrocentrism   The unwarranted claims about the past sometimes advanced under the rubric of Afrocentrism face an uncertain future. On one hand, they are institutionalized in many curricula and have influential supporters; furthermore, many nonblacks hesitate to oppose them for fear of giving offense or of being labeled as racists. Nonblacks may also support them in the hope that they will actually encourage African American youngsters' school achievement. On the other hand, more voices, including those of black scientists and academics, are speaking out in opposition. The works of Ortiz de Montellano, Graves, and others hold a promise of school curricula that are ethnically relevant *and* scientifically sound.

Cult Archaeology   The heterogeneous collection of beliefs grouped under the heading of cult archaeology will probably see an upsurge in publicity as we approach the year 2000 and the new millennium. Various New Age and religious groups will proclaim that apocalyptic or wondrous events—the end of the world or the arrival of a fleet of extraterrestrials—are just around the corner. If present trends in television and other mass media continue, awareness of and acceptance of these claims will probably grow. On the other hand, modest improvements in science education may have offsetting effects.

Perhaps the greatest effect that those who study the human past can have is by following Williams's advice in Chapter 9: work to tell the real story of the human past in the media and the schools, as well as in higher education. The more that people know about this amazing story, and the scientific methods by which we recover it, the less they will be attracted to a counterfeit past.

Notes

1. Gallup and Bezilla (1994) report the following results of a national poll (with a margin of error of plus or minus 3 percentage points) conducted in June 1993:

"Which of the following statements comes closest to your views on the origins and development of human beings?"

God created human beings in the last 10,000 years or so 47%
God guided evolution over millions of years 35%
Humans evolved over millions of years without God playing a part 11%
No opinion 7%

Thus, among those with an opinion, almost exactly equal percentages accept human evolution or reject it in favor of direct divine creation. Among those accepting human evolution, most believe that it was divinely guided.

2. There are, however, ongoing creationist attempts to defend in court the ability of creationist public-school science teachers to teach their beliefs in class, on the grounds of academic freedom (e.g., Scott 1994b).

3. We use the term "spokesmen" literally; to our knowledge, there is only one woman (Nell Seagraves of the Creation Science Research Center) among prominent creationist authors or lecturers.

4. Ironically, the antievolutionary arguments of Islamic creationists in Turkey are borrowed almost entirely from U.S. Christian creationists, with the willing help of the Institute for Cre-

ation Research (Edis 1994). Antievolutionism may be one of the few issues that these groups can agree on.

5. One variety of cult archaeology which may exhibit different associations from those we discuss here is the extreme Afrocentrism described by Ortiz de Montellano. Like other cult archaeology, it suggests rejection of conventional science—indeed, extending to general alienation from predominantly white society. Like creationism, it suggests a totalizing worldview, though one of racial identity rather than religion. However, the instrument used in this study did not measure Afrocentric belief.

References

Argüelles, Jose
1987 The Mayan Factor: Path beyond Technology. Santa Fe, N. Mex.: Bear Co.
Armey, Dick
1994 Freedom's choir. Policy Review 67:27–34.
Aronowitz, Stanley
1988 Science as Power: Discourse and Ideology in Modern Society. Minneapolis: University of Minnesota Press.
Asch, Solomon E.
1951 Effects of group pressure on the modification and distortion of judgment. In Harold Guetzkow, ed., Groups, Leadership and Men. Pittsburgh: Carnegie University Press.
Basil, Robert, ed.
1988 Not Necessarily the New Age. Buffalo, N.Y.: Prometheus Books.
Charfi, Farida Faouzia
1994 When Galileo meets Allah. New Perspectives Quarterly 11:30–32.
Chippendale, Christopher
1994 Stonehenge Complete. Rev. ed. New York: Thames and Hudson.
Cole, J. R.
1980 Cult archaeology and unscientific method and theory. In Michael B. Schiffer, ed., Advances in Archaeological Method and Theory, vol. 3, pp. 1–33. New York: Academic Press.
1990 Reply to Michlovic. Current Anthropology 31:390.
1993 Noah's Ark on CBS. NCSE Reports 13(1):4, 6.
Cremo, Michael A., and Richard L. Thompson
1994 Forbidden Archaeology: The Hidden History of the Human Race. San Diego: Govardham Hill.
Davis, Percival, and Dean H. Kenyon
1989 Of Pandas and People. Dallas: Haughton.
1993 Of Pandas and People. 2d ed. Dallas: Haughton.
Dawkins, Richard
1995 Putting away childish things. The Skeptical Inquirer 19(1):31–36.
Doherty, Joe, Elspeth Graham, and Mo Malek, eds.
1992 Postmodernism and the Social Sciences. New York: St. Martin's Press.
Edis, Taner
1994 Islamic creationism in Turkey. Creation/Evolution 14(1):1–12.
Eldredge, Niles
1982 The Monkey Business: A Scientist Looks at Creationism. New York: Washington Square Press.
Eve, Raymond A., and Francis B. Harrold
1991 The Creationist Movement in Modern America. Boston: Twayne Publishers.
1992 Scientific creationism and the politics of lifestyle concern in the United States. In

B. Misztal and A. Shupe, eds., *Religion and Politics in Comparative Perspective*, pp. 97–109. Westport, Conn.: Praeger.

1993 The influence of group processes on pseudoscientific belief: Knowledge industries and the legitimation of threatened lifestyles. In E. Lawler, B. Markovsky, J. O'Brien, and K. Heimer, eds., *Advances in Group Processes*, vol. 10, pp. 133–162. New York: JAI Press.

Eve, Raymond A., Francis B. Harrold, and John Taylor

1995 Differential etiology of pseudoscientific beliefs: Why creationists don't go to psychic fairs. Paper presented at the Annual Meeting of the American Association for the Advancement of Science, Atlanta, February 16–19.

Feder, Kenneth

1990a *Frauds, Myths and Mysteries: Science and Pseudoscience in Archaeology.* Mountain View, Calif.: Mayfield.

1990b Reply to Michlovic. *Current Anthropology* 31:390–391.

1994 Review of *Forbidden Archaeology*, by Stephen Williams. *Geoarchaeology* 9:337–340.

1995 Ten years after: Surveying misconceptions about the human past. *Cultural Resource Management* 18(3):10–14.

Fox, Robin

1992 Anthropology and the "teddy bear" picnic. *Society* 30(1):47–55.

Fuerst, Paul A.

1984 University student understanding of evolutionary biology's place in the creation/evolution controversy. *Ohio Journal of Science* 84:218–228.

Futuyma, Douglas J.

1983 *Science on Trial: The Case for Evolution.* New York: Pantheon.

Gallup, George, Jr., and Robert Bezilla

1994 The battle over the beginning. *Fort Worth Star-Telegram*, January 2, p. C5.

Gardner, Martin

1988 *The New Age: Notes of a Fringe Watcher.* Buffalo, N.Y.: Prometheus Books.

1995 Science vs. beauty? *The Skeptical Inquirer* 19(2):14–16, 55.

Genoni, Tom, Jr.

1995 Science literacy: The good news and the bad. *The Skeptical Inquirer* 19(1):5–6.

Gish, Duane

1985 *Evolution: The Challenge of the Fossil Record.* El Cajon, Calif.: Creation-Life Publishers.

Godfrey, Laurie R., ed.

1983 *Scientists Confront Creationism.* New York: Norton.

Goode, Erich

1992 *Collective Behavior.* Fort Worth: Harcourt Brace Jovanovich.

Gove, H.E.

1990 Dating the Turin Shroud—An assessment. *Radiocarbon* 32:87–92.

Graves, Joseph L., Jr.

1992 Materialist philosophy, evolutionist biology, and African-American students: I. Statement of the problem. In Charles E. Butler, ed., *New Directions for African-American Scholarship and Research: Colorizing the "Canon."* Proceedings of the National Research Conference on African American Studies, University of Oklahoma, pp. 22–42. Norman: University of Oklahoma.

1993 Evolutionary biology and human variation: Biological determinism and the mythology of race. *Sage Race Relations Abstracts* 18(3):4–34.

Graves, Joseph L., Jr., and Joanne Leigh

In press Materialist philosophy, evolutionary biology and African-American students: II. Empirical evidence. In *Race and a Global Society.* Proceedings of the Third National Conference on African American Studies, Norman, Oklahoma, November 1993.

Gross, Paul R., and Norman Levitt

1994 *Higher Superstition: The Academic Left and Its Quarrels with Science.* Baltimore: Johns Hopkins University Press.

Harding, Sandra

1986 *The Science Question in Feminism.* Ithaca, N.Y.: Cornell University Press.

1991 *Whose Science? Whose Knowledge? Thinking from Women's Lives.* Ithaca, N.Y.: Cornell University Press.

Harrold, Francis B., and Raymond A. Eve

1990 Reply to Michlovic. *Current Anthropology* 31:391–393.

Hoare, Rodney

1994 *The Turin Shroud Is Genuine.* London: Souvenir Press.

hooks, bell

1992 Columbus: Gone but not forgotten. *Z Magazine*, December, 25–28.

Huyghe, Patrick

1994 UFO update: The rise, fall, and afterlife of Erich von Däniken's theory of extraterrestrial gods. *Omni* 16(8):77.

IEA (International Association for the Evaluation of Educational Achievement)

1988 *Science Achievement in Seventeen Countries: A Preliminary Report.* Oxford: Pergamon Press.

Kehoe, Alice

1990 Reply to Michlovic. *Current Anthropology* 31:393.

Kitcher, Philip

1982 *Abusing Science: The Case against Creationism.* Cambridge: MIT Press.

Kolata, Gina

1994 Coincidences most times aren't. *The Skeptic* (Newsletter of the North Texas Skeptics) 8(11):1–2.

Larson, Edward

1985 *Trial and Error: The American Controversy over Creation and Evolution.* New York: Oxford University Press.

1989 *Trial and Error: The American Controversy over Creation and Evolution.* Updated ed. New York: Oxford University Press.

Larson, Erik

1994 Instead of evolution, a textbook proposes "intelligent design." *Wall Street Journal*, November 14, pp. 1, A7.

Lawson, Anton, and John Weser

1990 The rejection of non-scientific beliefs about life: Effects of instruction and reasoning skills. *Journal of Research in Science Teaching* 27:589–606.

Longino, Helen

1990 *Science as Social Knowledge.* Princeton: Princeton University Press.

Luff, Tracy L.

1990 Wicce: Adding a spiritual dimension to feminism. *Berkeley Journal of Sociology* 35: 91–105.

McGowan, Chris

1984 *In the Beginning . . .* Buffalo, N.Y.: Prometheus Books.

McGowan, John

1991 *Postmodernism and Its Critics.* Ithaca, N.Y.: Cornell University Press.

Markovsky, Barry, and Shane Thye

1992 Building theories in structural social psychology. Paper presented at the American Sociological Association Annual Meeting, Pittsburgh.

Marty, Martin E., and R. Scott Appleby
1992 *The Glory and the Power: The Fundamentalist Challenge to the Modern World.* Boston: Beacon Press.
Matsumura, Molleen
1994a Legislative loopholes and Trojan horses. *NCSE Reports* 14(2):3, 7.
1994b Evolution in an election year. *NCSE Reports* 14(3):3, 10.
Michlovic, Michael G.
1990 Folk archaeology in anthropological perspective. *Current Anthropology* 31:103–107.
Miller, Jon D.
1987 The scientifically illiterate. *American Demographics* 9(6):26–31.
Misztal, Bronislaw, and Anson Shupe
1992 Making sense of the global revival of fundamentalism. In Bronislaw Misztal and Anson Shupe, eds., *Religion and Politics in Comparative Perspective,* pp. 3–9. Westport, Conn.: Praeger.
Montagu, Ashley, ed.
1984 *Science and Creationism.* New York: Oxford University Press.
Morris, Henry M.
1984 *The Biblical Basis for Modern Science.* Grand Rapids, Mich.: Baker.
Nelkin, Dorothy
1982 *The Creation Controversy: Science or Scripture in the Schools.* New York: Norton.
Nickell, Joe
1989 Unshrouding a mystery: Science, pseudoscience, and the Cloth of Turin. *The Skeptical Inquirer* 13:296–299.
Numbers, Ronald
1992 *The Creationists: The Evolution of Scientific Creationism.* Berkeley: University of California Press.
O'Connor, John J.
1994 TV's infatuation with the mystical. *New York Times,* June 30, p. 20.
Piattelli-Palmarini, Massimo
1994 *Inevitable Illusions: How Mistakes of Reason Rule Our Minds.* New York: John Wiley and Sons.
Porterfield, Amanda
1987 Feminist theory as a revitalization movement. *Sociological Analysis* 48:234–244.
Ringel, Faye
1994 New England Neo-Pagans: Medievalism, fantasy, religion. *Journal of American Culture* 17(3):65–68.
Ruse, Michael
1982 *Darwinism Defended: A Guide to the Evolution Controversies.* Reading, Mass.: Addison-Wesley.
Schultz, Ted, ed.
1989 *The Fringes of Reason: A Whole Earth Catalog.* New York: Harmony Books.
Scott, Eugenie
1994a The struggle for the schools. *Natural History* (July): 10–13.
1994b Peloza case remanded to District Court. *NCSE Reports* 14(2):1, 7, 9.
Shankar, Ganga, and Gerald Skoog
1993 Emphasis given evolution and creationism by Texas high school biology teachers. *Science Education* 77:221–233.
Shanks, Michael, and Christopher Tilley
1992 *Re-Constructing Archaeology: Theory and Practice.* 2d ed. London: Routledge.
Sherif, Muzafer, and O. J. Harvey
1952 A study in ego-functioning: Elimination of stable anchorages in individual and group situations. *Sociometry* 15:272–305.

Singer, Barry, and Victor A. Benassi
1981 Occult beliefs. *American Scientist* 69:49–55.
Stempien, Richard, and Sarah Coleman
1985 Processes of persuasion: The case of creation science. *Review of Religious Research* 27(2): 169–177.
Stiebing, William H., Jr.
1984 *Ancient Astronauts, Cosmic Collisions, and Other Popular Theories about Man's Past.* Buffalo, N.Y.: Prometheus Books.
Tarzia, Wade
1994 *Forbidden Archaeology*: Antievolutionism outside the Christian arena. *Creation/Evolution* 14(1):13–25.
Taylor, Charles A.
1992 Audience, expertise and authority: The evolving creationism debate. *Quarterly Journal of Speech* 78:277–285.
Toumey, Christopher P.
1994a *God's Own Scientists: Creationists in a Secular World.* New Brunswick, N.J.: Rutgers University Press.
1994b God's own scientists. *Natural History* (July):4–9.
Walters, Laurel Sharper
1995 World educators compare notes. *The National Times*, December/January, 38–39.
White, John
1990 *The Meeting of Science and Spirit: Guidelines for a New Age.* New York: Paragon House.
Williams, Stephen
1992 *Fantastic Archaeology: The Wild Side of North American Prehistory.* Philadelphia: University of Pennsylvania Press.

Appendix:
The Student Opinion Questionnaire

The following questionnaire is part of a study of the ideas students have about several scientific and other topics. It is divided into two parts. The first part concerns some background on yourself (but we do NOT want your name or student number—you will remain anonymous). In the second part we will ask your opinions on a number of topics. Please answer all items on the accompanying computer sheets as best you can. Please be truthful—we are really interested in what you think. Thank you very much for participating in this study!

SECTION I

1) Age:
   a) 22 or under
   b) 23–29
   c) 30–39
   d) 40 and above
2) Class standing: (select one)
   a) Freshman
   b) Sophomore
   c) Junior
   d) Senior
   e) Other
3) Area of academic major: (select one)
   a) Anthropology
   b) Other Social/Behavioral Sciences (Political Science, Sociology, Social Work, Urban Studies, Criminal Justice, Psychology)
   c) Humanities (Art, English, Foreign Languages, Philosophy, General Studies, History, Music, Journalism, Communications, Physical Education)
   d) Engineering, Computer Science
   e) Business Administration
   f) Architecture/Environmental Design
   g) Natural/Physical Sciences (Biology, Biochemistry, Chemistry, Geology, Physics, Microbiology, Mathematics, Medical Technology, Pre-Med, Nursing)
   h) Other

4) Sex:
   a) Male
   b) Female
5) Grade Point Average on the 4-point scale: (select one)
   a) 0.0–0.99
   b) 1.0–1.99
   c) 2.0–2.49
   d) 2.5–2.99
   e) 3.0–3.49
   f) 3.5–4.0
6) Outside of class requirements, how many books do you read per year?
   a) 0-2
   b) 3–10
   c) over 10

For Nos. 7–15, please tell us whether you have taken a college-level course in each of the following areas by selecting (a) for YES and (b) for NO.

7) Anthropology (except Archaeology)
8) Archaeology
9) Astronomy
10) Biology
11) Chemistry or Physics
12) Geology
13) History
14) Logic
15) Psychology
16) Religious Studies
17) Race: (select one)
   a) White
   b) Black
   c) Hispanic
   d) Asian
   e) Other
18) Mother's education: (select most advanced level completed)
   a) Elementary school
   b) High school
   c) Technical or trade school
   d) College/University
   e) Graduate or professional school (medical, law, etc.)
19) Father's education (select most advanced level completed)
   a) Elementary school
   b) High school
   c) Technical or trade school
   d) College/University
   e) Graduate or professional school (medical, law, etc.)
20) Where did you grow up, mostly? (select one)
   a) In the country (rural area)

b) In a small town/city (pop. below 50,000)
c) In a medium-size metro area (50–500,000 people)
d) In a large metro area (over 500,000 people)
21) In what country or area did you grow up? (select one)
   a) U.S.A.
   b) Britain
   c) Europe (except Britain)
   d) Africa (except Middle East)
   e) Asia (except Middle East)
   f) Middle East
   g) Canada
   h) Latin America
   i) Other
22) If you grew up in the U.S.A., in what region was this? (select one)
   a) Texas
   b) California
   c) Pacific West (WA, OR, AK, HI)
   d) Mountain (MT, ID, WY, NV, UT, CO, AZ, NM)
   e) West North Central (ND, SD, NE, KS, IA, MO, MN)
   f) South Central (OK, AR, LA, MS, AL, TN, KY)
   g) South Atlantic (FL, GA, SC, NC, VA, WV, MD, DE)
   h) Middle Atlantic (NY, PA, NJ)
   i) East North Central (WI, IL, IN, OH, MI)
   j) New England (ME, VT, NH, MA, RI, CT)
23) If you lived in the U.S.A. during the past FIVE YEARS, in what region was this? (select one)
   a) Texas
   b) California
   c) Pacific West (WA, OR, AK, HI)
   d) Mountain (MT, ID, WY, NV, UT, CO, AZ, NM)
   e) West North Central (ND, SD, NE, KS, IA, MO, MN)
   f) South Central (OK, AR, LA, MS, AL, TN, KY)
   g) South Atlantic (FL, GA, SC, NC, VA, WV, MD, DE)
   h) Middle Atlantic (NY, PA, NJ)
   i) East North Central (WI, IL, IN, OH, MI)
   j) New England (ME, VT, NH, MA, RI, CT)
24) What is your religious affiliation? (select one)
   a) Roman Catholic
   b) Eastern Orthodox
   c) Jewish
   d) Latter-Day Saints
   e) Moslem
   f) Protestant
   g) None
   h) Other
25) If Protestant, what denomination? (select one)

    a) Baptist
    b) Churches of Christ
    c) Jehovah's Witnesses
    d) Episcopal
    e) Lutheran
    f) Methodist
    g) Presbyterian
    h) Pentecostal
    i) Foursquare Gospel
    j) Other

26) How important is religion in your life? (select one)
    a) Unimportant
    b) Somewhat important
    c) Very important

27) About how often do you attend church in a year? (select one)
    a) Never
    b) Twice
    c) 10 times
    d) 30 times
    e) 50 times
    f) 100 times

28) Religiously, which of the following terms describes you best? (select one)
    a) Fundamentalist
    b) Conservative
    c) Moderate
    d) Liberal
    e) Nonreligious

29) How important is politics in your life? (select one)
    a) Unimportant
    b) Somewhat important
    c) Very important

30) Which of the following best describes your political philosophy? (select one)
    a) Conservative
    b) Moderate
    c) Liberal
    d) Radical

31) Were you taught about evolution in your high school biology course(s)?
    a) Yes, and creation was taught along with it
    b) Yes, and creation was NOT taught along with it
    c) No

32) Which of the following best agrees with your conception of the modern theory of evolution? (select one)
    a) Man evolved from an apelike ancestor in Africa

      b) Evolution occurred because differing individual organisms left different numbers of offspring

      c) Evolution involved a purposeful striving toward higher forms (steady progress from microbes to man)

      d) Evolution occurred because the strong eventually eliminated the weak

33) Do you think the modern theory of evolution has a valid scientific foundation? (select one)

      a) Yes, because it is possible to test many hypotheses of evolutionary theory

      b) Yes, even though we can never test hypotheses about events in the past

      c) No, because we can never be sure about events in the past

      d) No, because evolutionary theory is based mainly on speculation, not hard scientific facts

      e) No, because it goes against my convictions

For Numbers 34–45, please tell us how often you watch or read each of the following, using the following scale:

      a) Never

      b) Rarely

      c) Sometimes

      d) Often

34) News programs on TV

35) Popular science magazines like *Discover* or *Science 85*

36) Daily newspapers

37) *National Enquirer, Star,* or similar papers

38) "In Search Of," "That's Incredible," "Ripley's Believe It or Not," or similar TV shows

39) Books reporting on UFOs, the Bermuda Triangle, ancient astronauts, or similar subjects

40) Science programs on PBS like "Nova" or "Cosmos"

41) Science fiction or fantasy books or stories

42) Books or essays by science writers like Carl Sagan

43) Professional scientific journals like *Science* or *Nature*

44) Books advocating creationism by Henry Morris, Duane Gish, etc.

45) Newsmagazines such as *Time*

For Numbers 46–59, please tell us how reliable a source of information you consider each of the following to be, using the following scale:

      a) Unreliable

      b) Somewhat reliable

      c) Very reliable

      d) I don't use this source

46) News programs on TV

47) Popular science magazines like *Discover* or *Science 85*

48) Daily newspapers

49) *National Enquirer, Star,* or similar papers
50) "In Search Of," "That's Incredible," "Ripley's Believe It or Not," or similar TV shows
51) Books reporting on UFOs, the Bermuda Triangle, ancient astronauts, or similar subjects
52) Science programs on PBS like "Nova" or "Cosmos"
53) Science fiction or fantasy books or stories
54) Books or essays by science writers like Carl Sagan
55) Professional scientific journals like *Science* or *Nature*
56) Books advocating creationism by Henry Morris, Duane Gish, etc.
57) Newsmagazines such as *Time*
58) Your college instructors
59) Your parents

SECTION II

Select the phrase after each statement that most clearly describes your belief about the statement. Possible choices are:
   a) Agree strongly
   b) Agree somewhat
   c) Disagree somewhat
   d) Disagree strongly
   e) Undecided; the available evidence is inconclusive
   f) Never heard of it/don't know enough to have an opinion

[Note: items marked with one asterisk were used to construct the Cult Scale discussed in Chapter 5; those marked with two asterisks were used in the creationism scale discussed in Chapter 6.]

60) The world is between 4 and 5 billion years old.
61) Aliens from other worlds are responsible for ancient monuments like the pyramids, which primitive people could not have built.
62) America was visited by Europeans long before either Columbus or the Vikings got here.
63) An ancient curse on the tomb of the Egyptian pharaoh King Tut actually killed people.
64) The Loch Ness "Monster" exists only in the imagination.
65) *UFOs are actual spacecraft from other planets.
66) Humanity came to be through evolution, which was controlled by God.
67) There is intelligent life somewhere out there in the universe.
68) **Adam and Eve, the first human beings, were created by God.
69) Time travel into the past is possible.
70) **There is a good deal of scientific evidence against evolution and in favor of the Bible's account of Creation.
71) Science has done far more good than bad for the world.
72) *"Bigfoot" (Sasquatch) is a real creature roaming the woods in the American Northwest.
73) One can believe in the Bible and Creation, OR in atheistic evolution; there is really no middle ground.

74) Reincarnation really happens.
75) Human beings biologically modern like they are today have been around for about 40,000 years.
76) Black magic really exists.
77) It is impossible to communicate with the dead.
78) Some people can predict future events by psychic power.
79) Claims that there is some mysterious force operating in the Bermuda Triangle are untrue.
80) The lost continent of Atlantis was the home of a great civilization.
81) The theory of evolution correctly explains the development of life on earth.
82) *Aliens from other worlds visited earth in the past.
83) The high civilizations of the Aztecs and Mayas were founded by Old World colonizers, such as the Egyptians.
84) Dinosaurs and humans lived at the same time, as is shown by finds of their footprints together.
85) **Everything written in the Bible is literally true.
86) Psychic power (ESP) has failed to prove helpful in finding and interpreting archaeological sites.
87) Our government is hiding information about the fact that UFOs are alien spacecraft.
88) Humans first evolved in North America and later spread to the rest of the world.
89) Astrology is an accurate predictor of future events.
90) Some races of people are more intelligent than others.
91) **God created humanity pretty much in its present form within the last 10,000 years or so.
92) One cannot read other people's thoughts by psychic powers.
93) Cars capable of very high mileage (over 100 MPG) can be built, but the oil companies are preventing this.
94) The story of the Great Flood and Noah's Ark, as told in the Bible, is symbolic rather than an actual event.
95) The Indians of the New World are descendants of the Lost Ten Tribes of Israel.
96) Science makes our way of life change too fast.
97) The Shroud of Turin has been proved to be the burial shroud of Christ.
98) Most scientists are atheists.
99) Evidence of Noah's Ark has been found on Mt. Ararat in Turkey.
100) Astrology is an accurate predictor of people's personalities.
101) *Ghosts really exist.
102) Humanity came to be through evolution, which occurred WITHOUT the help of God.
103) Most scientists today believe that the modern theory of evolution is a valid scientific theory.
104) The theory of evolution should be taught in public schools as an explanation of origins.

105) **The Bible's account of creation should be taught in public schools as an explanation of origins.
106) Sex education should be taught in public schools.
107) I have a clear understanding of the meaning of scientific study.
108) A woman should have a right to a legal abortion.
109) Science and religion often contradict each other.
110) I believe in the ERA to guarantee women equal rights.
111) I think prayer should be allowed in public schools.
112) Good science education is a top priority for our schools.
113) Finally, which college/university do you attend?
    a) University of Texas at Arlington
    b) Texas Christian University
    c) Central Connecticut State University
    d) Occidental College
    e) University of Southern California
    f) Other

THANK YOU VERY MUCH!

Contributors

JOHN COLE received his Ph.D. in anthropology from Columbia University. He has published widely on topics in archaeology, cult archaeology, and the history and ethnography of creationism and science. He is a senior research associate at the Institute for the Study of Human Issues and editor of both NCSE Reports and Creation/Evolution.

GEERTRUIDA C. DE GOEDE is social sciences librarian-bibliographer at the University of Texas at Arlington Libraries. She received her M.L.S. degree at the University of British Columbia and has worked with the literature of social, medical, and legal concerns at the Legislative Library of British Columbia and the University of Texas Southwestern Medical Center Library in Dallas. She is past president of the Tarrant County Association of Law Librarians.

SUZANNE KNUDSON ENGLER has a degree in anthropology from UCLA, with a background in Palestinian archaeology, archaeological method and theory, and archaeological dating techniques. Her research interests also include historical archaeology and folk medicine in seventeenth-century Virginia. She teaches at El Camino College.

RAYMOND A. EVE is associate professor of sociology at the University of Texas at Arlington. He received his Ph.D. from the University of North Carolina at Chapel Hill. His research interests center on child and adolescent socialization and on the interface between socialization and social control, with particular stress on collective behavior and social movements. He is coauthor (with Francis Harrold) of *The Creationist Movement in Modern America*.

KENNETH L. FEDER is professor of anthropology at Central Connecticut State University. The founder and director of the Farmington River Archaeological Project, he is also a member of the Education Subcommittee of the Committee for the Scientific Investigation of Claims of the Paranormal (CSICOP) and a consulting editor of its journal, *The Skeptical Inquirer*. He is the author of a number of books, including *Frauds, Myths, and Mysteries: Science and Pseudoscience in Archaeology*.

LAURIE GODFREY received her Ph.D. from Harvard University, specializing in physical anthropology and primatology. Currently professor of anthropology at the University of Massachusetts in Amherst, she has published extensively on primate anatomy and evolution (including fieldwork in Madagascar), evolutionary theory, and modern antievolutionism. She is a member of the board of directors of the National Center for Science Education and editor of *Scientists Confront Creationism*.

THOMAS GRAY is associate professor of psychology at Concordia University in Montreal. An experimental psychologist, he has published in areas ranging from social psychology to the brain and behavior. His current research interests involve people's conceptions of what constitutes good evidence for beliefs and how they critically assess the information they receive.

FRANCIS B. HARROLD is associate professor of anthropology at the University of Texas at Arlington. An archaeologist, he received his Ph.D. from the University of Chicago. His principal area of research and publication is the archaeology of early humans in Europe. He has done fieldwork and museum research in France, Spain, Portugal, Albania, and the United States. He is coauthor (with Raymond Eve) of *The Creationist Movement in Modern America*.

LUANNE HUDSON received her Ph.D. from the University of California at Los Angeles. She has taught anthropology and archaeology at the University of Southern California and is currently adjunct professor of anthropology at Occidental College. Her primary research foci are in Mesoamerica and modern material culture studies. These professional specialties, plus an avid love of science fiction, combined to interest her in the study of pseudoscientific beliefs.

ALICE B. KEHOE is professor of anthropology at Marquette University in Milwaukee. Since receiving her Ph.D. from Harvard University, she has done much research and publication on the archaeology and ethnology of American Indians of the Northern Plains, on the history of archaeology, and on scientific creationism. She is author of *American Indians: A Comprehensive Account*, now in its second edition.

BERNARD ORTIZ DE MONTELLANO is professor of anthropology at Wayne State University. Born in Mexico, he received his Ph.D. in organic chemistry from the University of Texas at Austin. He has done research in Aztec culture and medicine, the scientific validation of folk medicine, and the teaching of science to ethnic minority youth. He is author of *Aztec Medicine, Health and Religion* and a founding member of the Society for the Advancement of Chicanos and Native Americans in Science.

WILLIAM H. STIEBING, JR., is professor of history at the University of New Orleans, where he teaches courses in ancient history and archaeology. He received his Ph.D. from the University of Pennsylvania and has participated in archaeological excavations in Jordan and Lebanon. He is the author of *Ancient Astronauts, Cosmic Collisions, and Other Popular Theories about Man's Past; Out of the Desert? Archaeology and the Exodus/Conquest Narratives* (1989); *Uncovering the Past: A History of Archaeology* (1993); and numerous articles in scholarly journals.

STEPHEN WILLIAMS received his Ph.D. in anthropology from Yale University and has done extensive research and publication on the archaeology of American Indians. He is Peabody Professor of American Archaeology and Ethnology, Emeritus, at Harvard University and Honorary Curator of North American Archaeology at the Peabody Museum. Director of the Peabody's Lower Mississippi Survey from 1958 to 1993, he is the author of *Fantastic Archaeology: The Wild Side of North American Prehistory*.